LIBRARY OF HEBREW BIBLE/
OLD TESTAMENT STUDIES

676

Formerly Journal for the Study of the Old Testament Supplement Series

D1570389

ART AS BIBLICAL COMMENTARY

Visual Criticism from Hagar the Wife of Abraham to Mary the Mother of Jesus

J. Cheryl Exum

t&tclark
LONDON · NEW YORK · OXFORD · NEW DELHI · SYDNEY

T&T CLARK
Bloomsbury Publishing Plc
50 Bedford Square, London, WC1B 3DP, UK
1385 Broadway, New York, NY 10018, USA
29 Earlsfort Terrace, Dublin 2, Ireland

BLOOMSBURY, T&T CLARK and the T&T Clark logo
are trademarks of Bloomsbury Publishing Plc

First published in Great Britain in 2019
Paperback edition first published 2021

Cover design: Tjaša Krivec
Cover image: The Repudiation of Hagar, c. 1615. Found in the Collection of Staatliche Museen, Berlin.
(Photo by Fine Art Images/Heritage Images/Getty Images)

A catalogue record for this book is available from the British Library.

A catalogue record for this book is available from the Library of Congress

ISBN: HB: 978-0-5676-8518-6
PB: 978-0-5677-0030-8
ePDF: 978-0-5676-8519-3
eBook: 978-0-5676-8785-2

Series: Library of New Testament Studies, volume 676

Typeset by Forthcoming Publications (www.forthpub.com)

To find out more about our authors and books visit
www.bloomsbury.com and sign up for our newsletters.

For

The Faculty of Theology at Uppsala University

Colleagues in the SBL and SOTS,
especially David, Ellen, Francis, Katie and Martin

and the many talented students who took my classes on the Bible and the Arts
at the University of Sheffield and audiences near and far who have listened to
these ideas and by their input helped me develop and refine them

CONTENTS

Part III
FROM EVE TO MARY

PREFACE

When I visit a museum, I gravitate to the wing where the Old Masters are on display, and after that I look for Pre-Raphaelite painting. I am always on the lookout for paintings of biblical scenes or characters. Because I know the biblical text, I find myself studying biblical paintings to see how they relate to the text – for example, what they focus on or leave out, emphasize or underplay – and asking myself how I feel that I, as a viewer, am being invited to judge the characters. If I am with a companion or a group, an animated discussion usually takes place, often lasting quite some time, and sometimes leading to being asked not to get so close to a painting by a museum attendant.

My fondness for the Old Masters and for European painting from the seventeenth and eighteenth centuries accounts for my preference for painting over other forms of visual culture and explains in part why the majority of my examples come from these artists and this period. These well-known works of art have become for me important exegetical conversation partners largely because of their narrative quality, about which I will have more to say in Chapter 1. Because they strike me as not simply showing a particular event from the Bible but telling a story of their own – a story inspired by the biblical version with which I am so familiar – I find it impossible to resist drawing comparisons between the text and the canvas. The results of such encounters are to be found in the chapters of this book.

I do not talk about teaching in this book, but biblical art is such an effective resource in the classroom that I would like to say a few words about it here. I taught 'The Bible and the Arts' for many years, and the classes were wonderful learning experiences for my students and for me. I first started looking at paintings of the expulsion of Hagar – the subject of three chapters of this book – with my students, and paintings of other figures discussed here – Eve and Adam, Delilah and Bathsheba – have been the subject of many stimulating class discussions. Nothing works so well in generating an animated and productive conversation about a text as basing the discussion on five or six paintings of the scene by different artists. And no writing assignment I have given has ever resulted in such outstanding and original essays or been so interesting and informative for me to read as the one for which students had to 'read' a painting of their choice against the text. To provide guidance for this assignment I developed the questions one might ask about the relation of a text and its visual representation that are listed in Chapter 1.

For the contributions it can make to both research and teaching, including biblical art in mainstream biblical studies can open new areas for enquiry and energise the field. It can also play a role in making biblical studies more interdisciplinary, which, in my view, has always been a desirable goal. To be sure, one does not expect artists, writers, or musicians to turn to biblical criticism for inspiration, but biblical scholars do have something to offer the wider worlds of art, literature, and music. We could contribute to the work of researchers in these specialized fields by bringing our particular, subject-specific angles of vision to bear on discussion of relationships between the Bible and the arts – and, particularly, the Bible as represented in the arts.

This book has been a long time in the making. It is a pleasure to take this opportunity to thank Martin O'Kane and Francis Landy, both of whom read the entire manuscript, and Karalina Matskevich and David Clines, who read parts of it, for their astute criticism and helpful advice along the way. Although I could not do justice to all their judicious comments and incisive questions, I have attended to them as best I could, and the book is better for it. Thanks also to Loveday Alexander and Philip Alexander for discussing issues raised by the Lucan text with me when I was working on Chapter 9. I also thank Duncan Burns for his patience with a difficult job of typesetting and for working with me so diligently to get the images right and Kathryn Harding for invaluable assistance with reading proofs.

Some of the material included in the present study had early outings at staff and postgraduate seminars at the University of Sheffield, and at the Centre for Reception History of the Bible at Oxford University and the Ehrhardt Seminar at Manchester University. Meetings of the Society of Biblical Literature, the Society for Old Testament Study, and the International Organisation for the Study of the Old Testament provided numerous opportunities for me to present ongoing work. I thank Southern Methodist University for the invitation to deliver the Tate-Willson Lectures in 2015, at which some of this material was presented, and Uppsala University for hosting me on several occasions to present papers. I am fortunate to have had so many opportunities to present my research and very grateful for the valuable feedback I received from all these audiences.

Portions of Chapters 1, 2 and 4 are drawn from 'Toward a Genuine Dialogue between the Bible and Art', in *Congress Volume Helsinki 2010*, ed. Martti Nissinen, VTSup, 148 (Leiden: Brill, 2012): 473–503. Chapter 2 also contains material from 'Lovis Corinth's *Blinded Samson*', *Biblical Interpretation* 6 (1998): 410–25; Chapters 3 and 5 include material from 'The Accusing Look: The Abjection of Hagar in Art', *Religion and the Arts* 11 (2007): 143–71, and 'Hagar *en procès*: The Abject in Search of Subjectivity', in *From the Margins 1: Women of the Hebrew Bible and Their Afterlives*, ed. Peter S. Hawkins and Lesleigh Cushing Stahlberg (Sheffield: Sheffield Phoenix, 2009), 1–16. An earlier version of Chapter 7 appeared in *Between the Text and the Canvas: The Bible and Art in Dialogue*, ed. J. Cheryl Exum and Ela Nutu (Sheffield: Sheffield Phoenix, 2007), 11–37, and of Chapter 8 in *Bible, Art, Gallery*, ed. Martin O'Kane (Sheffield: Sheffield Phoenix, 2011), 69–96. A slightly different version of the discussion of Rossetti's *Ecce Ancilla Domini* in Chapter 9 appears in *Let the Reader Understand: Studies in Honor of Elizabeth Struthers Malbon*, ed. Edwin K. Broadhead (London: T&T Clark, 2018), 241–52. I thank the publishers for permission to use this material.

About Translations and Transliterations

Translations from the Hebrew are mine and transliterations are not scientific. Throughout this book I refer to biblical narrators as 'he', since men were responsible for preserving the tradition and, even if some of its authors were women, the world view of the Bible is the dominant androcentric world view of the times. Upper case is used for 'god' only when used as if it were the proper name for the deity as a biblical character.

LIST OF FIGURES

Part I

VISUAL CRITICISM

1

VISUAL CRITICISM:
BIBLICAL ART AS BIBLICAL COMMENTARY

The Bible has played an inspirational role in art for centuries, and art has, in turn, influenced the way the Bible is read. Indeed, what many people know or think they know about the Bible often comes more from familiar representations of biblical texts and themes in the arts than from study of the ancient text itself. In teaching and lecturing I have often encountered the supposition that Eve is alone in the garden of Eden when tempted by the serpent, and, having eaten the forbidden fruit (which is usually wrongly identified as an apple), goes in search of Adam in order to give him a bite of it. A painting in which Eve appears without Adam, such as Spencer Stanhope's *Eve Tempted*, discussed below in Chapter 8, encourages this misconception. In Western society, an image of a woman alone with a serpent or an apple or both is readily identifiable as Eve and perpetuates the age-old view that Eve, not Eve and Adam together, is responsible for the 'Fall'.[1]

Not only will our knowledge of the biblical text influence the way we view, say, a painting of a biblical scene, our reading of the biblical text is also likely to be shaped by our recollection of that painting. This is the case for some readers, I believe, with paintings of Bathsheba at her bath, which I discuss in Chapter 6. The iconographic tradition of Bathsheba displaying herself to view has probably played no small role in giving credence to the assumption one not infrequently encounters that she planned to be seen by King David as he strolled on his roof in the evening.[2]

1. See Katie B. Edwards, *Admen and Eve: The Bible in Contemporary Advertising* (Sheffield: Sheffield Phoenix Press, 2012), and the discussion in Chapter 8 below.

2. A view taken up by film, through which it has entered popular culture; e.g. *David and Bathsheba* (dir. Henry King, 1951), *King David* (dir. Bruce Beresford, 1985), on which see J. Cheryl Exum, *Plotted, Shot, and Painted: Cultural Representations of Biblical Women*, 2nd rev. ed. (Sheffield: Sheffield Phoenix Press, 2012), 28–32, 49–53.

This book is about visual art as it relates to biblical texts. It is as much concerned with biblical exegesis as it is with biblical art and it seeks to show, by means of a range of examples, the contributions an approach I call *visual criticism* can make to biblical exegesis and commentary.[3] My specific focus is on one of many forms of visual art, paintings of biblical scenes, and because all of my examples except three are of easel painting,[4] throughout this book I use the terms 'art' and 'painting' interchangeably. With the burgeoning interest in reception studies in recent years, we are now witnessing a growing emphasis on the Bible and art and a greater methodological diversity.[5] Various approaches are open to the critic

3. Though I deal here almost exclusively with painting, I consider the kind of approach I take here to be applicable *mutatis mutandis* to other forms of visual art, including film, as well as to literary retellings and musical renditions of the text, as illustrated by Paul M. Joyce and Diana Lipton, *Lamentations through the Centuries* (Oxford: Wiley-Blackwell, 2013). I have raised questions similar to those I ask here about art for film ('Do You Feel Comforted? M. Night Shyamalan's *Signs* and the Book of Job', in *Foster Biblical Scholarship: Essays in Honor of Kent Harold Richards*, ed. Frank Ritchel Ames and Charles William Miller [Atlanta, GA: Society of Biblical Literature, 2010], 251–67); music ('Any Dream Will Do? Joseph from Text to Technicolor', *Biblical Reception* 2 [2013]: 202–26); and a combination of literature, music and film in 'Samson and His God: Modern Culture Reads the Bible', in *Words, Ideas, Worlds: Essays in Honour of Yairah Amit*, ed. Athalya Brenner and Frank H. Polak (Sheffield: Sheffield Phoenix Press, 2012), 70–92, and in 'Why, Why, Why, Delilah?', in *Plotted, Shot, and Painted*, 209–75. For an application to a stained-glass window, see Fiona C. Black and J. Cheryl Exum, 'Semiotics in Stained Glass: Edward Burne-Jones's Song of Songs', in *Biblical Studies/Cultural Studies: The Third Sheffield Colloquium*, ed. J. Cheryl Exum and Stephen D. Moore (Sheffield: Sheffield Academic Press, 1998), 315–42. For an application to sculpture, see J. Cheryl Exum, 'The Accusing Look: The Abjection of Hagar in Art', *Religion and the Arts* 11 (2007): 165–68. Studies of the Bible and film flourish, while music is an area that has lagged behind; see, however, the important studies of Helen Leneman, *The Performed Bible: The Story of Ruth in Opera and Oratorio* (Sheffield: Sheffield Phoenix Press, 2007); Leneman, *Love, Lust, and Lunacy: The Stories of Saul and David in Music* (Sheffield: Sheffield Phoenix Press, 2010); Leneman, *Moses: The Man and the Myth in Music* (Sheffield: Sheffield Phoenix Press, 2014); Siobhán Dowling Long, *The Sacrifice of Isaac: The Reception of a Biblical Story in Music* (Sheffield: Sheffield Phoenix Press, 2013); Deborah W. Rooke, *Handel's Israelite Oratorio Libretti: Sacred Drama and Biblical Exegesis* (Oxford: Oxford University Press, 2012).

4. The exceptions are figs. 6.14, 6.15 and 6.16.

5. John F. A. Sawyer, 'A Critical Review of Recent Projects and Publications', *Hebrew Bible and Ancient Israel* 1 (2012): 298–326; Alison Gray, 'Reception of the Old Testament', in *The Hebrew Bible: A Critical Companion*, ed. John Barton (Princeton, NJ: Princeton University Press, 2016), 405–30; Diane Apostolos-Cappadona,

working in this area. One might focus on how an artist has interpreted the text in the light of social, cultural and personal factors that influenced the artist.[6] Or the subject could be approached by way of the cultural history of biblical traditions, examining ways that, over time, cultural attitudes and interests shape not only the meanings people find in biblical stories but also the way those stories are retold in the arts for a wider public.[7] Traditionally art historians have not shown much interest in the interpretation of the biblical text. For example, in *Fractured Families and Rebel Maidservants*, Christina Petra Sellin provides a fascinating study of representations of Hagar in art, a topic I consider at length in the present study, but her focus is on social and cultural influences on the artists and she is not really concerned with the biblical story itself. The presence of art historians along with biblical scholars in a recent collection on *The Art of Visual Exegesis* is a welcome development and, one hopes, a harbinger of future collaborative projects.[8] Studies jointly authored by biblical scholars and art critics, while still fairly rare, offer unique perspectives and insights into paintings with a biblical dimension.[9]

'Religion and the Arts: History and Method', *Brill Research Perspectives in Religion and the Arts* 1 (2017): 1–80.

6. An excellent example is Christine Petra Sellin, *Fractured Families and Rebel Maidservants: The Biblical Hagar in Seventeenth-Century Dutch Art and Literature* (New York: T&T Clark, 2006).

7. This approach is well illustrated by Colleen M. Conway, *Sex and Slaughter in the Tent of Jael: A Cultural History of a Biblical Story* (Oxford: Oxford University Press, 2017), and Katherine Low, *The Bible, Gender, and Reception History: The Case of Job's Wife* (London: T&T Clark, 2013), both of whom are particularly interested in the ways (changing) ideas about gender influence literary and artistic versions of the biblical material. See also Claudia V. Camp, 'Illustrations of the Sotah in Popular Printed Works in the Seventeenth – Nineteenth Centuries', in *A Critical Engagement: Essays on the Hebrew Bible in Honour of J. Cheryl Exum*, ed. David J. A. Clines and Ellen van Wolde (Sheffield: Sheffield Phoenix Press, 2011), 90–115.

8. Vernon K. Robbins, Walter S. Melion and Roy R. Jeal, eds., *The Art of Visual Exegesis: Rhetoric, Texts, Images* (Atlanta, GA: SBL Press, 2017).

9. E.g. Jane Boyd and Philip F. Esler, *Visuality and Biblical Text: Interpreting Velázquez' Christ with Martha and Mary as a Test Case* (Florence: Leo S. Olschki Editore, 2004); Heidi J. Hornik and Mikeal C. Parsons, *Illuminating Luke: The Infancy Narrative in Italian Renaissance Painting* (Harrisburg, PA: Trinity Press International, 2003); Hornik and Parsons, *Illuminating Luke: The Public Ministry of Christ in Italian Renaissance and Baroque Painting* (New York: Continuum, 2005); Hornik and Parsons, *Illuminating Luke: The Passion and Resurrection Narratives in Italian Renaissance and Baroque Painting* (London: T&T Clark, 2007); Hornik and Parsons, *Acts of the Apostles through the Centuries* (Chichester, West Sussex, UK:

'Visual exegesis' is a term that appears to be gaining currency in reception studies. Although the approach I am advocating here draws on visual exegesis in reaching some of its conclusions, it has a different goal. I understand 'visual exegesis' in the sense given it by Paolo Berdini, who uses it to describe the dynamics of an artist's visualization of a text in its historical circumstances. A painting, Berdini points out, visualizes a reading, not a text, and it is this reading, together with the social and political context that enables it, and the effect of the text through the image on the viewer that visual exegesis describes.[10] As Martin O'Kane similarly explains it, visual exegesis 'centres on how the painter "reads" the text, the role of the viewer in interpreting the image, and emphasises the powerful dynamic at work between image and viewer'.[11] The term is used with a range of meanings by the contributors to *The Art of Visual Exegesis*. The biblical scholars are concerned mainly with visual *material* culture contemporary with the New Testament and the light it sheds on New Testament texts, an important but altogether different enterprise from mine in its historical orientation, while the art historians are primarily interested in the reception of the Bible in later Christian art.

Closer to my approach is that of Paul Joyce and Diana Lipton, who, in their commentary on Lamentations, use an approach they call 'reception exegesis', the aim of which is to illuminate and interrogate the biblical text by bringing it into dialogue with a 'receiving text' selected from a range of genres.[12] The term 'reception exegesis', however, does not suit

Wiley Blackwell, 2016). In an important interdisciplinary study of the Bible and visual culture, art historian John Harvey asks what happens when the text becomes an image, and makes text and image partners in the ensuing conversation; *The Bible as Visual Culture: When Text Becomes Image* (Sheffield: Sheffield Phoenix Press, 2013).

10. Paolo Berdini, *The Religious Art of Jacopo Bassano: Painting as Visual Exegesis* (Cambridge: Cambridge University Press, 1997).

11. Martin O'Kane, '*Wirkungsgeschichte* and Visual Exegesis: The Contribution of Hans-Georg Gadamer', *Journal for the Study of the New Testament* 33 (2010): 148. He continues, 'It also describes the beholder's new encounter with the corresponding biblical text made possible by the image. Understanding the process at work between a biblical painting and its viewer – and seeing this process in parallel terms to what happens between a biblical text and its reader – allows us to appreciate how the painting of a biblical subject presents the viewer with a biblical event that impacts on his or her life.'

12. Joyce and Lipton, *Lamentations through the Centuries*. Also similar to the approach I have in mind is the work of Martin O'Kane, *Painting the Text: The Artist as Biblical Interpreter* (Sheffield: Sheffield Phoenix Press, 2007), who draws the biblical text and art into a fruitful relationship that reveals the important role art can play in influencing the viewer's understanding and appreciation of the text.

my project because it places too much emphasis on the Bible's reception in the arts, whereas I propose to shift the focus away from artists and their historical circumstances to the work of art in and of itself – a visual representation of the text that exists in the present and continues to affect and to produce meanings for its viewers (just as the text does for its readers).

As a biblical scholar whose primary interest is the biblical text and its interpretation, I want to know what a work of art can teach me about the biblical text. 'Visual criticism' is my term for an approach that addresses this question by focusing on the narrativity of images – reading them as if, like texts, they have a story to tell – and reading an image's 'story' against the biblical narrator's story. Whereas critique of the biblical text has not been a major emphasis in reception studies, visual criticism, as its name indicates, is not just an interpretative aid but a critical tool.[13] Differences between the visual narrative and the verbal narrative can point to problematic aspects of the text and help us 'see' things about the text we might have overlooked, or enable us to see things differently, or even make it impossible for us to look at the text again in the same way.[14] Of course, not every text lends itself to visual representation, and not every painting lends itself to narrative analysis. Still, there are many biblical paintings that have a 'story' to tell. I am arguing, therefore, for adding visual criticism to other criticisms (historical, literary, form, rhetorical, etc.) in the exegete's toolbox – for making visual criticism part of the exegetical process, so that, in biblical interpretation, we do not just look at the text and at the commentaries on the text but also at art as commentary.

Telling the 'story' – the fabula or diegesis – in different media poses different representational issues. Consider, for example, a biblical story and an artist's rendition of it. The biblical writer has to make decisions

See also Andrea M. Sheaffer, *Envisioning the Book of Judith: How Art Illuminates Minor Characters* (Sheffield: Sheffield Phoenix Press, 2014); Christine E. Joynes, 'A Place for Pushy Mothers? Visualizations of Christ Blessing the Children', *Biblical Reception* 2 (2013): 117–33.

13. What Linda Nochlin said some years ago about art historians 'for the most part reluctant to proceed in anything but the celebratory mode' and about 'the notion of art history as a positive rather than a critical discipline' seems to me to apply to biblical exegetes and the discipline of biblical studies as it is most widely practised; *The Politics of Vision: Essays on Nineteenth-Century Art and Society* (Boulder, CO: Westview Press, 1989), 56–57.

14. Particularly influential on my thinking about the narrativity of images and the relation of 'verbal narrative' and 'visual narrative' is Mieke Bal, *Reading 'Rembrandt': Beyond the Word–Image Opposition* (Cambridge: Cambridge University Press, 1991), from whom I borrow these terms.

about how to *tell* the story. The result is the text. The artist has to decide how to *show* the story, and the result is the painting. As Berdini puts it, 'The painter reads the text and translates his [*sic*] scriptural reading into a problem in representation, to which he offers a solution – the image'.[15] It may be that the painter is not particularly concerned with the text at all, but simply relies on conventions established by earlier, well-known paintings of the story, or bases the work on recollection of the biblical story and versions of it circulating at the time. Or a painting might be inspired by the text's afterlife in literature, as in the case of Jean-Jacques Henner's painting of the Levite and his dead wife, discussed below in Chapter 9, which owes its dramatic impact to a poem by Rousseau. Their own religious beliefs could play a significant role in influencing painters, as could reading the text and meditating on it or consulting theological or ecclesiastical sources, as Renaissance artists often did. Artists who painted the same subject more than once did not always show the same attitude to it.[16] A painter might be commissioned to paint a particular scene in a particular way, and political and economic concerns, not to mention the goodwill of patrons, often played a role in the choice of subject matter.[17] Such matters may contribute to visual critical analysis, but they are neither its primary objective nor necessarily relevant for its practice.

Regardless of the factors that may have influenced an artist's decision to paint a particular scene in a particular way, because the representational issues are different for text and image, the results, as I seek to show in the following chapters of this book, draw attention to different aspects of the story. As will become clear from my examples, I am interested specifically in the relation between verbal narrative and visual narrative, and in using the visual narrative as a commentary on the verbal narrative, regardless of the circumstances surrounding the origins of the text or the origins of the painting.

Artists can be keen textual interpreters, intentionally or unintentionally drawing our attention to textual tensions or problems or possibilities or depths not immediately apparent to readers. When artists paint a biblical scene, they must make decisions, not just about matters such as what the

15. Berdini, *The Religious Art of Jacopo Bassano*, 35.
16. Compare e.g. the paintings of Abraham, Hagar and Ishmael by Fabritius in figs. 3.1 and 3.8; Stom's different versions of Sarah presenting Hagar to Abraham in figs. 4.1, 4.3 and 4.5; and the different attitudes to Delilah in paintings by Rubens in figs. 8.3 and 8.4 below. Conway gives an interesting example of two drawings, one of which offers a positive, the other a negative portrayal of Jael, by the same artist, Maarten van Heemskerck (*Sex and Slaughter in the Tent of Jael*, 57–61).
17. Such issues are stressed by Conway, *Sex and Slaughter in the Tent of Jael*.

characters look like, how they should be dressed (in contemporary garb or however the artist imagined people in biblical times would have dressed), and where the scene takes place, but, more important for critical purposes, about what to show, what aspects of the scene or story to emphasize and what to leave out. In analysing a visual representation of a biblical text we might therefore want to ask what specific textual clues an artist picks up on in order to present a particular interpretation and whether an artist's interpretation might help us see something in the text we might have missed. We might be interested in ways biblical art can help us appreciate the richness or complexity of the text, or we might want to use the work of art to help us interrogate the text and vice versa. We might even revise our critical stance toward a biblical text as a result of our encounter with its artistic representation – and in the next chapter I offer two examples of this from my own experience. But regardless of whether or not a work of art persuades us to change our views about the text, our vision will have been enlarged, and that is a worthy goal in any intellectual pursuit.

Any conversation involving the text and its artistic representation is a three-way one. It is the critic – the critic as reader and the critic as viewer – who determines the questions, the angle of vision, as is the case in all interpretation. The critic plays a greater or lesser role, depending on inclination, in identifying the key issues. Like interpretation of texts, interpretation of images is not disinterested; the answers we find are shaped by the questions we ask, and the questions are framed in our own particular socio-historical context. For me, staging a meaningful conversation between the text and the canvas is often a matter of identifying an interpretative crux – a conundrum, gap, ambiguity or difficulty in the text, a stumbling block for interpretation or question that crops up repeatedly in artistic representations of it – and following its thread as it knits the text and painting together in complex and often unexpected ways. It might be a matter of identifying a problem that the artist has inherited from the text and considering how the artist's strategies for handling the problem relate to the textual strategies for dealing with it.[18] Or the visualization may raise issues not evident in the text and thus send us back to the text with

---

18. See e.g. Hugh S. Pyper, 'Love beyond Limits: The Debatable Body in Depictions of David and Jonathan', and Martin O'Kane, 'The Biblical Elijah and His Visual Afterlives', 38–59 and 60–79 respectively in *Between the Text and the Canvas: The Bible and Art in Dialogue*, ed. J. Cheryl Exum and Ela Nutu (Sheffield: Sheffield Phoenix Press, 2007); Johannes Taschner, 'Mit wem ringt Jakob in der Nacht? Oder: Der Versuch, mit Rembrandt eine Leerstelle auszuleuchten', in *Beyond the Biblical Horizon: The Bible and the Arts*, ed. J. Cheryl Exum (Leiden: Brill, 1999), 109–22.

a different set of questions.[19] Or, in the process of representing a biblical story, a painter may have difficulty maintaining a particular point of view over competing points of view, just as biblical narrators are sometimes at pains to promote a particular position at the expense of others (as, for example, the privileging of Abraham's point of view over Hagar's, discussed in Chapter 3). If a biblical narrator has to struggle to affirm a particular ideology, does the artist inadvertently reinscribe the difficulty, or recognize it or resolve it or treat it in an entirely different way?

In applying visual criticism to the biblical text, it is not a question of how the artist 'got it right' or 'got it wrong' but rather of pursuing connections between image and text to see where they will lead. Questions we might ask include:

To what features of the biblical text does a visual representation draw our attention?

What aspects does it ignore or underplay?

Does the artist respond to a perceived gap in the text or to questions unanswered by the text?

Does the artist add something to the biblical text? Does she or he, for example, magnify something that is not very important in the biblical version?

Does the visual representation illuminate dimensions of the biblical account in new and important ways, either positively or negatively?

Is the artist's attitude to the subject the same as that of the biblical text?

Does a painting attempt to represent the biblical story or to reshape it to fit certain interests, or does it reuse its themes in order to oppose it?

---

19. See e.g. O'Kane, *Painting the Text*, especially 107–59; Ela Nutu, 'Framing Judith: Whose Text, Whose Gaze, Whose Language?', in Exum and Nutu, eds., *Between the Text and the Canvas*, 117–44; Christine E. Joynes, 'Visualizing Salome's Dance of Death: The Contribution of Art to Biblical Exegesis', in Exum and Nutu, eds., *Between the Text and the Canvas*, 145–63; Rachel Nicholls, '"What kind of woman is this?" Reading Luke 7.36–50 in the Light of Dante Rossetti's Drawing *Mary Magdalene at the Door of Simon the Pharisee*, 1853–89', in *From the Margins 2: Women of the New Testament and Their Afterlives*, ed. Christine E. Joynes and Christopher C. Rowland (Sheffield: Sheffield Phoenix Press, 2009), 114–28.

Whose point of view does the artist represent and how does this compare to the presentation of point of view in the biblical version?

Does the artist involve the viewer in the painting? If so, how?

Is the viewer invited to identify with a particular character or see a scene through a particular character's eyes? If so, does the artist identify the viewer with the same character the biblical writer encourages the reader to identify with?

Does the painting alert us to something important that the biblical writer has left out or attempted to gloss over?

Does the visualization enable or perhaps force us to 'see' something we may have disregarded in the verbal narrative?

Does it, by what it emphasizes or downplays, shed light on the biblical narrator's ideology?

How are our assumptions about biblical characters influenced, or even shaped, by our encounters with their visual counterparts, and how does this affect the way we read their stories?

How does our knowledge of a text affect our interpretation of a painting based on it?

Visual criticism is an approach, not a prescriptive method, and these are only examples of the kinds of questions a critic might want to bring to the material at hand, guidelines for thinking about the relationship between text and image. The interests of the critic, the nature of the material being studied and the case one wants to make will determine the approach that works best in each individual case.[20] I am guided by different sets of questions in different chapters of this book. Because my

---

20. For a range of approaches that bring the Bible into productive dialogue with biblical art, see the articles in J. Cheryl Exum and David J. A. Clines, eds., *Biblical Reception* 1 (2012), 2 (2013) and 3 (2014) (Sheffield: Sheffield Phoenix Press) and in J. Cheryl Exum and David J. A. Clines, eds., *Biblical Women and the Arts*, *Biblical Reception* 5, guest editor Diane Apostolos-Cappadona (London: Bloomsbury, 2018). Ellen van Wolde brings another area of enquiry, cognitive linguistics, into the study of biblical art; see 'The Bow in the Clouds in Genesis 9.12–17: When Cognitive Linguistics Meets Visual Criticism', in Clines and van Wolde, eds., *A Critical Engagement*, 380–400.

interest is in biblical art as commentary, matters of concern to art historians (and often to reception history studies), such as conventions, trends and developments in the history of art, social and cultural influences that shaped an artist's interpretation, and the way viewers in the artist's time would have understood these paintings, are not relevant for the questions I want to raise about the text and its visual representations. In general, I do not devote much attention to the relation of an artist's work to the artist's life; in Chapter 2, however, in the case of Lovis Corinth, I discuss this relationship in detail. The reason for this is that the more I looked at Corinth's painting of *The Blinded Samson* and many other paintings in Corinth's œuvre reproduced in the outstanding exhibition catalogue, the more I became fascinated by the artist. The wealth of information we have about Corinth, including his autobiography, was another factor that led me to pursue investigation of the man and of his work.

In the case of Artemisia Gentileschi, in contrast, another painter who interested me very much as one of three women artists whose works appear in this book and about whose life much has been written, I chose not to approach the paintings I use in Chapters 6 and 7 in relation to her life. My reason for this decision was that I wanted to avoid the practice one finds so often of reducing the originality of her art by explaining it in reference to one particular event in her life – a significant event to be sure, but not the only influence on her art.

I mentioned above that our knowledge of the biblical text will invariably affect the way we view a painting or other visual representation of a biblical scene. Obviously the better one knows the biblical story the better equipped one is to analyse and to appreciate an artistic representation of it.[21] If one does not know the Bible, one might not, for example, recognize a painting as a biblical painting, and in some cases even knowing the Bible is no help in identifying the topic of certain biblical paintings. The Victoria and Albert Museum changed the title of Rembrandt's painting of *The Dismissal of Hagar* to *The Departure of the Shunammite Woman* only to change it back in the light of additional evidence.[22] Does Rembrandt's *The Jewish Bride* represent Isaac and Rebekah? Is his *David Sending Away Uriah* really David and Uriah, or are the two main figures Haman and Ahasuerus (and who is the third figure)? Sometimes, however, our

21. Knowing the biblical languages is also a great advantage; see e.g. John F. A. Sawyer, 'Interpreting Hebrew Writing in Christian Art', in Clines and van Wolde, eds., *A Critical Engagement*, 355–71.

22. Laura Greig Krauss, 'Restoring Hagar: Rembrandt van Rijn's Painting *Abraham Dismissing Hagar and Ishmael* in the Victoria and Albert Museum, London', *Biblical Reception* 1 (2012): 65–87.

knowledge of the biblical story can inhibit our freedom in interpretation, causing us to read a work of art according to convention and predetermined notions of what it is 'about'. Thus there are advantages in taking a painting as our starting point for interrogating the biblical story.[23]

As is the case with texts and their authors, the interpretation an artist wishes to present to the viewer may not be the same interpretation that an individual viewer discovers in the image. Viewers, like readers, play an active role in interpretation, in activating and creating meanings. In reading paintings in terms of their narrativity, I am advocating a reader-response criticism of art. '[S]ince viewers bring their own cultural baggage to images', Mieke Bal reminds us, 'there can be no such thing as a fixed, predetermined, or unified meaning. In fact, the very attempts to fix meaning furnish, among other things, the most convincing evidence for this view.'[24] Nanette Salomon, in an article on Artemisia Gentileschi's paintings of Susanna's bath, discussed below in Chapter 6, offers an example of competing interpretations of a painting by art historians (professional viewers) that forcefully illustrates the viewer's role in interpreting art. Referring to a classic study by Mary Garrard,[25] she observes of Gentileschi's 1622 painting:

> Garrard initially felt that Artemisia could not have painted this *Susanna* because she saw the figure as too seductive... The catalogue authors saw the same figure as spiritual in her appeal to God... Each reading has some validity. Together they are a sobering reminder of how personal vision is and of what we are doing when we 'do' art history.[26]

The role of viewers as readers of art is especially evident when it comes to facial expressions of figures in a painting, which are often very difficult to decipher, and not infrequently difficult even to see well. The postures

23. Well illustrated by Bal, *Reading 'Rembrandt'*; for an example, see J. Cheryl Exum, 'Is This Naomi?', in *Plotted, Shot, and Painted*, 161–207. Taking the painting I discuss (Calderon's *Ruth and Naomi*) as his starting point, Martin O'Kane offers an additional perspective by examining representations of Islam in European biblical art and the role of artists in constructing an imagined visual world of the Bible for Western viewers; 'The Bible in Orientalist Art', in Clines and van Wolde, eds., *A Critical Engagement*, 288–308.

24. Mieke Bal, *Looking In: The Art of Viewing* (London: Routledge, 2001), 71.

25. *Artemisia Gentileschi: The Image of the Female Hero in Italian Baroque Art* (Princeton, NJ: Princeton University Press, 1989).

26. Nanette Salomon, 'Judging Artemisia: A Baroque Woman in Modern Art History', in *The Artemisia Files: Artemisia Gentileschi for Feminists and Other Thinking People*, ed. Mieke Bal (Chicago: University of Chicago Press, 2005), 45.

of figures can also be ambiguous, as can the relationship among different figures in a painting – all leaving room for multiple meanings to be revealed in them.

As noted above, I read the paintings discussed in the following chapters in terms of their narrativity, concentrating on the interaction between visual and verbal narration. In visual representations of biblical narratives, the story is often compressed, with various elements of the story represented in one moment in time, which can sometimes lead to ambiguities different from, but not wholly unlike, the ambiguities we encounter in the biblical text. Paintings of the appearance of the divine messenger to Hagar in the wilderness, discussed in Chapter 5, provide an example. They cannot show the scene as described in the text because they must place all three characters – Hagar, the angel and Ishmael – in close proximity in order for the subject to be recognizable. The result is a different 'story' from the one told by the text, but how different? Happily, both texts and their visual representations have a way of eluding our attempts to fit them into moulds, of destabilizing our interpretations and inviting new ones. They can surprise us. The contribution visual criticism can make to biblical interpretation can best be illustrated with concrete examples, to which let us now turn.

2

THE BLINDED SAMSON AND *SCENE FROM THE*
SONG OF SONGS:
PAINTINGS THAT CHANGED MY MIND

Having argued in the previous chapter that biblical art can direct our
attention to aspects of the biblical text we had not 'seen' before and can
fruitfully influence our interpretation by raising new or different, and often
challenging, sets of critical questions, I offer here a personal testimony to
the value of visual criticism. The two paintings discussed below illustrate how an encounter with a painting led me to change my thinking
about biblical texts to which I have devoted considerable attention over
the course of my academic career, the story of Samson in Judges 13–16
and the Song of Songs. What makes interpretation of texts such an intellectually stimulating and pleasurable experience is that it is ongoing,
never static. To find long-held scholarly positions challenged and deeply
affected by works of art has not only been intellectually exciting and
broadening, it has also firmly persuaded me of the importance of making
visual criticism part of the interpretative process. It is with the hope that
my experience might persuade others to include visual criticism in their
exegetical repertory that I offer the following examples.

Unlike other paintings discussed in this book, no woman appears
in my first example, Lovis Corinth's *Blinded Samson*. But as the other
paintings I include in this chapter by way of comparison illustrate –
paintings in which the woman held responsible for the hero's downfall,
Delilah, does appear – the absence of the woman in *The Blinded Samson*
is what accounts largely for the powerful impact this painting has on the
viewer (as does the absence of any other characters, such as a temple full
of Philistines). The second example, Gustave Moreau's *Scene from the
Song of Songs*, like the paintings of Hagar brought to Abraham's bed by
Sarah discussed in Chapter 4 and paintings discussed below in Chapter 6,
invites the viewer to behold the woman as the object of a scene designed
to appeal principally to the prurient interests of an assumed heterosexually
oriented male spectatorship.

Lovis Corinth's Blinded Samson

A painting of the blinded and shackled Samson by the turn-of-the-century German artist Lovis Corinth (1858–1925) opened for me a dimension of the biblical story of Samson that I was previously unable to entertain seriously, namely, its tragic character. This transformation of a scholarly position I have long held, brought about by confrontation with a modern work of art, has been instrumental in shaping my views about the role biblical art can play in biblical commentary.

Lovis Corinth was prolific by any account; he produced around a thousand oil paintings (many of which are large canvasses) and some three thousand drawings, watercolours, and prints.[1] His *Blinded Samson*, painted in 1912, the year after he had suffered a severe stroke from which he never fully recovered, is widely considered to be autobiographical. At the time of his stroke, Corinth was already an acclaimed artist, whose works were widely exhibited, and a successful figure in the art world at large (he was president of the Berlin Secession, and had published essays and a book on painting).[2] The stroke, which left him partially paralyzed, changed his life as well as his style of painting. A number of works begun when he was able to paint again deal with suffering and distress. *The Blinded Samson* was his first large painting after his stroke. It is based on a sketch made some twenty years earlier,[3] and one sees immediately the differences, particularly in the rather expressionless face of the earlier Samson and his less contorted body. Around the same time as *The Blinded Samson*, Corinth also did a sketch of a tormented *Job and His Friends*

---

1. An excellent source for information about Corinth is the splendid catalogue from the Corinth exhibition of 1996 and 1997, shown at the Haus der Kunst, Munich, the Nationalgalerie, Berlin, the Saint Louis Art Museum, and the Tate Gallery, London: *Lovis Corinth*, ed. Peter-Klaus Schuster, Christoph Vitali and Barbara Butts; catalogue of paintings, Lothar Brauner and Andrea Bärnreuther; catalogue of drawings, watercolours and prints, Barbara Butts; with further contributions by Andrea Bärnreuther et al. (Munich: Prestel Verlag, 1996).

2. *Das Erlernen der Malerei. Ein Handbuch von Lovis Corinth*, 3rd ed. (Berlin: Paul Cassirer, 1920 [originally published 1908]; repr. Hildesheim: Gerstenberg Verlag, 1979). He later published his *Gesammelte Schriften* (Berlin: Fritz Gurlitt Verlag, 1920) and a *Selbstbiographie* (Leipzig: Hirzel, 1926). Corinth knew the Bible well and painted numerous biblical scenes. In *Das Erlernen der Malerei*, 88–92, he discusses biblical and classical themes as important sources for painting. 'Prachtvolle Erzählungen findet man im Alten Testament' [One finds splendid stories in the Old Testament], he observes (89).

3. Barbara Butts, 'Drawings, Watercolours, Prints', in Schuster, Vitali and Butts, eds., *Lovis Corinth*, 340 (the sketch, she notes, is incorrectly dated 1913).

and a watercolour of *Ecce Homo*, which he painted in oil in the year of his death. *Job and His Friends* is a highly autobiographical work based on Corinth's confident *Self-portrait with Glass* (1907),[4] and he used the bony right hand of Job for Samson's groping right hand.[5] The similarities of *Ecce Homo* (1925), another large oil canvas, to *The Blinded Samson* are marked, especially the strong impression made by the bright red blood dripping from the crown of thorns (like the blood from Samson's eyes), the shackled figure who has clearly suffered indignity, and the profound sense of physical and spiritual suffering conveyed by the facial expressions. It is not difficult to see in these works, and especially in *The Blinded Samson*, Corinth's sense of his own brokenness and his anguish at the reduction of his powers.[6]

The idea of Samson as a tragic hero is not new, either in art or in biblical criticism.[7] Scholars have described Samson as tragic, as comic, and as tragicomic, but by and large the grounds for these claims have not been well developed.[8] I have argued at length that the amoral, witty, libidinous, uncontrollable, destructive and beneficial Israelite champion is a comic hero, who exhibits many of the contradictions associated with

---

4. Ibid., 366. Corinth painted a self-portrait every year, around the time of his birthday, as a kind of introspective exercise. In the *Self-portrait with Glass* (cat. 69), the artist, whose massive frame is naked to the waist, stares self-confidently at the viewer. Lothar Brauner observes of the self-portrait, 'It portrays a man whose identity rests in his physical power, who is in every inch aware of this power and who is unable to imagine not being able to impose his will through calling upon it' (Schuster, Vitali and Butts, eds., *Lovis Corinth*, 173).

5. Butts, 'Drawings, Watercolours, Prints', 340.

6. Corinth was known in his youth for his physical strength; he was heavy-set (and a heavy drinker), married to a woman some twenty years younger than he, a prolific and successful artist who threw himself into his work. The stroke cut him down in the prime of his life, and adjusting to suddenly imposed physical limitations was difficult.

7. Milton sought to make Samson a tragic hero in *Samson Agonistes*, but even here the inherent comic plot line he inherited from the biblical version defeats the realization of the tragic vision. In spite of the hero's death, *Samson Agonistes* ends in restoration, with Manoah explaining why 'Nothing is here for tears, nothing to wail...' and the chorus affirming, 'All is best, though we oft doubt'.

8. John Vickery ('In Strange Ways: The Story of Samson', in *Images of Man and God*, ed. Burke O. Long [Sheffield: Almond Press, 1981], 58–73) argues that Samson is a tragic hero; W. Lee Humphreys (*The Tragic Vision and the Hebrew Tradition* [Philadelphia, PA: Fortress Press, 1985], 68–78) finds Samson more pathetic than tragic; James L. Crenshaw (*Samson: A Secret Betrayed, a Vow Ignored* [Atlanta, GA: John Knox Press, 1978], 129) suggests that the story be viewed as a tragicomedy.

the well-known trickster figure, and that the matrix of the Samson story is best described as comic, which does not necessarily mean that we like the way the story ends (thus I also use the designation 'classic' for the Samson story to avoid the associations with something funny that 'comic' often calls to mind).[9] In spite of Samson's suffering and death, I argue, the story, which ends with Samson's relationship to God restored through prayer and with Samson serving as the instrument of a great victory for Israel's god over the god of the Philistines, exemplifies the classic vision, a vision that can tolerate distress and suffering because life – that is, Israel's life – goes on. I also point to literary techniques, such as repetition going nowhere (as in Samson's recurrent skirmishes with the Philistines and his repeated weakness for women) and a heavy use of ironic punning that distinguish this narrative from the high seriousness of tragic style.

A major cause of Samson's failure to achieve true tragic status is to be found in his character. Indeed, as is typical of comic heroes, Samson undergoes little or no character development. He does not learn from his mistakes,[10] nor is he explicitly held morally accountable for them.[11] He bounds recklessly from one adventure to the next, undaunted and indefatigable until he meets his nemesis, Delilah, and he betrays no sense of his mission to 'begin to deliver Israel from the Philistines' (Judg. 13.6). I have never been able to see the biblical Samson as a sympathetic character, chiefly because of his insouciance and lack of awareness (but

9. *Tragedy and Biblical Narrative: Arrows of the Almighty* (Cambridge: Cambridge University Press, 1992), 16–44. The tragic and classic visions, although fundamentally opposed, are not mutually exclusive. As Susanne Langer points out, 'The matrix of the work is always either tragic or comic; but within its frame the two often interplay' (*Feeling and Form* [New York: Scribner's, 1953], 334). The classic vision is Murry Krieger's designation for the affirmative alternative to the tragic vision. The classic vision acknowledges the tragic but refuses it, opting instead to accept, without illusion and without despair, the imperfections of the human condition (Krieger, *Visions of Extremity in Modern Literature*. Vol. 2, *The Classic Vision: The Retreat from Extremity* [Baltimore, MD: Johns Hopkins University Press, 1971], 4, 42, 47–51; see also Exum, *Tragedy and Biblical Narrative*, 18–19, 157 n. 10).

10. For a different view, see Yair Zakovitch, '∪ and ∩ in the Bible', in *Tragedy and Comedy in the Bible*, ed. J. Cheryl Exum (Decatur, GA: Scholars Press, 1984), 111.

11. This is not to discount implicit judgments, and numerous commentators conclude that Samson is guilty of failing to live up to his Nazirite calling.

also because I do not like what he does: terrorize his enemies[12] and chase after foreign women).[13] We may find him exuberant, spontaneous and amusing, but there is nothing especially appealing about him, nothing that allows him to win our respect.[14] As Lee Humphreys observes, Samson's choices 'rather too narrowly serve his self-interests'.[15] Even his dying prayer is for vengeance. It takes a *deus ex machina*, typical of comedy, to provide the narrative with a satisfying closure. When God gives Samson the strength to pull down the temple and allows him to die together with his victims, it is not because Samson deserves it but simply because God chooses to grant Samson's prayer ('O Lord God, remember me, please, and strengthen me, please, just this once, O God, that I may be avenged upon the Philistines for one of my two eyes', Judg. 16.28; 'Let me die with the Philistines', Judg. 16.29).

Comedy can serve, as it does in Judges 13–16, as an outlet for aggression and release from antisocial instincts. These rowdy tales in which the mighty champion of the underdog Israelites gets the better of the militarily superior Philistines are, as James Wharton perceptively describes them, 'resistance stories'.[16] Central to a reading of the Samson story as embodying a comic or classic vision is the acceptance of the narratorial

---

12. On Samson as a terrorist, see J. Cheryl Exum, 'The Many Faces of Samson', in *Samson: Hero or Fool?*, ed. Erik Eynikel and Tobias Nicklas (Leiden: Brill, 2014), 17–20; Joseph R. Jeter, Jr., *Preaching Judges* (St Louis, MO: Chalice Press, 2003), 116.

13. The women are not necessarily Philistine (only Samson's wife from Timnah is referred to as a Philistine); they are simply 'other', which makes them 'foreign'; see J. Cheryl Exum, *Fragmented Women: Feminist (Sub)versions of Biblical Narratives*, 2nd ed. (London: Bloomsbury T&T Clark, 2016), 47–50.

14. Compare, for example, King Lear, who is initially such an unsympap thetic character that one would like to see him have his comeuppance; yet not just by breaking him, but by showing the effects of his *hamartia* on his character, Shakespeare makes us forget his folly and feel sympathy.

15. Humphreys, *The Tragic Vision*, 69.

16. James A. Wharton, 'The Secret of Yahweh: Story and Affirmation in Judges 13–16', *Interpretation* 27 (1973): 48–65 (esp. 53–54). As Barbara Babcock-Abrahams observes of this kind of tale, '[I]t would perhaps be better to call both this type of tale and persona by the literary term "picaresque" which combines with the notion of trickery and roguish behavior the idea of the uncertain or hostile attitude of an individual to existing society and an involvement in narrative focussed on movement, within and beyond that society' ('"A Tolerated Margin of Mess": The Trickster and His Tales Reconsidered', *Journal of the Folklore Institute* 11 [1975]: 159); see also Susan Niditch, 'Samson as Culture Hero, Trickster, and Bandit: The Empowerment of the Weak', *Catholic Biblical Quarterly* 52 (1990): 608–24; Gregory Mobley, 'The

point of view that sees God as controlling events according to a plan: 'His father and his mother did not know that it was from Yahweh, for he was seeking an occasion against the Philistines' (Judg. 14.4). Samson is the instrument of a divine plan that, though unusual, does not appear inscrutable. The classic vision can embrace suffering and death in the larger context of restoration: God, who earlier had 'left him' (16.20), intervenes in response to Samson's prayers; Israel, through Samson, is victorious over their Philistine oppressors; and Samson wins even greater glory through his heroic death ('the dead that he killed at his death were more than those he had killed in his life', 16.30). Significantly, Samson does not die by his own hand; it is not his own strength that enables him to destroy the temple and take his own life but rather God's empowering of him. In the end, then, it is God who controls life and death,[17] and, for readers of the story, there is perhaps a certain security in that knowledge. The story does not threaten our assumptions about the nature of things. Or does it?

As I suggested in *Tragedy and Biblical Narrative*, an interpretation of the Samson story along tragic lines is not unthinkable:

> If God's behind-the-scenes activity through Samson inspires our confidence, the classic vision prevails. If, however, we choose to foreground hostile transcendence by focusing on Samson as a *victim* of forces beyond his control, our interpretation no longer finds accommodation in the classic vision... Everything that happens to Samson seems determined by God without his knowledge or consent, leaving Samson with little, if any, control over his own life... One might argue that Samson's role as Yahweh's instrument against the Philistines, because it was unwitting and because he was not offered a choice, is no compensation for his personal loss, his blindness, humiliation, and death. Perhaps most disturbing is the fact that Samson is dispensable in God's plan.

I was, however, unable to convince myself that, in the absence of any struggle against fate or awareness of fatedness, Samson could be viewed as a tragic figure, and thus could not sustain a reading along these lines.[18]

Wild Man in the Bible and the Ancient Near East', *Journal of Biblical Literature* 116 (1997): 217–33. Gregory Mobley (*Samson and the Liminal Hero in the Ancient Near East* [New York: T&T Clark, 2006]) surveys a range of attempts to categorize Samson, with emphasis on Samson's complexity and liminal status.

17. In 15.19, God gives Samson water so that 'he lived'; in 16.30 God grants Samson death; see Exum, *Tragedy and Biblical Narrative*, 33–34.

18. Against my contention that Samson displays no tragic awareness, David Gunn argues that Samson is aware of his place in God's plan and does struggle against it; 'Samson of Sorrows: An Isaianic Gloss on Judges 13–16', in *Reading between*

And I felt no more than a perfunctory sympathy for poor Samson until I saw Corinth's *Blinded Samson* (fig. 2.1). Corinth's painting has given me a new perspective on the biblical hero, a vision of Samson as tragic and as truly deserving of sympathy. I shall not be able to read the story of Samson ever again without calling to mind Corinth's haunting image of anguish and brokenness, regardless of how I choose to let that image affect my interpretation at any given time.

Fig. 2.1. Lovis Corinth, *The Blinded Samson*, 1912, Nationalgalerie, Berlin

Texts: Intertextuality and the Hebrew Bible, ed. Danna Nolan Fewell (Louisville, KY: Westminster John Knox Press, 1992), 225–53. Although Gunn sheds light on the tragic dimension of the Samson story by reading it intertextually in the light of Deutero-Isaiah, especially the 'servant' passages, his argument about Samson's self-awareness rests too heavily on speculation about what Samson may have thought and felt.

Corinth's depiction of suffering and desolation in *The Blinded Samson* is profoundly unsettling. I find the painting overwhelming. When I first saw it, I knew I had to write about it, but I hardly knew how, so intense and real is the misery conveyed by the anguished face and the distorted human frame groping its way toward the viewer. The canvas is large (130 × 105 cm), which adds to its capacity to overwhelm the viewer. It does not offer a full view of Samson: the painting ends at the knees; the top of Samson's head touches the top of the canvas, while his hair and two fingers of his left hand extend beyond its borders. This is suffering that exceeds all bounds; it cannot be contained within the confines of the canvas, and we, the viewers, are too close for comfort.

There is nothing so hard to communicate as the experience of pain. In *The Body in Pain*, Elaine Scarry discusses this 'most radically private of experiences' in terms of the difficulty a person in physical pain has in describing to another exactly what her or his pain is, and of attempts at creating a language for pain so it can enter into the realm of shared discourse.[19] In considering the arts, Scarry speaks of '[the] isolated play, [the] exceptional film, [the] extraordinary novel that is not just incidentally but centrally and uninterruptedly about the nature of bodily pain'.[20] Corinth's painting is such an exceptional rendering of the experience of pain in the visual arts. *The Blinded Samson* conveys both bodily and spiritual anguish with an incredible immediacy. I, for one, cannot view it without wincing. One senses the pain in the hero's massive, contorted body, squeezed uncomfortably within the door frame (not the pillars of the temple, as one might at first think). His hands, in chains, reach out helplessly, groping with outstretched fingers (with the fingers of the oversized left hand grasping around the corners of the canvas); his head is thrust forward from hunched shoulders. With a few savage brush strokes, Corinth shows us what remains or has grown back of Samson's hair after the shaving, sticking out in disordered clumps. The facial expression is particularly harrowing. Rather than hiding the gouged-out eyes, the bloodstained bandage draws attention to the dark and dimly visible eye sockets, while fresh drops of bright red blood fall down Samson's face. Samson's agony is concentrated in the remarkable mouth, set as though the big, uneven teeth are holding back a cry.[21]

19. Elaine Scarry, *The Body in Pain: The Making and Unmaking of the World* (New York: Oxford University Press, 1985), 6.

20. Ibid., 10.

21. The closed mouth in the sketch of 1912 gives an entirely different, far less disturbing impression.

I see in this painting a Samson totally alone, with no resources left to him, a Samson dispensable in God's plan; in other words, a tragic Samson. This is not just a Samson who has been betrayed into the hands of his enemies by the woman he loved, as we have in numerous paintings, but much more: a Samson broken not by mere mortals (Delilah and the Philistines are nowhere in sight) but by the forces of the universe – a Samson abandoned by his god.

There are other paintings of Samson that come close to this tragic effect, but do not quite succeed. Rembrandt's famous painting of *The Blinding of Samson*, for example, dramatically conveys the hero's agony (fig. 2.2). Rembrandt shows us the gouging of Samson's right eye, the spurting blood, and the teeth gritted in pain. One of two other paintings Corinth did of Samson, *The Arrest and Blinding of Samson* (1907), is modelled on it (fig. 2.3).[22]

Fig. 2.2. Rembrandt van Rijn, *The Blinding of Samson*, 1636,
Städelsches Kunstinstitut, Frankfurt-am-Main

22. The third (in a private collection) is a painting of 1893, showing the Philistines, led by Delilah, approaching Samson, asleep in his tent. I have not seen a reproduction of it.

Fig. 2.3. Lovis Corinth, *The Arrest and Blinding of Samson*, 1907,
Landesmuseum, Mainz

Two important differences between these paintings and *The Blinded Samson* lessen their tragic impact for me. One is the presence of so many people in the paintings in comparison to *The Blinded Samson* who stands alone, expressing symbolically the isolation typically experienced by tragic heroes. Rembrandt gives us a crowd of people, but there is distance between the figures; Corinth has crammed them more closely together, with the result that his painting seems overcrowded. Rembrandt's *The Blinding of Samson* and Corinth's *The Arrest and Blinding of Samson* are scenes of violence; indeed, the Philistines appear even more brutal in Corinth's painting. But whereas Rembrandt forces us to witness the very moment when Samson's eye is being gouged out, in Corinth's version Samson has not yet been blinded. There is, however, an allusion to the blinding in the blood flowing from the eye of the figure on the floor in the foreground. In striking contrast to all this savage activity, violence in

The Blinded Samson is mediated to the viewer through Samson's abused body, a body in pain.

The other feature that diminishes the tragic impact of the Rembrandt painting and Corinth's based on it is the presence of the treacherous Delilah, a feature that enables, if not encourages, the viewer to blame the woman.[23] In the Rembrandt, Delilah holds Samson's shorn locks in one hand and the scissors in the other. These two signs of her guilt arrest attention by virtue of being silhouetted against the one source of light in the picture. Because of the uniform colouring and shading of *The Arrest and Blinding of Samson*, Corinth's Delilah is not immediately so conspicuous as Rembrandt's, who is moving into the light. Unlike Rembrandt's Delilah, whose blue dress associates her with the bluish light of the world outside, Corinth's Delilah is naked, and thus more brazen – and therefore more culpable. From a superior position, perched above the fray and looking down triumphantly at the strong man she has rendered helpless, she is the embodiment of the *femme fatale*, the woman deadly to man, if there ever was one.[24] As in Rembrandt's painting, the composition constructs a line from Delilah to Samson, so that the viewer's attention is shared between them and the moral that love blinds is easily drawn.

Blaming the woman, which is what most paintings of Delilah implicitly do, allows the viewer to hold Samson less accountable (he is responsible for his own undoing in the biblical account, for he does not have to tell Delilah the secret of his strength). And, more important, the tacit accusation of the woman deflects attention from the other character who, in the biblical account, shares responsibility for Samson's extreme agony: the deity. We might recall that in the Bible Delilah disappears from the narrative after betraying Samson into the hands of the Philistines. Her reaction to the blinding, if she witnessed it – as in Rembrandt's *The Blinding of Samson* and Corinth's *The Arrest and Blinding of Samson* – is a connection the reader must supply.[25] In *The Blinded Samson*, Delilah

23. See the discussion of Delilah below in Chapter 8.

24. There are others in Corinth's corpus. Corinth was inspired by Oscar Wilde's play to paint two versions of an extraordinary Salome (in 1899 and 1900), where the voluptuous *femme fatale*, her breasts exposed, leans over the platter on which John the Baptist's head lies, and with her bejewelled fingers forces open his eye so that, though dead, he will be forced to behold her.

25. Is the connection self-evident? A different interpretation altogether, one that seeks to redeem Delilah, can be found in Cecil B. DeMille's 1949 film, *Samson and Delilah*, starring Victor Mature and Hedy Lamarr. In DeMille's version (screenplay by Jesse Lasky, Jr. and Fredric Frank), Delilah leaves the tent before the blinding takes place and knows nothing about it until later; indeed, the blinding violates the

has disappeared without a trace as completely as she does in the biblical story. Gone, too, are the Philistine captors. No one is left to compete with Samson for the viewer's attention in this painting, and even the surroundings lack almost all detail, so that there is no visual escape for the viewer, nowhere else to fix attention except on the broken hero.[26] Because here Samson stands so very alone and helpless in the inhospitable world, we can only blame God, in other words, the forces of the universe beyond our ken.

In *The Blinded Samson*, a drop of blood appears to have fallen on or be falling in front of Samson's chest on the left side, about at his heart. Is this an allusion to Corinth's stroke? If the sketch of *Job and His Friends* is based on Corinth's *Self-portrait with Glass*, perhaps I am not unjustified in being reminded here of another of Corinth's self-portraits, *Self-portrait with Model* (1903; cat. 56), in which Corinth appears with his young wife Charlotte Berend-Corinth as a back-view nude leaning against his chest, while he, at the height of his powers, stares at his reflection.[27] To me, Samson's face somewhat resembles Corinth's, and his build even more so, for Corinth, too, was a heavy-set man. Also similar is the colouring in the two paintings, with their preference for shades of amber and green. Charlotte Berend-Corinth wrote of *The Blinded Samson* that 'there might well be a considerable autobiographical content to this work!'[28] Was Corinth, like Samson, contemplating suicide? Apparently he often did,[29]

spirit but not the letter of her agreement with the Philistines that 'no drop of his blood shall be shed; no blade shall touch his skin'; see, further, Exum, *Plotted, Shot, and Painted*, 229–66.

26. The doorknob and keyhole alert us to the fact that Samson is standing in a door frame and not in the temple between the two pillars. The fresh drops of blood on his face and the open door behind him suggest that he has just been released from the prison for the Philistines' amusement and is only at this moment revealed to the viewer. There are many details about the other figures in the other paintings that compete for the viewer's attention; for a fascinating reading of the Rembrandt painting, see Bal, *Reading 'Rembrandt'*, 326–46.

27. The fact that Corinth painted so many self-portraits makes us particularly aware that he is looking at himself in a mirror. In this painting, he has not corrected the left-right reversal of the mirror image.

28. Charlotte Berend-Corinth, *Lovis* (Munich, 1958), 157, cited by Brauner in *Lovis Corinth*, 202.

29. After an exhibition of his works by the Nationalgalerie in 1923, marking Corinth's sixty-fifth birthday, he wrote, 'Ich war nicht wenig erstaunt, daß alle Welt mich aus meinen Arbeiten einen starken Lebensbejaher nannte. In der Tat war ich, ich kann wohl sagen seit meiner Kindheit, von schwerster Melancholie heimge-sucht. Es ist kein Tag vergangen, an welchem ich es nicht besser fand, aus diesem

and many of his paintings reveal a preoccupation with the theme of mortality. The painting of the blinded and shackled Samson, in any event, gives the viewer the impression of a suicide desired but postponed.[30]

Looking through the catalogue of Corinth's paintings, even an amateur can tell how the stroke influenced his style; the later paintings, for example, are more impressionistic.[31] Critics remark on the role possibly played by the partial paralysis of his left hand and tremors in his right, with which he painted, as did Corinth himself:

> Auch im Juli 1923 machte eine Ausstellung in der National-Galerie meinen Ruf bedeutender. Die Kritiker lobten mich weit über Gebühr. Ich möchte mich über einen Ausdruck verteidigen, den mir die Presse vorwarf: 'Virtuosität'. Krankheiten, eine linksseitige Lähmung, wie ein ungeheures Zittern der rechten Hand, durch Anstrengung mit der Nadel verstärkt und durch frühere Exzesse von Alkohol hervorgerufen, verhinderten schon eine handwerkliche kalligraphische Mache in meinen Arbeiten. Ein fortwährendes Streben, mein Ziel zu erreichen, das ich in dem Grade niemals erreichte, hat mein Leben vergällt und jede Arbeit endete mit Depressionen, dieses Leben noch weiter führen zu müssen![32]

> [Also in July 1923 an exhibition in the National Gallery enhanced my reputation. The critics praised me far more than I deserved. I want to defend myself against one accusation that the press levelled against me: 'virtuosity'. Illness, paralysis on the left side and a debilitating trembling of the right hand, increased by efforts with the engraving needle and brought on by earlier excess of alcohol, made a technically precise execution in my work impossible. A constant striving to reach my goal that I never fully achieved made my life bitter and every work ended with depression over having to continue with this life.]

Leben zu verscheiden. Nur eines war der Unterschied: ich habe es nicht getan!' (*Selbstbiographie*, 171). [I was not a little surprised that the world called me an incorrigible sybarite on the basis of my work. In fact, I would say that since my childhood I have been plagued by melancholy. Not a single day has passed that I did not find it better to leave this life. The difference is: I did not do it.]

30. I am borrowing here the title of the review of the Tate exhibit, 'Impressions of a Suicide Postponed', by Peter Vergo in the *Times Literary Supplement* (14 March 1997): 18.

31. The range of Corinth's style makes it difficult to fit into the categories of Impressionism or Expressionism. After his death, his work was removed from museums as part of the Nazi campaign against 'degenerate art'; it has taken time for his reputation to be re-established.

32. *Selbstbiographie*, 168.

But the differences cannot be adequately accounted for simply by attributing them to the physical or psychological results of his illness. Corinth also speaks of a change of attitude to form:

> Noch einmal sehe ich Bilder, mit welchen ich mich in der Jugend abgequält habe und an die ich meine Hoffnungen gesetzt hatte. Ich denke an die Zeiten, die dann kamen, und in denen ich glaubte, anders malen zu müssen. Ich sehe deutlich eine Änderung meines Vortrages, ein größeres Betonen der Formen... Überblicke ich das Ganze, so scheint es mir doch wie aus einem Guß... Stets habe ich nach meiner Überzeugung gehandelt, und niemals bin ich vom Pfade des mir richtig Erscheinenden abgewichen.[33]

> [I still see paintings on which I laboured in my youth and on which I set my hopes. I think of the time that came afterwards, during which I thought I should paint differently. I see clearly a change in my execution, a greater emphasis on form... Considering the whole, it does seem to me all of a piece... I have always acted on my conviction and I have never strayed from the path of what seemed to me right.]

Ironically, though Corinth's haunting image showed me a tragic dimension to the biblical Samson, there are suggestions that Corinth saw in Samson a symbol of the challenge to struggle against suddenly imposed physical limitations. In that case, the painting could be said to represent more the classic than the tragic vision. Not surprisingly, his near encounter with death caused Corinth to reassess his life.

> Im Dezember 1911 hatte ich einen Krankheitsanfall auszuhalten, der mich dem Tode nahe brachte... Das ganze Leben strich an mir vorbei, ein Leben, welches doch wertvoller erschien jetzt im alleinigen Ringen, als in Jugend und Kraft. Es zwang mir Rechenschaft ab. Hiob rief mir zu: Gürte deine Lenden wie ein Mann – ich will dich fragen, lehre mich! 'Wo warst du, als ich dich erschaffen?' So soll mir nochmals der Weg beleuchtet werden. Eine Spanne winzig kurz erschien sie mir.[34]

> [In December 1911 I suffered an attack of illness that brought me near death. My whole life passed before me, a life that seemed more precious

---

33. 'Januar 1913, Lovis Corinths Vorwort im Ausstellungskatalog', in *Lovis Corinth: Eine Dokumentation*, ed. Thomas Corinth (Tübingen: Verlag Ernst Wasmuth, 1979), 166.

34. Corinth, *Selbstbiographie*, 123. In a letter to his son, Thomas, dated December 1911, Corinth wrote, 'Mit meinen Augen habe ich den Tod gesehen; ich habe ihn gesehen und geglaubt, daß mein Leben beendet gewesen ist' (*Lovis Corinth: Eine Dokumentation*, 152). [I have seen death with my own eyes; I have seen it and believed that my life has come to an end.]

now, straining solitarily, than when I had youth and strength. It called me to account. Job called to me: Gird up your loins like a man – I will question you; declare to me! 'Where were you when I created you?' So my path was once more clear. An incredibly brief span it seemed to me.]

Lothar Brauner writes of *The Blinded Samson* that 'the powerful, but drastically abused figure is shown feeling his way forwards with renewed determination and an energy that threatens to burst the confines of the composition'.[35] Is there determination here, the will to persevere and overcome? Perhaps Corinth had in mind Samson's victory in the temple, yet to occur. Of the Job sketch made around the same time, Corinth's son Thomas observed a number of parallels: between Job's suffering and Corinth's illness; between Job's restoration and Corinth's hope for recovery; between the blessings and success both enjoyed in later life.

> Corinth wählte wohl dieses Thema, weil er eine Parallele sah zwischen seiner Krankheit und dem Leiden des Hiob... Lovis Corinth hoffte es wohl und so geschah es auch, daß er nach dem Tiefpunkt der Krankheit und schwerer körperlichen und seelischen Leiden, ähnlich Hiob, wieder von Gott ausgezeichnet wurde; Lovis stieg, von seiner Krankheit nur zeitweise unterbrochen, dann auf noch größere künstlerische Höhen.[36]

> [Corinth chose this theme because he saw a parallel between his illness and the suffering of Job... Lovis Corinth hoped – and so it happened – that, after the nadir of his illness and severe bodily and spiritual suffering, like Job he would be favoured by God; only temporarily broken by his illness, Lovis rose to even greater artistic heights.]

It would be absurd to expect that, when he resumed painting after his stroke, Corinth's mental state as reflected in his paintings would be

---

35. Brauner, *Lovis Corinth*, 202. As my comments indicate, it is not determination and energy that I observe here, though I can see how the painting could be interpreted this way.

36. 'Bericht von Thomas Corinth', in Thomas Corinth, ed., *Lovis Corinth: Eine Dokumentation*, 156. Corinth's *Selbstbiographie*, in contrast, gives the impression that he was often depressed and suicidal. The *Selbstbiographie* is, however, not a detailed account of Corinth's life but more a series of impressions about events; in the forward Corinth notes that he 'habe nur immer weiter geschrieben, ohne viel auf das Vorgehende zu achten' [simply kept writing without paying much attention to the preceding]. Perhaps when he was depressed he tended to write about it. On the last page of the *Selbstbiographie* is Corinth's sketch of himself as a man of sorrows. The unsettling sketch is reminiscent of *Ecce Homo*, which, in turn, bears similarities to *The Blinded Samson*.

transparent and uncomplicated. We should not be surprised to find both tragic and classic aspects in *The Blinded Samson*, just as both are present in the biblical story on which it is based. Reflecting on the biblical Samson in the light of Corinth's Samson, I have come to the conclusion that, even if the story is not tragic, the hero himself is, in his unsought role as an instrument of no consequence in a divine vendetta against the Philistines. The poet W. H. Auden observed that had the *Iliad* been written in the first person by Achilles or by Hector, it would be a comedy, not a tragedy. This observation interests me more than the question whether or not Auden was right. In the same vein, I propose that if the Samson story in Judges 13–16 had been told in the first person by Samson, it would be a tragedy, not a comedy.

Gustave Moreau's Scene from the Song of Songs

In Gustave Moreau's *Scene from the Song of Songs*, the text is visualized in a shockingly brutal way (fig. 2.4).

Fig. 2.4. Gustave Moreau, *Scene from the Song of Songs*, 1853,
Musée des Beaux-Arts, Dijon

The painting, commissioned in 1852 for the Dijon Museum of Fine Arts and painted in 1853, is based on Song 5.7, in which the female protagonist describes her harsh treatment at the hands of the city watchmen when they encounter her in the street, searching for her lover. The description of the painting I found on the Web is interesting in view of paintings of Sarah presenting Hagar to Abraham discussed in Chapter 4 below. It reads: 'The scene is based on the biblical episode of the Sulamite [*sic*] who, not seeing her beloved return, leaves the city at night to find him, but is attacked and raped by the guards'.[37] It is not unusual for descriptions of biblical art to get the biblical story wrong, but this is wrong in almost every respect. The mention of 'rape', however, creates a connection, even if an erroneous one, with the rape of Hagar, and Moreau depicts an assault that could easily end in rape.

In the text, the scene belongs to the woman's account of a night-time visit by her lover, seeking admittance to her chamber:

5.2   I was sleeping but my heart was awake.
            Listen! My lover is knocking!
        Open to me, my sister, my friend,
            my dove, my perfect one,
        for my head is drenched with dew,
            my locks with mist of the night.
3   I have taken off my robe.
            Am I to put it on again?
        I have washed my feet.
            Am I to get them dirty?
4   My lover reached his hand into the opening,
            at which my body thrilled.
5   I rose to open to my lover,
            and my hands dripped myrrh,
        my fingers, flowing myrrh,
            on the handles of the bolt.
6   I opened to my lover,
            but my lover had turned and gone.
        I swooned because of him.
        I sought him but I did not find him,
            I called him but he did not answer me.
7   *The watchmen found me,*
            those who go the rounds of the city,
            they struck me, injured me,
        took my wrap from me,
            the watchmen of the walls.

37. www.artedossier.it/en/art-history/artist/moreau-gustave/.

8   I place you under oath, women of Jerusalem:
             if you find my lover,
         what will you tell him?
             That I am faint with love.
         . . . .
6.1   Where has your lover gone,
             most beautiful of women?
         Where has your lover turned,
             that we may seek him with you?
2   My lover has gone down to his garden,
             to the beds of spices,
         to graze in the gardens
             and to gather lilies.
3   I am my lover's and my lover is mine,
             he who grazes among the lilies.

Commentators generally agree that Song 5.2–6.3 is a unit,[38] and thus the
account ends happily, for we discover that the woman knows where her
lover is: in his garden among the lilies; in other words, with her.[39] The
transitions in the text are abrupt and the precise meaning of the key v. 7
is difficult to determine. In v. 6, the woman recounts how she 'opens' to
her lover,[40] only to discover that he has gone. She seeks him but does not
find him, calls him but he does not answer. Next (v. 7) she describes the
beating, without bothering to mention that she has gone out into the city
streets in search of him, as in the parallel account in 3.1-5. Then, just as
suddenly, in v. 8 she addresses the women of Jerusalem as though nothing
out of the ordinary has happened, placing them under oath to tell her lover
that she is lovesick, if they should come across him (one wonders how
many people are out in the streets at night).

38. I have omitted from the translation above 5.9-16, where the women of
Jerusalem ask the woman what makes her lover so special and she replies with a
metaphoric description of his body, in effect conjuring him up through praising him.
For the translation and further discussion, see J. Cheryl Exum, *Song of Songs: A
Commentary* (Louisville, KY: Westminster John Knox Press, 2005), 183–210.

39. The woman is a lily (2.1) and a garden (4.12–5.1), and her beloved goes down
to his garden to feed among the lilies (6.2–3).

40. There is no door; on double entendre in this passage, see J. Cheryl Exum,
'In the Eye of the Beholder: Wishing, Dreaming, and *double entendre* in the Song of
Songs', in *The Labour of Reading: Desire, Alienation, and Biblical Interpretation*, ed.
Fiona C. Black, Roland Boer and Erin Runions (Atlanta, GA: Scholars Press, 1999),
71–86; Exum, *Song of Songs*, 190–92.

The critical problem we face with v. 7 is that the text is ambiguous regarding the severity of the watchmen's attack. The verb *hikkah* can mean either to strike or to beat (see, e.g., Num. 22.23, 25; Job 16.10; Prov. 19.25; Exod. 5.14, 16; Jer. 20.2; 37.15 [*nkh* in the *hiphil*]), and *patsa'* can mean to wound or injure. This leaves us with the question, did the watchmen strike the woman, perhaps only once, which resulted in some degree of bodily harm, or did they beat her, seriously injuring her?[41] In addition, it is not clear what type of garment the watchmen take from her. The term I have translated 'wrap', *redid*, occurs elsewhere only in Isa. 3.23, in a list of finery worn by Jerusalem women. It may refer to a veil or light cloak.[42] Earlier in her account, the woman says that she has undressed for bed (v. 3). If she is half-naked except for this garment, as, for example, Michael Fox supposes,[43] then in terms of its portrayal of sexual aggression Moreau's painting is not so far off the mark as one might initially think, especially if we take the verse to mean that the watchmen beat the woman and seriously injure her. Even if this wrap is not an essential piece of clothing, for the watchmen to strip it off her is a contemptuous act of exposure.

Moreau visualizes the scene as a sexual attack. The figures are largely in the shadows, except for the light that falls on the woman's hands and arms, with which she seeks to defend herself, and her torso, and on the exposed upper body of the watchman in front. The darkness that envelops the characters in this night-time scene lends a sinister effect to the painting and requires the viewer to look closely to try to read the facial expressions. The watchmen are tearing at the woman's clothes. They look like revellers, with the one in front holding up what appears to be a goblet of wine. Whether from drunkenness or excitement, he has let the goblet tilt, and some wine spills out. One of the watchmen is leering over the woman's shoulder, while lifting part of her garment with his left hand and

41. Striking someone can result in serious injury, and often death (Exod. 21.12, 18-20; 22.1; Deut. 25.2-3, 11; cf. Prov. 23.13). The combination of striking and wounding appears also in 1 Kgs 20.37, where a prophet has a man strike him so that he can use a bandage to disguise himself as a wounded soldier in order to prevent the king from recognizing him, but here, too, the severity of the beating is not clear.

42. LXX renders *theristron* a light summer garment or veil, here and in the Isaiah passage, a term it also uses for *tsa'iph*, 'veil', in Gen. 24.65 and 38.14, 19.

43. Michael V. Fox, *The Song of Songs and the Ancient Egyptian Love Songs* (Madison: University of Wisconsin Press, 1985), 146; cf. Gianni Barbiero (*Song of Songs: A Close Reading*, trans. Michael Tait [Leiden: Brill, 2011], 264), who assumes she would have been naked in bed or perhaps covered with a mantle.

grabbing at it with his right. She turns her face away from him, holding on to her garment with one hand and trying to push his hand away with the other. The watchmen in the foreground on the right and left of the painting also grasp greedily at the woman's clothing. It is difficult to tell what the watchman in the background on the right is doing. It is unimaginable for the woman pictured here to ignore this experience in order to engage in a playful conversation with her friends about her lover, as the woman in the text does.

The subject of Moreau's painting is the one verse from the Song of Songs in which violent behaviour is described and the woman is its object,[44] a verse that provides artists with an opportunity to paint a salacious scene by appealing to the Bible. Moreau's visualization of Song 5.7 is important for my argument that art can influence the way we interpret a text because it calls attention to a textual detail that has the power to disrupt traditional, sanguine readings of the Song. It asks us to consider the possibility that all is not well in the garden of erotic delights.

The verse represented in Moreau's painting is actually something of a conundrum in Song of Songs interpretation, and Moreau has visualized it in a way we may not like but cannot ignore. Because what happens in Song 5.7 seems out of place in the idyllic world of the Song, this verse has long been a stumbling block for commentators. Typically they endeavour to downplay the violence of the scene, an interpretative move that leads Fiona Black to counter, 'The "finding" and stripping, beating and "wounding" of a woman at night by a group of men is extremely suggestive of rape... and this is a possibility that should not be excluded from this scene'.[45] The watchmen here, unlike the watchmen in the similar episode in 3.1-5, behave surprisingly, and the text offers no justification for their outrageous behaviour. Commentators have offered various expla-nations for it. Some propose that they abuse the woman because they take

---

44. The only other possible candidate is Song 1.6; see below. Another work of art, a stained glass window by Edward Burne-Jones, also draws attention to the disruptive effect of Song 5.7 by giving it a prominent place among twelve panels showing scenes from the Song; see Black and Exum, 'Semiotics in Stained Glass'; Fiona C. Black, 'Nocturnal Egression: Exploring Some Margins of the Song of Songs', in *Postmodern Interpretations of the Bible*, ed. A. K. M. Adam (St Louis, MO: Chalice Press, 2001), 93–104.

45. Black, 'Nocturnal Egression', 101; cf. Fiona C. Black, *The Artifice of Love: Grotesque Bodies in the Song of Songs* (London: T&T Clark, 2009), 192 n. 13: 'If [she is] raped, however, the fear would doubtless not be articulated in the jubilant spirit in which the poem seems to be written'.

her to be a prostitute, but there is no actual evidence to support this view.[46] Others favour a psychological interpretation of the event. Leo Krinetzki, for example, finds the abusive encounter 'psychologically necessary' as a way of testing the strength of love,[47] and Duane Garrett views vv. 2-7 as a representation of the trauma of the woman's loss of virginity.[48]

Because in v. 2 the woman tells us, 'I was sleeping but my heart was awake', many commentators view what happens in the following verses as a dream. Hans-Peter Müller proposes that the beating is the result of the woman's bad conscience regarding the hidden desires expressed in her dream.[49] Similarly, both Ilana Pardes and Donald Polaski liken what happens in v. 7 to an anxiety dream, in which the dreamer, who has internalized patriarchal standards and judgments, disciplines herself for her forbidden wishes.[50] Interpreting v. 7 as a punishment dream has the unfortunate effect of shifting the blame from the watchmen to the woman by making her responsible for her abuse.

The question for me is not 'Is this a dream?' Where would the dream end and what? – reality? – begin? We are dealing with a poem, not an account of events in the lives of real lovers. Does it make a difference if we say a character in the poem is recounting a dream? Would that make what is described in this verse any less problematic? The question for me is, Why did the poet, whose creations the lovers are and whose poem is a carefully crafted work of art, choose to depict such an outrageous incident in a love poem?

In Song 3.8, the guard surrounding Solomon's litter as it makes its way across the steppe is armed 'against the terrors of the night'. It is debated what the dangers are. But the procession encounters no dangers. It is the woman who faces danger at night. The beating by the watchmen, like the only other case of aggression against the woman in the poem, the anger

---

46. See the discussion in Exum, *Song of Songs*, 197–98.

47. Leo Krinetzki, *Das Hohe Lied: Kommentar zu Gestalt und Kerygma eines alttestamentarischen Liebesliedes* (Düsseldorf: Patmos, 1964), 183.

48. Duane Garrett, *Song of Songs* (Nashville, TN: Thomas Nelson, 2004), 204, 214.

49. Hans-Peter Müller, *Das Hohelied* (Göttingen: Vandenhoeck & Ruprecht, 1992), 56.

50. Ilana Pardes, '"I Am a Wall, and My Breasts like Towers": The Song of Songs and the Question of Canonization', in *Countertraditions in the Bible: A Feminist Approach* (Cambridge, MA: Harvard University Press, 1992), 137–39; Donald C. Polaski, '"What Will Ye See in the Shulammite?" Women, Power and Panopticism in the Song of Songs', *Biblical Interpretation* 5 (1997): 78–79.

of her brothers in 1.6, is a blind motif, a potential story that leaves the reader to ponder what, if anything, its significance might be. Perhaps both are evidence of patriarchal constraints, attempts to control the woman, to keep her from stepping out of bounds. The brothers' mistreatment of their sister is not so explicitly represented as that of the watchmen, but neither experience seems to affect the woman very much. She is not deterred by the watchmen's ruthless behaviour, and her quest for her lover ends successfully (6.1-3). Moreover, we need to take into account the pervasiveness of double entendre in the woman's story. What happens in 5.2-6 can be read on different levels: the literal, as a missed encounter, and the erotic, as a veiled account of coition.[51] In the course of her account of the night's events, it transpires that the woman knows where her lover is – in his garden (6.2) – which means that her search for him is not to be taken too seriously, for the garden is both the woman herself and the place where the lovers take their pleasure in each other.

Recognizing double entendre in these verses, while important for understanding the development of the poem, does not mean that the beating should be dismissed as insignificant any more than calling it a dream does. Although the woman is unaffected by her encounter with the watchmen, it is not so easy for modern readers to dismiss it. Nor should it be. The question remains, what are we to make of her scandalous treatment at their hands, however brief and inconsequential it may appear? Moreau's painting offers one answer: Song 5.7 is about humiliation, abuse and a sexual attack. This interpretation, however, is at odds with the positive way the poet deals with the female character in the rest of the Song.

Perhaps the woman's abuse by the watchmen illustrates love's willingness to suffer. This has seemed to me a plausible explanation ever since I saw a BBC television programme called 'The Hamar Trilogy' about the Hamar women of southwest Ethiopia. The women are ritually beaten at a young man's coming of age ceremony, and, according to one of the women interviewed, participating in the ceremony shows you love him enough to suffer for him. The theme of love willing to undergo trials appears in some ancient Egyptian love poetry, where, in fact, we find a young woman prepared to be beaten for her lover's sake:

---

51. As noted above, there is no door; the erotic suggestiveness of vv. 2–6 is heightened by the absence of a direct object: first, the man's request, 'open to me', v. 2; then the woman's intention 'to open to my lover', v. 5, followed by the act itself, 'I opened to my lover', v. 6; see, further, Exum, *Song of Songs*, 192–96.

My heart is not yet done with your lovemaking,
      my (little) wolf cub!
            Your liquor is (your) lovemaking.
I <will not> abandon it
      until blows drive (me) away
           to spend my days in the marshes,
(until blows banish me)
to the land of Syria with sticks and rods,
      to the land of Nubia with palms,
           to the highlands with switches,
      to the lowlands with cudgels.
I will not listen to their advice
      to abandon the one I desire.[52]

The willingness to brave hardship for love's sake is not limited to women in the Egyptian love poems. In another Egyptian love poem, a young man crosses a river in spite of the strong currents and a crocodile in order to be with his beloved on the other side of the river bank.[53] In the Song, however, the man does not undergo suffering for love's sake, and the fact remains that it is a woman whom the poet represents as abused by men in a role of authority.[54]

Some scholars compare the woman's treatment by the watchmen to the ordeals suffered by the goddess in the accounts of the descent of Inanna or Ishtar to the netherworld, in which seven items of the goddess's dress and ornamentation are removed one by one at each of the seven gates to the underworld before she is hung out to die.[55] When I wrote my commentary on the Song of Songs, I did not think this possible parallel merited serious consideration. By drawing attention to an incident that is discordant, disruptive of the basically idyllic picture of love in the Song of Songs, Moreau's painting has led me to reconsider the connection of Song 5.7 to this ancient Near Eastern epic and what that connection might mean for

---

52. P. Harris 500, Group A: No. 4, translated by Fox, *The Song of Songs and the Ancient Egyptian Love Songs*, 10.

53. Cairo Love Songs, Group A: No. 20D; Fox, *The Song of Songs and the Ancient Egyptian Love Songs*, 32.

54. This disparity may well reflect the different expectations ancient Israelite society had for men's and women's behaviour; see Exum, *Song of Songs*, 25–28: 'The Song and Conventional Gender Relations'.

55. For a poetic response that connects Song 5.7 to the Descent, see Yael Cameron Klangwisan, *Jouissance: A Cixousian Encounter with the Song of Songs* (Sheffield: Sheffield Phoenix Press, 2015), 169–76.

interpretation of the Song. Both protagonists are endangered when they cross a threshold. The woman in the Song leaves the safety of her chamber to go outside what is usually considered the woman's domain into the city streets; Inanna/Ishtar dares to enter the netherworld. Both protagonists have clothing taken from them. Both are vulnerable, and both are mistreated. If the poet is alluding to the Descent, what is the significance of the allusion?

Clearly Song 5.7 expresses anxiety, but not over fantasies or forbidden desires. The woman is anxious about not finding her lover. Her anxiety and vulnerability resonates with what is in my view the source of anxiety for the poet as distinct from the anxieties the poet ascribes to the lovers. The poet is concerned about death; that is, the fact that lovers, real lovers, die, and their love dies with them.[56] What if the loved one cannot be found and does not answer because the loved one is no more, like Inanna in the underworld?[57] How can this love be preserved? The poet's answer to this question is the poem, which immortalizes a vision of love as ongoing, never-ending, strong as death – a vision that lives on so long as the poem is read. That this is the poet's aim is apparent from Song 8.6-7, which *tells* us that love is strong as death. Even more important is the way the poem *shows* that love is strong as death, preserving it on the page before us by means of such features as the *illusion of immediacy*, which creates the impression that the action is taking place in the present, unfolding before the reader;[58] *conjuring*, whereby the lovers materialize and dematerialize through speech in an infinite deferral of presence; the *invitation to the reader* to enter into a seemingly private world of eroticism; the *blurring of distinctions* between anticipation, enjoyment of love's delights, and satisfaction (and so between past, present, and future); and the *refusal to reach closure* so that the poem can begin again with desire *in medias res*.[59]

56. The lovers' anxieties are different from the poet's: the man is anxious about the effect the woman has on him; she, about his elusiveness (Exum, *Song of Songs*, 15–17). On the complexity of the woman's anxiety, see Kathryn Harding, '"I sought him but I did not find him": The Elusive Lover in the Song of Songs', *Biblical Interpretation* 16 (2008): 43–59.

57. This is the kind of anxiety captured in Wordsworth's first Lucy poem ('Strange fits of passion have I known'), when, while he is travelling to Lucy's cottage, the thought crosses his mind, '"O mercy!" to myself I cried, "If Lucy should be dead!"'

58. Created not just by presenting the lovers in the act of addressing each other but also through a preference for participles, imperatives, vocatives, together with other grammatical forms that suggest present time.

59. On the way these poetic strategies function to immortalize the poet's vision of love, see Exum, *Song of Songs*, 3–13 *et passim*.

Correspondences between the Song and ancient Near Eastern love poems indicate that the poet drew on a rich cultural tradition of love poetry,[60] and so a familiarity with other ancient Near Eastern textual traditions such as the Descent on the part of the poet and some among the poem's audience is plausible. The menace of death looms large in the account of Inanna's, or Ishtar's, Descent to the Netherworld. If Song 5.7 is an allusion to the Descent, the disrobing of the woman and her abuse by the watchmen could be seen as a foreshadowing of death. Song 5.7 would then provide a trace of the poet's anxiety about death in advance of the climactic affirmation about death's power compared to that of love in Song 8.6.[61] The poet, whose voice never intrudes upon the poem, expresses this anxiety through the voice of the female lover, the introspective character in the poem. In 5.7 she recounts a frightening experience reminiscent of Inanna's, and in 8.6 she urgently wants to be remembered, to be a seal upon her lover's heart as a testimony to the strength of love. In contrast to the many things the poem's lovers have to say about their love, Song 8.6-7 is the only observation about the nature of love in general in the Song, making it indispensable for appreciating the poet's agenda.

Moreau's painting stimulated my thinking about these connections; it led me to look at the text differently. And is that not what we, as scholars, want: to be challenged to look at our material from new angles, whether or not we are persuaded by the results? Even if I am wrong in suggesting that Song 5.7 alludes to Inanna/Ishtar's Descent to the Netherworld and presages the anxiety about death that we find in Song 8.6-7, the disruptive power of this verse will affect my ongoing interpretation of the Song. And I owe that, in part at least, to Gustave Moreau's *Scene from the Song of Songs*.

60. How original the Song may be we cannot be sure, since so little ancient Near Eastern love poetry has survived. In my view, the Song's distinctiveness lies in the way it uses the tradition, selecting, refining, developing, and combining elements from a rich and varied poetic repertory to create a particular vision of love. On the similarities between the Song and ancient Near Eastern love poetry, as well as differences, see Exum, *Song of Songs*, 47–63.

61. That death and decay are what the poem urgently seeks to suppress becomes evident through a deconstructive reading, as compellingly illustrated by Christopher Meredith, '"Eating Sex" and the Unlovely Song of Songs: Reading Consumption, Excretion and D. H. Lawrence', *Journal for the Study of the Old Testament* 42 (2018): 341–62.

Part II

HAGAR

3

THE ABJECTION OF HAGAR

I begin this enquiry into the place of Hagar in the biblical story of Abraham and his family with the expulsion – or what I shall call, borrowing the term from Julia Kristeva, the 'abjection' – of Hagar and her son Ishmael from Abraham's household, recounted in Gen. 21.8-14. I begin with the abjection because it is the key moment in Hagar's story (insofar as one can speak of a minor character as having a 'story'). It is also, for the storyteller and his audience, of crucial significance for Israel's sense of itself as a chosen people. The two other events that concern Hagar take place before and immediately after this one. Hagar's first appearance in the larger story, in Gen. 16.1-16, serves to explain how Hagar came to be in Abraham's household in the first place, and her flight from Abraham's house and return to it prepares the reader for the expulsion in Genesis 21, as we shall see. Hagar's encounter with the divine messenger in the steppe country[1] (Gen. 21.15-21) is a necessary resolution to the abjection, for were the story to end at v. 14, with Hagar and Ishmael cast out with meagre provisions, readers would not only be left wondering what happened to them but perhaps also discomfited, if not scandalized, by the way they are treated.

For all the emotional tension the abjection of Hagar and Ishmael from the Abrahamic family suggests, the story in Gen. 21.8-14 is remarkably restrained. This is not the case in art, where the expulsion is a popular theme (no doubt because it is such an emotional, powerful and disturbing subject) and we find it depicted with a good deal of attention to the possible feelings of the various characters – not only Abraham, Hagar and Ishmael but often Sarah and Isaac as well, although in the text Sarah

---

1. The conventional rendering in English, 'wilderness', is misleading. Hebrew *midbar* is uncultivated, mostly uninhabited land; land used only for grazing. I use 'wilderness' in this chapter and in Chapter 5, however, in keeping with the traditional titles of paintings, 'Hagar in the Wilderness' or 'The Wilderness Rescue', used of Hagar's encounter with the messenger in the steppe after the abjection.

and Isaac are not present when Abraham sends Hagar and Ishmael away. In particular, when artists visualize the scene, they offer viewers what the text withholds, Hagar and Ishmael's point of view, with the result that the viewer, unlike the reader, is openly invited to feel sympathy for them. When Hagar is pictured as directing her look at Abraham, the look inevitably accuses. The accusing look exposes Abraham as cruel and unfeeling, and viewers are likely to find his action difficult to comprehend, if not morally reprehensible.

Abraham is more than just a character in the story, he represents the nation Israel, whose 'father' he is. I refer to the story in Gen. 21.8-14 as the abjection of Hagar, as well as using the traditional nomenclature 'expulsion' or 'dismissal' of Hagar, because of the way Abraham so abruptly and forcefully jettisons Hagar and Ishmael in an attempt to construct for himself (Israel) a distinct, separate identity from his kin, the Ishmaelites, personified in their eponymous ancestor, Abraham's son Ishmael. What Abraham/Israel does in Gen. 21.8-14 could be described, in the psychological terminology of Julia Kristeva, as abjecting a part of his self.[2] In the book of Genesis, Israel is – again to borrow a term from Kristeva – a *sujet en procès*, a subject in process/subject on trial, never able but zealously striving to create stable boundaries between itself and the world around it.[3] A central concern of the patriarchal stories is the issue of Israel's identity: who belongs to the 'chosen people' and who does not? Israel alone receives the special promises of God, while its relatives – the Ishmaelites, the Edomites, the Ammonites, the Moabites, the Midianites, the Arameans – are excluded. Throughout Genesis, Israel is continually defining itself over against its neighbours, whose relation to Israel is described in terms of complex family relationships.[4]

2. Julia Kristeva, *Powers of Horror: An Essay on Abjection*, trans. L. S. Roudiez (New York: Columbia University Press, 1982), 1–7 *et passim*.

3. On the use of genealogies to mark the boundary between Israel and the other, see Ronald Hendel, *Remembering Abraham: Culture, Memory, and History in the Hebrew Bible* (Oxford: Oxford University Press, 2005), 10–12.

4. Indeed, Israel's struggle to define itself against its neighbours is one that continues beyond Genesis; one could say it is a central concern of the Bible. It surfaces forcefully in Ezra–Nehemiah, where Jewish men are instructed to divorce their foreign wives, and it is possible that the Genesis stories took their final shape around the same time as Ezra–Nehemiah (fifth to fourth century BCE) and are influenced by its exclusivist ideology; for different assessments of this influence, see R. Christopher Heard, *Dynamics of Diselection: Ambiguity in Genesis 12–36 and Ethnic Boundaries in Post-Exilic Judah* (Atlanta, GA: Society of Biblical Literature, 2001), 16–22, 174–77; Mark G. Brett, *Genesis: Procreation and the Politics of Identity* (London: Routledge, 2000), 61–85.

Israel as a Subject in Process in the Book of Genesis

Whereas I borrow from Kristeva the notions of abjection and subject in process, or on trial (*le sujet en procès* carries both meanings), I do so not because I rely on or espouse her psychoanalytic theory, but because these concepts seem to me particularly well suited for describing the dynamics I see at work in the narrative. For Kristeva, literature is a way of working through abjection, a way of guarding the borders, of keeping the abject at bay, which is what I am suggesting here about the way the narratives in Genesis function.[5]

According to Kristeva, abjection is an ongoing process, begun when the infant begins to develop a sense of self, whose borders it seeks to establish by abjecting or rejecting what seems to be a part of itself but what it also perceives as threatening the fragile boundaries of its self (initially the mother's body). But abjection is more than a stage through which the subject passes on the way to some other stage. 'Imaginary uncanniness and real threat', the abject is always with us. It is whatever 'disturbs identity, system, order. What does not respect borders, positions, rules. The in-between, the ambiguous, the composite.'[6] There is no such thing as a fixed and stable 'I'. Rather, the subject is always in process, never finished, never complete and never able to create stable boundaries between itself and the 'other'.

Can we speak of *Israel* as a subject in process, an 'I' seeking to establish itself in relation to the world around it? The biblical narrator encourages us to do so, and thereby invites a psychoanalytic literary reading of the story, by personifying Israel in the figures of Israel's ancestors, the patriarchs and matriarchs. Who constitutes the 'self' that calls itself 'Israel', the chosen people, the people of the covenant? Who is not part of this 'self'?[7]

The 'father' of Israel, Abraham, is introduced in Genesis 11 and becomes in Genesis 12 the bearer of the divine promise.[8] Like the infant, for whom, according to Kristeva, the first thing to be abjected

5. Kristeva, *Powers of Horror*, 207–10 *et passim*.

6. Ibid., 4.

7. This is a historical, as well as a psychological, question: what different peoples made up ancient 'Israel'? What were their origins and how did they come together? What interests me here is the biblical construction of Israel's origins, how the biblical writers explain 'Israel'.

8. Throughout this chapter and the next ones, I use the names Abraham and Sarah. The biblical text uses Abram and Sarai until ch. 17, where God changes their names to Abraham and Sarah. Abram probably means 'the (divine) father is exalted'; the name Abraham is given the meaning 'father of a multitude' in Gen. 17.5. Sarah, meaning 'princess', is a variant of Sarai.

is the mother's body, the place of origin that is both 'self' and 'other', Abraham's first step in forging his identity is to separate himself from his origins, his ancestral home in Mesopotamia: 'Go from your country and your kindred and your father's house to the land that I will show you' (Gen. 12.1).[9] To Abraham God promises land (the land of Canaan), numerous descendants (as numerous as the stars of heaven and the sand on the seashore, Gen. 15.5; 22.17) and a blessing that Abraham can confer upon others ('I will bless those who bless you, and those who slight you I will curse', Gen. 12.3).[10] This promise is passed on from father to son: to Isaac (Gen. 26.3-5), to Jacob (Gen. 28.13-14; 35.11-12) and to Jacob's sons, the eponymous ancestors of the twelve tribes of Israel (Gen. 49).[11]

Others, both distant and close relations, are excluded: Moab and Ammon, the children of Abraham's nephew Lot by his own daughters;

---

9. In speaking of 'Israel' as a 'self', I refer to the people as a whole, the chara acters who personify them (Abraham, Sarah, Isaac, Jacob, etc.), their god, and their spokesperson, the narrator. 'People who hear "voices" listen to split-off parts of themselves', as Francis Landy observes in a study of Gen. 22, a story closely related to the expulsion of Hagar and Ishmael, namely, Abraham's near-sacrifice of his other son, Isaac. Or, to put it differently, as Landy does: 'The voice is experienced externally, as the voice of God, and yet is an inner voice, since the narrative has hypostatized in it its creative and questioning drive, and since every outer voice, especially a disembodied one, corresponds to some inner reality. Otherwise it could not be heard.' See Francis Landy, 'Narrative Techniques and Symbolic Transactions in the Akedah', in *Signs and Wonders: Biblical Texts in Literary Focus*, ed. J. Cheryl Exum (Atlanta, GA: Society of Biblical Literature, 1989), 2; repr. in Francis Landy, *Beauty and the Enigma and Other Essays on the Hebrew Bible* (Sheffield: Sheffield Academic Press, 2001), 123–58.

10. The meaning of the last part of 12.3 is uncertain. Possible readings include: 'in you all the families of the earth shall be blessed' or 'by you all the families of the earth shall bless themselves' (i.e. they will say 'may we be blessed like Abraham') or 'all the families of the earth will find blessing in you'; see Claus Westermann, *Genesis 12–36: A Commentary*, trans. John J. Scullion (London: SPCK, 1985), 151–52; Gordon J. Wenham, *Genesis 1–15* (Waco, TX: Word Books, 1987), 265, 277–78; Keith N. Grüneberg, *Abraham, Blessing and the Nations: A Philological and Exegetical Study of Genesis 12:3 in Its Narrative Context* (Berlin: W. de Gruyter, 2003). This third part of the promise receives less attention in the narrative than the first two parts.

11. On the 'promises to the fathers', see Martin Noth, *A History of Pentateuchal Traditions*, trans. Bernhard W. Anderson (Englewood Cliffs, NJ: Prentice-Hall, 1972), 54–58; Claus Westermann, *The Promises to the Fathers: Studies on the Patriarchal Narratives*, trans. David E. Green (Philadelphia, PA: Fortress Press, 1980); David J. A. Clines, *The Theme of the Pentateuch*, 2nd ed. (Sheffield: Sheffield Phoenix Press, 1997), 30–50.

the Ishmaelites, the subject of our story; and Abraham's sons by Keturah, among them Midian, who at one point in the narrative seems to be confused with the Ishmaelites (Gen. 37.25-28).[12] Abraham's grandson Jacob (who receives the name 'Israel') must separate himself from his uncle Laban (Aramea/Mesopotamia), who threatens to include Jacob, his wives and his children in his – Laban's – extended family: 'The daughters are my daughters, the children are my children', he maintains (Gen. 31.43).[13]

Although Egypt, represented in our story by Hagar, is not related to Israel by ties of blood, it nevertheless presents a threat to Israel's self-identity. As a powerful nation, a civilization with an advanced culture and an influential force in the ancient Near East, its attractions are obvious. Israel must protect its self against the appeal of Egypt (absorption into the desired 'other') if it is to maintain its boundaries. Indeed, at the end of Genesis, the boundaries between Israel and Egypt are nearly dissolved when Joseph/Israel is virtually assimilated into Egypt as Zaphenath-paneah, an Egyptian official with an Egyptian wife (Gen. 41.45). Only abjection on a major scale, the exodus, enables Israel to assert its ideal of itself as separate, 'a holy nation' chosen by God (Exod. 19.6).[14] Already in Genesis 12, which prefigures the exodus story, we find a flirtation with assimilation into Egypt when famine causes Abraham to settle in Egypt, where he passes Sarah off as his sister and she is taken into the harem of the pharaoh – only for them to be sent away when God afflicts Pharaoh and his house with plagues. Israel's brief sojourn in Egypt on this occasion provides, as rabbinic tradition records, an explanation for how Sarah came to have an Egyptian servant, Hagar.[15] 'Hagar the Egyptian' is how the biblical narrator introduces her in both Genesis 16 and 21 to foreground her foreignness, her exclusion from the 'self' that is Israel. Hagar the Egyptian is desirable as a surrogate mother because Sarah is infertile; whether or not she is ever an object of Abraham's sexual desire is a matter about which the text is silent.[16]

---

12. Note that we are told that Abraham 'sent them away *from his son Isaac*', Gen. 25.6.

13. On the conflict between patrilocal and uxorilocal marriage in Genesis and the threat Jacob's possible assimilation into his maternal uncle's family poses to Israel's identity, see Exum, *Fragmented Women*, 88–90.

14. See Diana Lipton, *Longing for Egypt and Other Tales of the Unexpected* (Sheffield: Sheffield Phoenix Press, 2008), 13–49.

15. For the view that Hagar was Pharaoh's daughter, see *Gen. Rab.* 45.1.

16. See Chapter 4 below on artistic representations of the scene of Sarah bringing Hagar to Abraham that depict Abraham's desire for the other, foreign woman.

The real threat to Israel's identity in Genesis 16 and 21, however, is not Hagar as representative of Egypt, the potentially desirable 'other', but Ishmael, the son she bears to Abraham, the 'father' of the Ishmaelites. The biblical narrator views the abjection of Hagar and Ishmael as necessary, since the Ishmaelites are a people separate from Israel and have no share in Israel's special covenant with God. But it is problematic as well because the Ishmaelites are also seen to be related to Israel. In Gen. 21.8-14, Ishmael and his mother are cast out of Abraham's household because Ishmael poses a threat to Israel's proper line of descent through Isaac, the son of Abraham's primary wife Sarah (Gen. 17.18-21; 21.12). Although Ishmael is the son of Abraham/Israel, his mother, Hagar, Abraham's wife of secondary rank, is an Egyptian, and the 'true' Israel cannot have a 'foreign' mother.[17] As one of the first in a series of abjections, or separations, in Genesis, the dismissal of Hagar and Ishmael is one of the most forceful. Why, we might ask, are Ishmael and Hagar so violently expelled? The answer would seem to be that the greater the challenge that the self perceives to its boundaries, the stronger its reaction ('I expel *myself*, I spit *myself* out, I abject *myself* within the same motion through which "I" claim to establish *myself*').[18] As Abraham's own flesh

17. For a pure line of descent to be maintained, Israel's mother should be from the same family line as the father. Endogamous marriage, the marriage of men to women from their own patriline, is the ideal in the patriarchal stories since it ensures that Israel will not have to share its inheritance with 'foreigners'; see Naomi Steinberg, *Kinship and Marriage in Genesis: A Household Economics Perspective* (Minneapolis, MN: Fortress Press, 1993), 10–14; Steinberg, 'The World of the Family in Genesis', in *The Book of Genesis: Composition, Reception, and Interpretation*, ed. Craig A. Evans, Joel N. Lohr and David L. Petersen (Leiden: Brill, 2012), 283–84, 286–94; Exum, *Fragmented Women*, 107–10. But who is 'foreign' or 'other' and who is not is not straightforward; the Bible does not give a clear rationale for including some and excluding others, a pattern established as early as the story of Cain and Abel in Gen. 4. Interestingly, whereas Hagar and her son are cast out, when Jacob has sons by his wives' servants, Bilhah and Zilpah, the women remain part of the extended family and their sons are absorbed into 'Israel'; see Exum, *Fragmented Women*, 122, 131–34.

18. Kristeva, *Powers of Horror*, 3, italics hers. In the patriarchal stories of Genesis only one other separation will be as traumatic, when Jacob usurps his brother Esau's blessing and thereby excludes him (that is, Edom) from the line of descent that constitutes Israel. In the story of Jacob's theft of the paternal blessing in Gen. 27 we encounter the powerful emotion lacking in our story—Isaac's anguish and Esau's tears—and the sympathy for the one disinherited, also denied to Hagar and Ishmael. In Esau's case, as well, a reconciliation takes place, a seeming resolution of the enmity between the brothers (Gen. 33.4-11) that will, however, never be truly resolved (cf. Gen. 33.14-17; Amos 1.11; Ps. 137.7).

and blood, Ishmael radically threatens the fragile boundaries of Israel's proper 'self': 'the son of this slave woman shall not be heir with my son Isaac' (Gen. 21.10).

The Accusing Look

Whereas the biblical narrator presents it as God's will that Israel trace its descent through Isaac, he nevertheless finds it difficult to justify the abjection of Abraham's other son, Ishmael, and his mother Hagar, a difficulty that has not gone unnoticed by readers.[19] Biblical scholars, though perplexed and sometimes unsettled by it, are rarely resistant readers of this story; rather, they have tended to accept its premise that the expulsion is divinely ordained and that Ishmael and Hagar have no part in God's plan for Israel.[20] Even though biblical scholarship has become increasingly critical of the story, particularly in the light of

19. For a survey of Jewish and Christian interpretations from ancient times to the Reformation, see John L. Thompson, *Writing the Wrongs: Women of the Old Testament among Biblical Commentators from Philo through the Reformation* (Oxford: Oxford University Press, 2001), 24–99. Of these early, precritical commentators Thompson writes that those who 'were moved to write at any length seem so moved in part because of the troubling nature of the story with its many unanswered questions, but also and often simply out of sadness and sympathy for Hagar' (99); see also John L. Thompson, *Reading the Bible with the Dead: What You Can Learn from the History of Exegesis that You Can't Learn from Exegesis Alone* (Grand Rapids, MI: Eerdmans, 2007), 13–32. Cf. Susan Niditch, 'Genesis', in *Women's Bible Commentary*, ed. Carol A. Newsom, Sharon H. Ringe and Jacqueline E. Lapsley, 3rd rev. ed. (Louisville, KY: Westminster John Knox Press, 2012), 35 ('This passage is a difficult one in biblical ethics... The author works hard to rationalize and justify the emotions and actions of Abraham and Sarah'); Walter Brueggemann (*Genesis* [Atlanta, GA: John Knox Press, 1982], 183) describes the narrator's difficulty well, though his comment makes it sound as though the characters have a will of their own rather than being the creations of a narrator and spokespersons for his ideology: 'The story knows what it wants to tell. Isaac is the child of the future. But the story has no easy time imposing its will on the characters... For some inscrutable reason, God is not quite prepared to yield easily to his own essential plot.'

20. Reading with the ideology of the text leads one to accept the narrator's consolation that God has a plan for Ishmael too. Whereas some scholars defend the actions of Abraham, others criticize Abraham and especially Sarah but are less inclined to be critical of God, as though he were not also a character in the story. Biblical scholars are even less likely to challenge or denounce the premise of the story, finding in the following events (vv. 15-21) evidence that God cares for Hagar and Ishmael.

feminist criticism,[21] it seldom provides the kind of forceful critique we find in art.[22] Some of the most influential readers of this text have been artists. Regardless of their beliefs about the rectitude of the expulsion, when artists paint the scene in which Abraham casts out Hagar and Ishmael they effectively divorce the abjection from its larger context and, consequently, from its ideology. Abraham sends away his wife and his son, with few provisions and with no thought of where they will go, and we see it on the canvas, stripped of its theological (ideological) trappings. This makes it much more difficult for viewers not well acquainted with the story to 'see' any justification for Abraham's treatment of Hagar and Ishmael.[23]

21. Feminist criticism of the Hagar narrative is extensive and growing; for a brief overview, see Thompson, *Writing the Wrongs*, 17–24; and for a comparison of six feminist interpretations (by Katie Cannon, Sharon Pace Jeansonne, Elsa Tamez, Phyllis Trible, Renita Weems and Delores Williams), see Richard D. Weis, 'Stained Glass Window, Kaleidoscope or Catalyst: The Implications of Difference in Readings of the Hagar and Sarah Stories', in *A Gift of God in Due Season: Essays on Scripture and Community in Honor of James A. Sanders*, ed. Richard D. Weis and David M. Carr (Sheffield: Sheffield Academic Press, 1996), 253–73. A classic, early study is Phyllis Trible, *Texts of Terror: Literary-Feminist Readings of Biblical Narratives* (Philadelphia, PA: Fortress Press, 1984), 9–35; see also Trible, 'Ominous Beginnings for a Promise of Blessing', in *Hagar, Sarah, and Their Children: Jewish, Christian, and Muslim Perspectives*, ed. Phyllis Trible and Letty M. Russell (Louisville, KY: Westminster John Knox Press, 2006), 33–69. Katheryn Pfisterer Darr includes rabbinic perspectives along with feminist ones in *Far More Precious than Jewels: Perspectives on Biblical Women* (Louisville, KY: Westminster John Knox Press, 1991), 132–63. A fascinating feminist postcolonial reading is offered by Judith E. McKinlay, 'Sarah and Hagar: What Have I to Do with Them?', in *Her Master's Tools? Feminist and Postcolonial Engagements of Historical-Critical Discourse*, ed. Caroline Vander Stichele and Todd Penner (Atlanta, GA: Society of Biblical Literature, 2005), 159–77; see also McKinlay, *Reframing Her: Biblical Women in Postcolonial Focus* (Sheffield: Sheffield Phoenix Press, 2004), 121–36. Like feminist criticism, postcolonial criticism provides models of reading subversively or deconstructively by showing how the text undermines its ideology of election and exclusion; in addition to McKinlay, see Brett, *Genesis*, 61–85.

22. An important exception is Yvonne Sherwood, 'Hagar and Ishmael: The Reception of Expulsion', *Interpretation* 68 (2014): 286–304.

23. Even if they are aware of the larger story, viewers' recollections are not usually the result of critical reading. Artists sometimes use compression to provide the viewer with other scenes from the story, such as the appearance of the angel to Hagar in the wilderness; see e.g. Jan Mostaert's painting of the expulsion discussed by Sellin, *Fractured Families and Rebel Maidservants*, 105–106.

In what follows my aim is to stage a conversation between the biblical text and some representative artistic renderings of it, a conversation that reveals the importance of visual criticism as an exegetical tool and the contribution biblical art can make to biblical interpretation.[24] Specifically, we shall be looking at how particular works of art handle unresolved questions, gaps, and other difficulties in the text, and how their treatment of the interpretative cruces that biblical scholars wrestle with, or sometimes simply avoid, might help us to see problems of interpretation and conventional solutions in a different light. Because developments or trends in the representation of the expulsion in art are not relevant for the questions I shall be asking, my discussion below deals with seventeenth- and eighteenth-century European paintings. Paintings of biblical scenes flourished in the seventeenth century, perhaps influenced by the large number of illustrated Bibles produced in the sixteenth century, which provided artists with a wealth of subject matter for inspiration.[25] The expulsion was a popular theme in art and there are many examples to choose from.[26] I selected these particular paintings because they are

24. My approach is the opposite of that of Phyllis Silverman Kramer, whose premise that art as exegesis 'should somehow mirror the Bible text' prevents her from allowing artists to engage in the process of interrogating the text; 'The Dismissal of Hagar in Five Art Works of the Sixteenth and Seventeenth Centuries', in *Genesis: A Feminist Companion to the Bible (Second Series)*, ed. Athalya Brenner (Sheffield: Sheffield Academic Press, 1998), 195. The five works Kramer discusses are paintings by Peter Paul Rubens and Jan Steen and engravings by Antonio Tempesta, Mozes van Uytenbrouck and Lucas van Leyden. All of them depict the expulsion in Gen. 21 except Rubens, who depicts the companion story in Gen. 16.

25. Many of my examples are from the United Provinces, where there was considerable interest in Old Testament themes and where Israel's deliverance from Egypt was frequently compared with the struggles of the Dutch against Spain; see Richard Verdi, *Matthias Stom: Isaac Blessing Jacob* (Birmingham: The Trustees of the Barber Institute of Fine Arts, 1999), 23.

26. For an important treatment of seventeenth-century Dutch paintings of Hagar, analysed in the light of contemporary Dutch religious literature and views, see Sellin, *Fractured Families and Rebel Maidservants*. Sellin comments on the enormous popularity of the expulsion scene (some seventy-five surviving paintings) in the northern Netherlands in the seventeenth century. The look and its accusatory power is a topic not addressed by Sellin in her study, though she stresses the sympathetic portrayal of Hagar in seventeenth-century Dutch painting; *Fractured Families*, 101–32. Another important resource is Yaffa England, 'The Expulsion of Hagar: Reading the Image, (Re)Viewing the Story', *Religion and the Arts* 22 (2018): 261–93. See also Anne Marijke Spijkerboer, 'Rembrandt und Hagar', in *Unless Some One Guide Me* [Festschrift K. A. Duerloo], ed. Janet W. Dyk et al. (Maastricht: Shaker, 2001), 21–31.

representative of the different combinations of the characters one finds in art (three, four, or all five of them) and because they allow us to compare the effect of Hagar's not looking at Abraham, or looking away, with her looking at him, all of which, I argue, accuse him and expose his guilt.

In Gen. 21.14 we have a case where the centrality of looking in art draws attention to the way point of view is handled in the text, thereby enabling us to 'see' more clearly what the biblical narrator does not want us to see. By making the ethical problem of the dismissal visible, artistic representations of the biblical text not only pose a challenge to much traditional biblical scholarship, they also provide an effective critical model for resistant readers who would take issue with the biblical ideology and question the necessity of the expulsion.[27]

27. I have in mind the kind of radical critique Carol Delaney offers of the related story of the near sacrifice of Isaac (Gen. 22), when she asks, 'Why is the willingness to sacrifice the child, rather than the passionate protection of the child, at the foundation of faith?', and invites her readers to 'imagine how our society would have evolved if protection of the child had been the model of faith' (*Abraham on Trial: The Social Legacy of Biblical Myth* [Princeton, NJ: Princeton University Press, 1998], 252–53). Cf. Louise Antony, 'Does God Love Us?', in *Divine Evil? The Moral Character of the God of Abraham*, ed. Michael Bergmann, Michael J. Murray and Michael C. Rea (Oxford: Oxford University Press, 2013), 40. In the case of the abjection, one might imagine what the effect of the story might have been if it were about inclusion rather than exclusion, a pressing question in these troubled times. For critical responses to Gen. 21 and 22 respectively, see Sherwood, 'Hagar and Ishmael: The Reception of Expulsion', and Yvonne Sherwood, 'Binding–Unbinding: Divided Responses of Judaism, Christianity, and Islam to the "Sacrifice" of Abraham's Beloved Son', *Journal of the American Academy of Religion* 72 (2004): 821–61. To be fair, the biblical writers are keenly aware of the complex relationship between deeds and their consequences, and often provide a kind of inner-biblical critique; see Joel Rosenberg, *King and Kin: Political Allegory in the Hebrew Bible* (Bloomington: Indiana University Press, 1986), 70–98. Genesis 22 is a case in point; on the parallels between Gen. 22, where Abraham almost kills his son Isaac, and Gen. 21, where he casts out his son Ishmael, see S. Nikaido, 'Hagar and Ishmael as Literary Figures: An Intertextual Study', *Vetus Testamentum* 51 (2001): 221–29; Brett, *Genesis*, 72–78; Jon D. Levenson, *The Death and Resurrection of the Beloved Son: The Transformation of Child Sacrifice in Judaism and Christianity* (New Haven, CT: Yale University Press, 1993), 104–10, 123–24. On parallels between Hagar the Egyptian slave oppressed by Israel and Israel's experience of slavery in Egypt, see Thomas B. Dozeman, 'The Wilderness and Salvation History in the Hagar Story', *Journal of Biblical Literature* 117 (1998): 28–43. In an unconventional, often highly speculative reading, Pamela Tamarkin Reis holds Hagar responsible for the ills that befall her (and Ishmael responsible in 21.9), but sees Israel's 400 years of oppression in Egypt and its laws concerning the treatment of the stranger (*ha-ger*) as God's form of restitution; 'Hagar Requited', *Journal for the Study of the Old Testament* 87 (2000): 75–109.

Like many artistic representations of it, the story of the abjection recognizes the power of looking. An act of looking turns a happy occasion, a feast in celebration of Isaac's weaning, into a portent of misery: 'Sarah *saw* the son of Hagar the Egyptian, whom she had borne to Abraham, playing' (Gen. 21.9). The text invites the reader to look, first through Sarah's eyes, then through Abraham's. But not through Hagar's.[28] Calling Hagar 'the Egyptian' draws attention to her foreignness. Already this designation of her as other, not properly belonging to the 'self' that is Israel, prepares for her abjection. The description of Ishmael as 'the son of Hagar the Egyptian', as though he were not also Abraham's son, represents Sarah's point of view, as becomes clear in the next verse, where, in language cold and distancing, Sarah tells Abraham to 'cast out *this slave* with *her son*, for *the son of this slave* shall not be heir with my son Isaac'. The biblical narrator presents expelling Hagar and Ishmael as Sarah's idea, and, even though God will take her side, Sarah seems jealous, petty and cruel. This is all the more the case because we are not told what so upsets Sarah about Ishmael on this occasion, whether it is simply the sight of him – a reminder of the threat he poses to Isaac's inheritance (Israel's identity) – or what he is doing. What is he doing?[29] Why 'playing' (*metsaheq*), a pun on the name Isaac (*yitshaq*), is so odious to Sarah is barely hinted at, not clarified.[30] Perhaps Ishmael is 'Isaacing', in Sarah's view threatening to

28. Although Hagar is the subject of looking in the companion story, Gen. 16 ('when she *saw* that she had conceived, her mistress was of little account *in her eyes*'), her look is suppressed in Gen. 21 until after the dismissal, when, alone with the child in the desert, the water Abraham gave her having run out, she does not wish to *see* the child die, and God opens her eyes so that she *sees* a well of water. Up until that point, when Hagar for a brief time becomes the subject of her own story, it is Israel's point of view, represented by Abraham and Sarah, that is important, not Hagar's; see Chapter 5 below.

29. For an approach to this question that brings the text in conversation with art, see Jaffa Englard, 'Ishmael Playing? Exegetical Understandings and Artistic Representations of the Verb *meṣaḥēq* in Genesis 21.9', *Biblical Reception* 2 (2013): 16–35.

30. Readers over the centuries have felt the need to fill this gap in the biblical narrative, since 'playing' seems insufficient as a reason for such a drastic reaction, and the meaning of the word is hard to pin down with any precision. The verb *tsahaq* occurs seven times in this particular verbal form, the *piel* (Gen. 19.14; 21.9; 26.8; 39.14, 17; Exod. 32.6; and Judg. 16.25). With an object, it can refer to mocking or ridiculing; without an object (as here) to playing, jesting, revelling, or performing to cause amusement. It can sometimes have a sexual sense, as when Abimelech sees Isaac engaging in sexual play (*metsaheq*) with his wife Rebekah (Gen. 26.8). *Genesis Rabbah* (fourth–fifth century CE) speculates whether 'playing' refers to sexual immorality (cf. the use of the term in Gen. 39.17), idolatry (cf. Exod. 32.6),

take Isaac's position as the legitimate heir. That Ishmael might become an 'Isaac', that is, part of the 'self' that is Israel, is reflected in the pun on Isaac's name.[31]

With Sarah to bear the brunt of the blame, the narrator is able to offer a more favourable picture of Abraham, to give him a different point of view from hers, perhaps one closer to the narrator's own.[32] It bears keeping in mind the complexity of point of view here. The characters Sarah and Abraham are both parts of the 'self' that is Israel; their different attitudes with respect to the abjection reveal the struggle within the self, and provide the narrator a means of working through the dilemma the expulsion presents for Israel. What Sarah calls for is 'exceedingly evil in Abraham's eyes'.[33] Why? 'Because of his son' (v. 11). In contrast to Sarah, Abraham sees Ishmael not as 'the son of this slave' but rather as '*his* son'. He has fatherly feelings toward Ishmael. Nothing, however, is said about his feelings for Hagar.

The narrator presents God as supporting Sarah's demand:

> Do not let it be evil in your eyes because of the boy and because of your slave. Do all that Sarah tells you, because your offspring shall be named through Isaac. I will make a nation of the son of the slave also, because he is your offspring (vv. 12-13).[34]

murder (cf. 2 Sam. 2.14), or mocking Isaac's claim to primogeniture (*Gen. Rab.* 53.11 [Freedman 1:470]). Christian commentators repeated these arguments; see Thompson, *Writing the Wrongs*, 55–56. The Hebrew lacks 'with Isaac her son'. The Greek translation and the Latin Vulgate, followed by most English translations, add the phrase, which has given rise to further speculation about the nature of this play.

31. George W. Coats (*Genesis, with an Introduction to Narrative Literature* [Grand Rapids, MI: Eerdmans, 1983], 153) proposes that Ishmael is playing the role of Isaac and thinks this implies disdain, like his mother's disdain for Sarah in 16.4; Jo Ann Hackett suggests that Ishmael is doing something 'to indicate he was just like Isaac, that they were equals' ('Rehabilitating Hagar: Fragments of an Epic Pattern', in *Gender and Difference in Ancient Israel*, ed. Peggy L. Day [Minneapolis, MN: Fortress Press, 1989], 21); numerous other scholars argue along these lines. Ishmael is otherwise passive in the story, apart from weeping (if he, and not Hagar, as the Hebrew text has it, is the one who weeps, 21.16); in one verse he grows up (21.20).

32. This is in keeping with an ideology that uses the matriarchs to carry out the disagreeable but necessary deeds for Israel to fulfil its destiny, thereby allowing the patriarchs to appear in a better light; see Exum, *Fragmented Women*, 132, 145–47 *et passim*; J. Cheryl Exum, 'Israel's Ancestors: The Patriarchs and Matriarchs', in *The Biblical World*, ed. Katharine Dell (Oxford: Routledge, forthcoming).

33. Often toned down in translations as 'very displeasing in Abraham's eyes'.

34. Both Ishmael himself and Abraham's descendants through Isaac are desig‌nated by the term 'offspring' (*zera'*), but *Israel* will trace its descent through Isaac.

Like Sarah, God speaks of Ishmael and Hagar impersonally as 'the boy', 'your offspring', 'the son of the slave' and 'your slave'. But whereas Sarah appears to lack the quality of mercy, God compensates for his harsh judgment by promising to make a great nation of Ishmael. The promise here, however, is not for the sake of the victims but because Ishmael is Abraham's offspring ('your seed', as opposed to the more intimate 'your son'). Ishmael will be the father of a nation. Just not the chosen nation. Perhaps Abraham is consoled by this promise; in any event, he silently acquiesces.[35] He abjects Hagar with a finality that is all the more palpable for the lack of any sign of emotion. One can imagine considerable pent-up emotion, and artists, as we shall see, are sensitive to how emotionally charged the scene is. But the text, v. 14, says simply:

> Early next morning Abraham took bread and a skin of water and gave them to Hagar. He placed them on her shoulder, with the child, and sent her away.

Although Ishmael is the reason for the dismissal, the narrator mentions him almost incidentally, along with the provisions Abraham gives Hagar when he sends her away. 'The child' seems like an afterthought, since the bread and water are mentioned first, as if the narrator would like to 'forget' about Ishmael. Skilfully, by making Hagar alone the object of the verb 'sent away', the narrator manages to avoid actually saying that Abraham casts out his own son. Where is Abraham sending Hagar, with 'the child', his child? And how are we to understand this portrayal of Abraham? What is a reader to think will happen to mother and child with such meagre provisions?[36]

By not giving the reader access to Hagar and Ishmael's point of view, the biblical narrator manages the reader's sympathy with Hagar and Ishmael, keeping it at a minimum. He struggles to justify the dismissal by focusing on the threat to Israel's identity, expressed both as Sarah's concern for Isaac's inheritance and the divine decision to make Isaac the heir to the promise, rather than on the actual expulsion, to which he gives the barest

---

35. Abraham does not plead for Ishmael as he did earlier ('O that Ishmael might live in your sight', 17.18) nor does he attempt to bargain with God, as he does for the inhabitants of Sodom and Gomorrah in Gen. 18. In Gen. 17, God responds to Abraham's plea by reserving the covenant for Isaac but nevertheless promising to make a great nation of Ishmael, thus setting the stage for Gen. 21.

36. Could not such a wealthy man as Abraham have given them more? is a question frequently asked by readers. Abraham gives gifts to his sons by Keturah when he sends them away so that Isaac will be his sole heir (Gen. 25.6), so why not to Ishmael?

attention possible (one verse, v. 14). He endeavours to make Abraham seem less cruel and more caring at Sarah's expense, and, having allowed the reader direct access to their points of view, their different attitudes to the dismissal, he recounts the dismissal itself in a detached and objective manner, as though observing the scene from afar. He never refers to Ishmael by name, and he avoids drawing attention to the severity of Ishmael's plight by barely acknowledging his presence in the expulsion scene. And he makes the abjection less difficult for readers to accept by assuring us that the son who is cast out will have a future as a great nation, albeit separate and over against the chosen people, Israel (21.13, 18; cf. 16.10).[37]

Justifying the expulsion is, in fact, so difficult that it takes the narrator two attempts to deal with it.[38] As Meir Sternberg describes the situation, '[F]aced with a task of persuasion that bristles with difficulty, the biblical narrator would rather go to extra compositional trouble than simply load the dice for or against the problematic character or cause'. First (Gen. 16) Hagar flees from Abraham's household while she is still pregnant with Ishmael. She flees of her own volition, to escape the harsh treatment she receives at Sarah's hand. She is sent back by God, only to be driven out years later, with her son (21.8-14). Of the differences in the accounts Sternberg observes:

37. As Danna Nolan Fewell notes, the conclusion of the story in vv. 15–21 is double-edged: 'On the one hand, we are told of God's presence with and protection of Ishmael and, by extension, his mother. And on the other hand that very notice of divine presence and protection *permits the reader to give no more thought to their welfare*'; 'Changing the Subject: Retelling the Story of Hagar the Egyptian', in *Genesis: A Feminist Companion to the Bible (Second Series)*, ed. Athalya Brenner (Sheffield: Sheffield Academic Press, 1998), 194 n. 23; italics mine.

38. The traditional (source critical) view saw the two accounts in Gen. 16 and 21 as variants and attributed the material in them to different sources; e.g. Hermann Gunkel, *Genesis*, 6th ed. (Göttingen: Vandenhoeck & Ruprecht, 1964), 226–33; John Skinner, *A Critical and Exegetical Commentary on Genesis*, 2nd ed. (Edinburgh: T. & T. Clark, 1930), 320–21; Gerhard von Rad, *Genesis: A Commentary*, trans. John H. Marks (Philadelphia, PA: Westminster Press, 1961), 226; E. A. Speiser, *Genesis* (Garden City, NY: Doubleday, 1964), 153–57; Bruce Vawter, *On Genesis: A New Reading* (London: Geoffrey Chapman, 1977), 248; Levenson, *The Death and Resurrection of the Beloved Son*, 82–110; Horst Seebass, *Genesis II: Vätergeschichte I (11,27–22,24)* (Neukirchen-Vluyn: Neukirchener Verlag, 1997), 91–94, 183–85; Hendel, *Remembering Abraham*, 37–40; Philip Y. Yoo, 'Hagar the Egyptian: Wife, Handmaid, and Concubine', *Catholic Biblical Quarterly* 78 (2016): 215–35. Increasingly, scholars are questioning this hypothesis, see e.g. T. D. Alexander, 'The Hagar Traditions in Genesis XVI and XXI', in *Studies in the Pentateuch*, ed. J. A. Emerton (Leiden: Brill, 1990), 131–48.

In each variation on the principle, the narrator so extends and divides his treatment as to lead up to a crucial scene that might otherwise *prove too much for the reader*: the first episode softens our response to the second by getting us used to the idea of the antagonist's deprivation or, more radically, splitting it into two gradated and differently motivated acts on the protagonist's part.[39]

All of these various narrative transactions reveal the narrator's unease about the treatment of Hagar and Ishmael, if not a sense of guilt. We need not ascribe to the biblical narrator a conscious sense of guilt to recognize that there is much to feel guilty about. Hagar is a servant, a slave. The use (and abuse) of Hagar by Sarah and Abraham in Genesis 16 looms in the background: we do not know how Hagar is affected by being given to Abraham by Sarah for the purpose of bearing a son who is to be reckoned as Sarah's son, for here too Hagar's point of view is suppressed. To cast her out with her child compounds the injury done to her.

Ignoring Hagar's point of view does not make the ethical problem of abjecting her go away, as paintings of the expulsion persistently remind us. A variety of cultural, social, religious or personal considerations will have influenced artists whose subject was this biblical story. They may have been following iconographic tradition or constrained by the requirements of their patrons or desirous of furthering their reputation (and receiving commissions) by putting their own stamp on the subject. Whatever led them to this subject, they had to decide how to represent both the scene – who is present, where are they and what are they doing? – and the characters – their ages, physical appearance, attire and, in particular, their reactions to what is happening. By drawing attention to Hagar and Ishmael's obvious distress, intentionally or not, artists call their treatment at Abraham's hand radically into question. Hagar and Ishmael become subjects instead of, as in the biblical story, objects ('this slave', 'the son of this slave', 'the boy', 'your slave'), and, as subjects of the story the painting tells, they are usually the centre of attention or they vie with Abraham and Sarah, and sometimes Isaac, for the viewer's attention. The more a particular painting arouses our sympathy for Hagar and Ishmael, the less we are able to comprehend Abraham's behaviour. Sarah is often included in paintings of the expulsion. Her presence serves to remind the viewer that she was the one who called for expulsion, and

39. Meir Sternberg, *The Poetics of Biblical Narrative: Ideological Literature and the Drama of Reading* (Bloomington: Indiana University Press, 1985), 494, italics mine. For a trenchant analysis of the two versions of the expulsion, see Karalina Matskevich, *Construction of Gender and Identity in Genesis: The Subject and the Other* (London: T&T Clark, 2019), 131–52.

thus allows Abraham, who opposed it, to appear in a better light. God is not included in any of the paintings discussed here, nor in post-sixteenth-century painting generally, which leaves Sarah without the divine support the biblical narrator gives her.[40] By focusing on the moment when Hagar and Ishmael are sent away – fixing in time before our eyes the very part of the story that the biblical narrator wants to pass over quickly – artists draw attention to Israel's responsibility for Hagar and Ishmael's plight, and often its insensitivity or its guilt, wherever their own sympathies might lie.

One cannot look at *Hagar and Ishmael* by Barent Fabritius without feeling Hagar's anguish and Ishmael's trepidation (fig. 3.1). Hagar is disconsolate, weeping upon Abraham's shoulder and clinging to him, and Ishmael has an apprehensive look on his face. Abraham supports Hagar with his right arm, but with his left hand he points with his finger into the distance, in what in the iconographic tradition is his typical gesture of dismissal. In Abraham's pose, Fabritius captures well on canvas the conflict within Abraham, who is distressed by the expulsion but yields to the divine command. Indeed Fabritius seems not only to invite sympathy for Hagar and Ishmael, but also for Abraham, who looks down at Hagar tenderly and perhaps with regret. He must send her away – the dismissing gesture is decisive – but he does not want to. By making this a highly emotional scene, Fabritius highlights the bond between Abraham and Hagar that the biblical text ignores, a bond that makes the expulsion all the more painful. Nevertheless, since Sarah is not represented in the painting, there is no one for the viewer to blame except Abraham.[41] Blaming Abraham is not unjustified, since only Abraham can send Hagar and Ishmael away. As a woman, Sarah does not have the authority to do it herself, which is why she tells Abraham to do it.[42]

40. Depictions of God would have been avoided in most post-sixteenth-century painting due to the widespread preference for realistic figures in art and the interest in portraying the story in human terms.

41. This is not to say that the viewer familiar with the story would not blame Sarah and perhaps even view her absence at this tender moment as a sign of her utter lack of empathy. God, who commands Abraham to do as Sarah tells him, is not represented in the painting either, but viewers, like readers, are likely to read with the ideology of the text and blame Sarah, who shows no pity, and not God, who promises to make a nation of Ishmael as well as Isaac.

42. Sarah clearly has power here (the ability to gain compliance with her wishes, to achieve her ends) but only Abraham, as a man and head of the household, has the authority to send his wife of secondary rank and their son away. Earlier (Gen. 16) Sarah achieves her goal by complaining to Abraham about Hagar's attitude toward her ('I am lowered in her eyes'), venting her anger on Abraham ('My wrong is upon you!... Yahweh judge between you and me!', 16.5).

Fig. 3.1. Barent Fabritius, *Hagar and Ishmael*, 1658,
Courtesy Metropolitan Museum of Art

Like many paintings of this scene, the inhospitable landscape underscores the cruelty of the dismissal and further arouses the viewer's
sympathy for Hagar and Ishmael's predicament. The colours of the
landscape reflect the mood. They are dark and muted. Apart from the
white of Abraham's turban and Hagar's headdress and sleeve, the only
colour that stands out is the red of Abraham's and Ishmael's clothing, the
only thing that connects father and son. The son looks on, and his gaze
in the painting invites the viewer to adopt his perspective and to imagine
his reaction to the emotionally fraught scene between his parents, a strong
contrast to the way the biblical narrative ignores him. There is a question
as to how old Ishmael would have been when Abraham sent him away.
Genesis 16.16 gives Abraham's age as eighty-six when Ishmael is born
and 21.5 reports that he is one hundred when Isaac is born. The expulsion
takes place after Isaac is weaned, and weaning typically took place about
three years after birth, which would make Ishmael sixteen or seventeen
when Abraham sends him away. But in Gen. 21.14, he seems to be an
infant, whom Abraham places on Hagar's shoulder along with the bread
and water and whom, in the sequel to the expulsion, his mother casts
under a bush because she does not want to watch him die of thirst in the
steppe (v. 15; cf. also v. 18).[43] Fabritius makes Ishmael a little boy, which
is how he is usually portrayed in paintings of the abjection. Awkwardly
holding the jug of water Abraham has given his mother, he stands alone
and looks on, a frightened, bewildered child, whose pained expression
and outstretched arm suggest that he, too, is in need of comfort. In his left
hand he holds a bow, foreshadowing his destiny (v. 20).

In Pieter Lastman's painting of the dismissal (fig. 3.2), Abraham's right
hand rests on Ishmael's head in a gesture of blessing,[44] and with his other
hand he grasps Hagar's arm. Although Lastman is relatively sympathetic
to Abraham, both Hagar's look, directed at Abraham, and her pose reveal
her bewilderment at being cast out. The look accuses, and her left hand
is stretched out in a pleading gesture that seems to say, Why?, How?, and
Where shall we go? Abraham returns her gaze, and one wonders how long
he can bear the eye contact. Ishmael is clearly distraught. His position
as the central figure in the painting, between his parents, together with
Abraham's solicitous gesture, reminds the viewer that he is Abraham's
son as well as Hagar's. Although his feet are planted firmly on the spot, he
has turned away from his parents toward the viewer, in a pose that draws

43. Scholars have traditionally explained the discrepancy as the result of different
sources used by the final redactor of Genesis.

44. According to Sellin (*Fractured Families and Rebel Maidservants*, 108), this
blessing gesture appears to be a sixteenth-century Dutch innovation.

the viewer's attention to him and elicits our sympathy. His hand is on his face as though he were weeping.

Fig. 3.2. Pieter Lastman, *The Dismissal of Hagar*, 1612, Kunsthalle Hamburg

The subjects' clothing, in particular Abraham's turban and ornate robe and Hagar's headdress, are characteristic of the orientalizing of biblical characters that takes place in paintings of this period, while the setting itself is more European than Near Eastern.[45] As is conventional in paintings of the expulsion, the landscape behind Hagar, her destination, is dark and unwelcoming, emphasizing the hopelessness of Hagar and Ishmael's situation. In contrast with the stark landscape on Hagar's side of the painting is a domestic scene in the background behind Abraham, in which Sarah and Isaac appear along with a maid milking a cow.

Similarly, against a very dark and foreboding backdrop, Willem van Mieris's Hagar looks pleadingly at Abraham, while pointing to Ishmael, as if to ask how a father could do such a thing to his own child (fig. 3.3). Abraham's outstretched hand fills the distance between him and Hagar, holding off mother and child. Bathed in light, Hagar, whose scant clothing suggests her vulnerability, immediately attracts the viewer's eye, even as she draws Abraham's and the viewer's attention to Ishmael. On the far side of the painting opposite Abraham, Ishmael is clearly more Hagar's child than Abraham's. His back is to the viewer, and we cannot tell

45. See O'Kane, 'The Bible in Orientalist Art', 290–95.

whether he is looking at his mother, as he is in many paintings, or at the wilderness that lies before him. Sarah is barely visible in the background behind Abraham to share the blame with Abraham, but she is so hard to see that a viewer could be forgiven for holding Abraham more responsible than Sarah for the expulsion.

Fig. 3.3. Willem van Mieris, *The Expulsion of Hagar*, 1724,
The Hermitage, St. Petersburg

A typical representation of the abjection, with Sarah and Isaac as visual clues to the subject matter, is Carlo Maratta's *The Banishing of Hagar and Ishmael* (fig. 3.4). Abraham is virtually chasing Hagar and Ishmael out, as if the sooner they have left his household the better. Hagar looks back pleadingly, and somewhat fearfully, or at least apprehensively, at the father of her child who is so vigorously thrusting them away, while Ishmael seems ready to embrace expulsion. In contrast to most portrayals of him, he does not seem distressed but rather points to the land beyond, bathed in light as though bearing promise, as if willingly accepting his future outside the Abrahamic household. Sarah and Isaac, the son for whose sake the expulsion is necessary, are in the background.

Fig. 3.4. Carlo Maratta, *The Banishing of Hagar and Ishmael*, 1670–1680, Church of St Francis, Sant' Agata de' Goti

The entire family also appears in *Hagar and Ishmael Banished by Abraham* by Flemish painter Pieter Jozef Verhaghen (fig. 3.5). The balanced composition is decentred by the unaccommodating wilderness, Hagar's destiny, on the right. Hagar, on whom the light falls, is the central figure in the family grouping and focus of the viewer's attention. On either side of her are the two children and beside them are Sarah and Abraham. Abraham, dressed in his oriental-looking elaborate white turban and red robes that suggest his prosperous status, does not look like the centenarian of the biblical account or the aged Abraham of many paintings. His beard has not yet turned grey, and he does not appear considerably older than Hagar. Sarah, who is often pictured as old, wrinkled and unattractive, appears rather youthful and comely, despite the fact that she wears drab clothing that conceals most of her features (in fact, she resembles Hagar). Since Abraham and Sarah do not look as though they are well past their child-bearing years, a viewer might wonder why it was necessary for Abraham to take Hagar as a wife in the first place. Hagar is young and pretty, which, together with her alluring attire – in particular the low-cut blouse that exposes her breasts and the sleeve that seems to have slipped off her shoulder – suggests the sexual attraction she possibly holds, or held, for Abraham.

Though Ishmael should be older than Isaac, the two children look about the same age. Ishmael, who holds onto his mother's hand as he often does in paintings of the expulsion, has one foot forward, as if he is already beginning his journey into the unknown. Interestingly, Abraham is on the side of Hagar with Ishmael and not on her other side, with Sarah and Isaac, a sign of his attachment to Hagar and Ishmael as well as a forceful reminder that he, Hagar and Ishmael form a family unit that he is now disavowing.[46]

Fig. 3.5. Pieter Jozef Verhaghen, *Hagar and Ishmael Banished by Abraham*, 1781, Koninklijk Museum voor Schone Kunsten, Antwerp

Balance in the composition extends to the gaze, and the artist manages to convey a good deal about the characters' possible feelings by the way he handles focalization. Abraham and Sarah are both looking at Hagar, as if they are uncertain how she is going to respond. Will she go willingly? Will she put up resistance? Abraham looks as though he is escorting Hagar out the door. He has one hand behind her back and with the other gestures toward the wilderness. There is a certain tentativeness in his pose: he is urging her on with his outstretched hand, not pointing her away insistently. Sarah's left arm is behind Hagar, and she too seems to be tentatively urging Hagar on her way. Hagar stands still; she has not

46. Abraham is placed between Sarah and Isaac, on one side, and Hagar and Ishmael, on the other, in the majority of sixteenth- to nineteenth-century paintings of the expulsion according to England, 'The Expulsion of Hagar'.

yet taken a step down from the threshold, unlike Ishmael, who has begun to move forward. She does not return either Abraham's or Sarah's gaze, but instead looks down at Isaac. She seems sad, perhaps resigned, but the look nevertheless accuses. This golden-haired, innocent-looking little boy, whose physical appearance marks him out as the favoured child, is the cause of her and her son's predicament. The children, one the bearer of the promise and the other abjected, look at each other. Their mutual gaze is open to interpretation. They seem not to understand the meaning of this fraught and decisive moment and appear to be sad to part. Yet Ishmael's look at Isaac, like that of his mother, accuses. Does his brother want them to go away? Sarah seems to be restraining Isaac, who strains to get a better look at his brother. With his left hand he may be pushing against the pillar to exert a counterforce against his mother's grip. Is this what prevents him from extending his hand to his brother? Any harmony we might imagine to exist between the brothers is illusory, since Isaac, in order to become the bearer of the promise, the true Israel, must separate himself from Ishmael.

Like the biblical narrator who uses Sarah to make Abraham look better, Verhaghen includes Sarah to share the blame. But he goes a step further. Although, in the biblical account, Isaac, or rather safeguarding Isaac's future as the true Israel, is the reason for the expulsion of Hagar and Ishmael, the biblical narrator is careful to keep Isaac in the background. The expulsion is Sarah's idea, supported by God and carried out by Abraham. Isaac is only an infant; the expulsion appears to take place soon after he is weaned, possibly the next day. Verhaghen, in contrast, involves Isaac by means of Hagar's and Ishmael's gaze at him. In spite of Abraham and Sarah's tentativeness, Hagar's apparent calm and the children's seeming lack of comprehension, the painting conveys a sense of melancholy at what is taking place. The gloomy surroundings provide an atmosphere of impending doom and impress upon the viewer the seriousness of the situation. Whereas the biblical account gives the reader little time to contemplate the abjection, the painting asks viewers to consider it from the perspective of all of the characters involved.

Another painting of the dismissal, Guercino's *Abraham Casting Out Hagar and Ishmael*, in which the protagonists appear as large half-figures, draws the viewer more closely into the proceedings (fig. 3.6). The artist has dispensed with the barren landscape we find in many paintings of the scene. A huge column and a foreboding cloudy sky form the backdrop, leaving nothing to vie with the characters for the viewer's attention. Guercino dramatically represents the division of the family by placing Abraham and Sarah on one side of the painting and Hagar and Ishmael

on the other. The pure line of Israel's descent through Isaac is vigilantly
guarded, with Abraham making a multi-layered gesture of dismissal. With
one hand he points determinedly into the distance, while his pointing
finger at the same time draws the viewer's attention to Ishmael. With his
other hand he makes a gesture of blessing that simultaneously holds Hagar
off, symbolically barring the way.[47] Ishmael weeps. His mother comforts
him. The handkerchief she holds in her hand appears frequently in the
iconographic tradition to show she has been weeping. Over her shoulder
she carries a bag containing the few provisions Abraham has given them.
Sarah has quite literally turned her back on the proceedings. Abraham and
Sarah's coldness, their lack of emotion, reflects the reserve with which
the biblical narrator presents the expulsion itself (21.14). The artist fills
the telling gap in the biblical narrative by supplying Hagar and Ishmael's
reactions.

Fig. 3.6. Guercino (Giovanni Francesco Barbieri), *Abraham Casting Out
Hagar and Ishmael*, 1657, Pinacoteca di Brera, Milan

47. Abraham's blessing that simultaneously bars the way is like the biblical
promises to Hagar about Ishmael's future: in spite of the seeming concern for the
outcasts, it nonetheless excludes Ishmael from the chosen people.

A viewer can readily sympathize with Hagar and Ishmael against the callous Abraham and Sarah. Abraham looks at Hagar, who returns his gaze with a look that expresses hurt and bewilderment, as if to ask, What have we done to deserve this? A look that accuses. Abraham's face is set and his pose conveys intransigence.[48] He is old, whereas Hagar is young and attractive, a typical contrast that inevitably invites us to read into Hagar's accusing look questions about his earlier sexual appropriation of her. Sarah appears to be older than Hagar because of the way she wears her hair and the wrinkles in her neck, but she has not yet turned grey and is not as old as Abraham.

Sarah, who has turned away, and Abraham, who sends Hagar away, share the blame, but Guercino leaves Isaac out of the conflict. Sarah's pose, with her back to the proceedings, makes it clear that, in the end, responsibility for the abjection rests with Abraham. Although she demanded the abjection, Sarah does not want to watch. Is it because she is unfeeling, or might we read into her pose feelings of guilt for setting this tragic event in motion?

The stern-faced Abraham, who does the dismissing, and Hagar, whose pleading look accuses him, provide the centre of dramatic interest in the painting. The considerable space between the faces of Hagar and Abraham is occupied only by Abraham's hand, raised in a gesture of repudiation. We cannot see the faces of Sarah and Ishmael, who stand at opposite borders of the painting, as far apart from each other as possible. It is hard to imagine that this pitiful little boy, crying on his mother's breast, was the cause of Sarah's demand for his and his mother's expulsion.

As these representative examples of paintings of the abjection reveal, the greater our sympathy for Hagar and Ishmael, the more critical we are likely to be of Abraham, who represents Israel. This is especially clear in Guercino's painting, where the unsympathetic poses of Abraham and Sarah seem to encourage the viewer to judge them through Hagar's accusing eyes. Even when we cannot see Hagar's face, we know that her gaze accuses. In Adriaen van der Werff's version of the expulsion (fig. 3.7), Abraham makes a gesture of blessing with one hand and of dismissal with the other. The expression on his face seems solicitous. Indeed, apart from Isaac, who is smiling, van der Werff appears to invite the viewer's sympathy for all the characters. Sarah's expression is particularly ambiguous. Her presence reminds the viewer of her role in the abjection, but she appears rather more sorrowful than self-satisfied at what she has brought about.

48. The eyes are hard to see, but to me they look cold. Reading facial expressions in paintings is, however, particularly difficult.

Fig. 3.7. Adriaen van der Werff, *The Dismissal of Hagar*, 1697,
Gemäldegalerie Alte Meister, Dresden

Against the stark unaccommodating landscape that lies ahead of them,
Hagar and Ishmael, upon whom light falls, stand out. They are dressed in
almost classical style, scantily clad and barefoot in contrast to the fully
clothed true family of Abraham, whose future, unlike theirs, is secure.
As in numerous paintings, Hagar holds a handkerchief as a sign she has
been weeping. Most striking is Ishmael, who stands between his father
and his mother and who looks back longingly. His pose captures dramatically his reluctance to leave, and he is barely holding on to his mother's

hand. Hagar looks at Abraham, while Ishmael's gaze is focused on Isaac, for whose sake he must be cast out. He looks as though he would gladly change places with Isaac or even *be* Isaac, which calls to mind the 'Isaacing' that provoked his dismissal (Gen. 21.9).

Granted that a painting like van der Werff's can elicit sympathy for Abraham and Sarah, is it possible for an artist to represent the dismissal in a way that does not accuse them of ill-treating Hagar and Ishmael? Yes, but it seems to me only by rendering the scene virtually unrecognizable or by departing noticeably from the way the biblical narrator tells the story.[49] Consider, for example, another painting of the scene by Fabritius, with whom we began. Like his *Hagar and Ishmael*, Fabritius's *Hagar and Ishmael Taking Leave of Abraham* is sympathetic to Abraham, but unlike that painting this one is almost as reticent as the biblical text with regard to the characters' emotions (fig. 3.8).

It is revealing to compare this painting with the earlier, influential work by Pieter Lastman, discussed above (fig. 3.2).[50] Unlike Lastman's painting, this one is not particularly fraught with anxiety. Fabritius follows Lastman in placing the three characters at a crossroad. His Abraham, whose right hand rests on Ishmael's head, is virtually identical to Lastman's, both in his pose and his attire. He is younger, however, and the Hagar and Ishmael of this painting differ significantly from Lastman's. Even if Lastman is somewhat sympathetic to Abraham, there is an accusation in his painting that is absent in Fabritius's. Whereas Lastman's Ishmael is clearly upset, Fabritius's Ishmael has his back to the viewer, so that we do not see any emotion. Moreover, the light that falls on Ishmael in Lastman's painting draws attention to the forlorn child, whereas the striking feature of Ishmael in Fabritius's painting is his head in the centre of the painting, upon which Abraham's hand rests in a gesture of blessing.

---

49. See, for example, the paintings discussed by Sellin that teach humility, obedience, and discipline by contrasting a 'bad' Hagar to a diligent Dutch maidservant (*Fractured Families and Rebel Maidservants*, 122–25). These paintings change the biblical story by adding another character, the good, hardworking servant; they show Hagar and Ishmael being cast out in the background, so that a viewer cannot see their faces well and thus sympathize with their point of view. Also interesting to compare are paintings discussed by Sellin that appear to ascribe the expulsion to sibling rivalry by including scenes of hostility between the brothers (104–6). They use compression to remind the viewer of Hagar's encounter with the angel in the wilderness (Gen. 21.15-21), reproducing the biblical narrator's strategy of making the abjection less problematic by showing the divine concern for the victims.

50. On Lastman's influence on later painters of the scene, including Rembrandt and his school, see Netty van de Kamp, 'Die Genesis: Die Urgeschichte und die Geschichte der Erzväter', in Tümpel, ed., *Im Lichte Rembrandts*, 30.

Fig. 3.8. Barent Fabritius, *Hagar and Ishmael Taking Leave of Abraham*,
ca. 1650–1660, Fine Arts Museums of San Francisco

Like the biblical narrator, Fabritius here seems protective of Abraham:
there is little to suggest any guilt on Abraham's part for sending his
wife and child away. The act of blessing replaces the telltale dismissing gesture that we find in the artist's *Hagar and Ishmael* (fig. 3.1), and
the colour scheme is warmer too. Abraham looks solicitously at Hagar.
Significantly, although Hagar has a solemn look on her face, she does
not look at Abraham in a way that is unmistakably accusatory nor does
she make a well-defined gesture of protest. It is not entirely clear that
the woman and child are being cast out. One could imagine that they are
going on a journey and the man is wishing them a safe return. 'Taking
leave' in the title makes the proceedings seem less disturbing. Were it not
for the title, a viewer might not recognize the subject. Viewers who know
the story, however, might well surmise that Hagar's look is accusing, and
perhaps see in the position of her left hand (it is hard to see) a trace of
unwillingness.

There is no one, definitive way of 'reading' biblical art any more than
there is a single, incontestable reading of the text. At the beginning of this
chapter, I called attention to the restraint shown by the biblical narrator in
recounting the abjection of Hagar and Ishmael compared to what happens

when the events in the narrative are shown through the medium of art. The critical perspective and insights visual criticism provides, when combined with textual analysis, make, in my view, a compelling case for including visual criticism in the repertory of approaches available to the biblical interpreter. Artistic representations of the abjection not only show us what the biblical text withholds, Hagar and Ishmael's point of view, thereby arousing our sympathy, they also point to something fundamentally wrong with the biblical picture: the removal (though not entirely successful and not without guilt) of responsibility from Abraham/Israel.[51] In the text, at God's command Abraham simply sends Hagar and Ishmael away. In art, we typically witness the pain, and tragedy, of a family being broken up, even if, like the biblical narrator, artists view the expulsion as a fait accompli.

Whereas the biblical text is concerned with drawing distinctions, with establishing Israel's identity as an independent 'self', visualizations of the abjection draw attention to the bonds that connect the characters and encourage the viewer to contemplate the meaning of these bonds and the obligations they imply. Captured on the canvas as in the process of being cast out, Hagar and Ishmael are still, if precariously, part of the extended family of Abraham/Israel, as if the abjection could be halted or the viewer cry 'Stop!' In the twenty-first century, when religious and ethnic divisions still tear societies apart, we might do well to consider the consequences of Abraham/Israel's exclusion of Hagar and Ishmael because he refuses to recognize the 'self' in the other, the connectedness of the human family. In the Bible, the boundaries Israel constructs for itself are tenuous and fragile. After his abjection, Ishmael lingers on the borders of the self that is Israel, returning 'home' to bury his father (Gen. 25.9) and occupying a space at the margins of Israel's subjectivity (Gen. 16.12; 25.18; 37.25-28, 36; Judg. 8.24; Ps. 83.6). Abjection is traumatic and comes at a price, as visual representations of Abraham casting out Hagar and Ishmael illustrate touchingly and compellingly. Why is the expulsion necessary? Why must there be a chosen people?

---

51. In 'The Accusing Look', 158–61, 165–68, I examine two works of art not treated here: Gabriel Metsu's painting *The Expulsion of Hagar* (1650–1655) and George Segal's sculpture *Abraham's Farewell to Ishmael* (1987). Sculpture is particularly interesting because the viewer can analyse it from different perspectives simply by moving around. And because this sculpture is life-size, the viewer can feel like a participant in the proceedings and can engage with the figures on different levels. There are four figures, Abraham, Sarah, Hagar and Ishmael. Interestingly the title does not acknowledge the women; they are like planets revolving around the sun, with the men as the fixed focal point in the centre.

4

THE RAPE OF HAGAR

Having considered the definitive event in the story of Hagar – her abjection, with Ishmael, from Abraham's household, which tackles the problem that Ishmael poses for Israel's self-understanding – let us turn now to the earlier account of Hagar's ill-treatment by Abraham and Sarah. Hagar is introduced in Gen. 16.1-2 as Sarah's Egyptian slave and the solution to the problem of her infertility. In Gen. 16.3-4, Sarah gives Hagar to Abraham as a wife in order to have a son through her. Whether the matriarchs' giving of their female servants to their husbands in order to have children through them, for which there is ancient Near Eastern evidence, was once a custom in Israel or is a legal fiction, the story takes the state of affairs for granted.[1] In their visualizations of this scene, usually with the title 'Sarah Presenting Hagar to Abraham', artists draw attention to narrative gaps in relation to a key issue, the rape of Hagar, and, related to it, the question of the patriarch's desire.

Rape is a serious accusation, and my use of the term 'rape' with reference to Gen. 16.4 is open to the charge of anachronism. In the patriarchal world of ancient Israel, what happens in this text would not have been regarded as rape.[2] In fact, there are many societies today that do not

1. For ancient Near Eastern evidence, see e.g. Tikva Frymer-Kensky, 'Patriarchal Family Relationships and Near Eastern Law', *Biblical Archaeologist* 44 (1981): 209–14; Westermann, *Genesis 12–36*, 239; Gordon J. Wenham, *Genesis 16–50* (Dallas, TX: Word Books, 1994), 7; see also the evidence adduced by Yoo ('Hagar the Egyptian'), who sees the story as informed by ancient Near Eastern customs. Some see it as a legal fiction; e.g. Rosenberg, *King and Kin*, 95; Levenson, *The Death and Resurrection of the Beloved Son*, 92–93; Heard, *Dynamics of Diselection*, 64; Exum, *Fragmented Women*, 121. Reis ('Hagar Requited', 78), citing Nahum Sarna's view that the text reflects a folk belief that a woman who is unable to conceive may become fertile herself by adopting a child, proposes that what motivates the matriarchs is not the intention to adopt the child but rather a superstitious or pious wish to have a child of their own as a reward from God for furthering his command to propagate.

2. Carol L. Meyers ('Was Ancient Israel a Patriarchal Society?', *Journal of Biblical Literature* 113 [2014]: 8–27) argues that 'patriarchy' is not an adequate or accurate description of ancient Israelite society and suggests 'heterarchy' as

recognize rape in marriage. But that does not prevent a modern commentator from raising the issue of rape with regard to this text. The point I want to underscore by doing so is that paintings of this scene require us to acknowledge the conspicuous sexual dimension of what biblical commentators frequently pass over without so much as a comment, or, in their reluctance to say much about the subject, refer to as the use, misuse or abuse of Hagar.[3] Whether or not the painters discussed below thought of their subject as rape is also not the issue. Polygamy was the subject of theological discussions in Europe in the seventeenth century, when all but one of the paintings discussed below were produced,[4] and Abraham's polygamy was often used as an example either for or against the practice.[5] The artists were surely aware of the titillating nature of their paintings, and they were painting for a competitive art market in which the theme of 'mercenary love' or 'unequal lovers' in compositions using three figures appealed to seventeenth-century Dutch tastes.[6] The issue in cases where rape is alleged is, was it against the victim's will?[7] By showing us what the biblical writer does not, Hagar's point of view, artists raise the question of force versus consent, though their answers may vary.

In Gen. 16.1-6, as in the account of the expulsion in Gen. 21.8-14, the biblical narrator depersonalizes Hagar by objectifying her. Hagar, the Egyptian slave, neither speaks to Abraham or Sarah nor is she spoken to by them. She is only spoken about and acted upon.[8] Sarah *takes* Hagar

---

a better model for 'accommodat[ing] the diversity of women's experiences and acknowledg[ing] their control of certain household and society-wide functions' (27). I use 'patriarchal' because it draws attention to the male-dominated power structure exhibited in biblical texts. Sarah has power in this story but authority (socially recognized power) rests with Abraham.

3. An important exception is Susanne Scholz, *Sacred Witness: Rape in the Hebrew Bible* (Minneapolis, MN: Fortress Press, 2010), 57–59.

4. Fig. 4.6 is from the eighteenth century.

5. Sellin, *Fractured Families and Rebel Maidservants*, 43–58.

6. Ibid., 70.

7. This too is an anachronistic question, but, I maintain, modern readers should be asking it of contemporary responses when dealing with this text. As Robert S. Kawashima points out, women did not have the power of sexual consent in biblical Israel; 'Could a Woman Say "No" in Biblical Israel? On the Genealogy of Legal Status in Biblical Law and Literature', *Association for Jewish Studies Review* 35 (2011): 2.

8. In Gen. 21 Hagar is referred to as an *'amah* and once as Abraham's *'amah*; in Gen. 16 she is Sarah's *shiphah*. Both terms refer to a female servant or slave, but may indicate that Hagar has a different status vis-à-vis Sarah and Abraham as well as a different status after the birth of the child; for problems and proposals, see

and *gives* her as a wife to Abraham (v. 3). Abraham *goes in to* her – an idiom for sexual intercourse[9] – and she becomes pregnant, something over which she has no control (v. 4). Hagar's point of view, how she feels about being given to Abraham as a wife for the purpose of bearing a son for Sarah, is withheld from the reader. The narrator does, however, confer upon her a degree of subjectivity in relating that, when she *sees* that she has conceived, her mistress loses esteem *in her eyes* (v. 4). But this will lead to her harsh treatment at the hands of Sarah, which, in turn, causes Hagar to flee. As we saw in Chapter 3 above, by representing Hagar as departing of her own volition, the narrator prepares the reader for her later expulsion by Abraham, who casts her out at Sarah's and God's insistence.

What happens between Hagar and Abraham when she becomes his wife, a wife of secondary status,[10] receives, like the one-verse description of the abjection of Hagar and Ishmael in Gen. 21.14, the barest narrative attention possible.

> Sarai the wife of Abram took Hagar the Egyptian, her slave (after Abram had lived in the land of Canaan ten years), and gave her to Abram her husband as a wife. He had intercourse with Hagar and she conceived (Gen. 16.3-4a).

The biblical text does not describe a scene in which Sarah personally leads Hagar to Abraham's bed, but one can see how easy it was for artists to render this succinct presentation as one scene. In it, Sarah becomes a procurer, as in this painting by Matthias Stom, or Stomer, as he is also known (fig. 4.1).[11]

Yoo, 'Hagar the Egyptian'. Because Hagar is a servant, it is not entirely unexpected that she is treated as an object and not as a person in her own right. Perhaps what *is* unexpected is the fact that, given Hagar's status, the biblical narrator later treats her as subject in 16.7-14 and 21.15-21.

9. *DCH* 2.113b.

10. There is no word for 'wife' in biblical Hebrew. The word used is *'ishshah*, 'woman'. This form of marriage, in which a woman other than a man's primary wife functions as a secondary wife of lower status, is known as polycoity. Steinberg points out that Sarah, as primary wife, has legal and economic rights not available to Hagar, a slave, who does not bring property into the marriage and whose marriage thus can easily be dissolved by her husband. Hagar's son's status is different, since he is considered a legitimate heir to his biological father Abraham and to Sarah, Abraham's primary wife; 'The World of the Family in Genesis', 289–90.

11. I am reminded of paintings of Delilah cutting Samson's hair while an old madam looks over her shoulder (e.g. Rubens's *Samson and Delilah* in the National Gallery, London, and his *The Capture of Samson* in the Alte Pinakothek, Munich, and Stom's *Samson and Delilah* in the Galleria Nazionale d'Arte Antica, Rome).

Fig. 4.1. Matthias Stom, *Sarah Leading Hagar to Abraham*, 1637–1639, Gemäldegalerie der Staatlichen Museen zu Berlin

By presenting the marriage as Sarah's idea, the biblical narrator allows Sarah to be blamed when the plan backfires. In addition, Abraham appears in a better light, less like the perpetrator of a crime of passion. Abraham may force himself upon Hagar but it is at Sarah's bidding. In Stom's painting, Hagar has a petrified, apprehensive look on her face. She seems to be looking past Abraham, as if in a daze, perhaps steeling herself for the ordeal to come. She holds her already partially opened dress around her protectively. Sarah's vacant, absent stare into space makes it seem as though she does not belong here, but her role as instigator of the rape is emphasized by the way she offers Hagar to Abraham with both hands. Abraham seems rather passive, a frail-looking old man with his hands by his sides. His partial nakedness suggests his vulnerability rather than his desire. It is difficult to decide exactly where he is looking. Possibly he looks at Hagar, but it appears more likely that he is looking at Sarah as if to ask if she really wants him to carry out this marriage arrangement.

The procurer is a common topos in art; see Sellin, *Fractured Families and Rebel Maidservants*, 77–78. Of Stom's painting above, Sellin observes, 'By incorporating this procuress type and formulaic elements from the "unequal lovers" theme, Stomer could make the intimate biblical scene all the more provocative, lively, and witty' (78). This painting shares many features with Stom's painting of *Isaac Blessing Jacob* in the Barber Institute of Fine Arts, Birmingham; see Verdi, *Matthias Stom*, 13, 37–38; O'Kane, *Painting the Text*, 120–27.

The upward open position of his left hand also hints at a hesitancy on his part. In this case, as in the biblical account, Abraham appears less culpable than Sarah, whose idea it is to use Hagar as a surrogate mother.

In a painting by Salomon de Bray (fig. 4.2), although we cannot see her face, it is apparent from her posture that Hagar is unwilling as she reluctantly enters Abraham's bed, urged on by both Abraham and Sarah. Like most painters of this scene, de Bray emphasizes the difference in age between the young, nubile Hagar and the old, unappealing Abraham and Sarah. Abraham and Sarah's advanced years play an important role in the biblical narrative, making their childless plight all the more desperate. When this age difference is dramatically visualized, it becomes increasingly difficult for a viewer to imagine Hagar being complicit in the marriage arrangement.

Fig. 4.2. Salomon de Bray, *Hagar Brought to Abraham by Sarah*, 1650, Agnes Etherington Art Centre, Queen's University, Kingston, Ontario, Canada

Hagar's pose in de Bray's painting conveys not only reluctance, but, even more strongly, humiliation and shame. For good reason. She is naked while Abraham and Sarah are fully clothed, and she is going to be raped. By focusing in on the moment that Hagar is brought to Abraham's bed for sex, freezing it in time and requiring the viewer to contemplate it, paintings of Sarah bringing Hagar to Abraham make the event more awkward for the viewer than the biblical narrator's simple 'Abraham went in to her' is for the reader.[12] It is hard to imagine a viewer not having a strong reaction to this painting. Titillation? Revulsion? Embarrassment? Pity? Outrage? Identification with the victim? There are many possibilities, but none involves overlooking what is taking place.

Abraham appears relatively passive in Genesis 16, as he is in the account of the abjection in Gen. 21.8-14. The biblical narrator reports only that he obeyed Sarah (v. 2) and had intercourse with Hagar (v. 4). Some paintings of the scene are noteworthy for pointing to something the biblical narrator has not simply glossed over, the rape, but ignored, the question of the patriarch's desire.[13] Another painting of the scene by Stom (fig. 4.3) shows an old, rather feeble Abraham stretching out his left hand as if to assure a young, sexually endowed Hagar that things will be all right, his open right hand ready to embrace her. She responds to his overture by placing a protective hand over her breast. Abraham's posture, supported by the look on his face, reveals his eagerness to have Hagar in his bed.

When Ishmael is born, Abraham is eighty-six years old (Gen. 16.16). In fig. 4.3, even more than in the painting by Stom discussed above (fig. 4.1), the viewer encounters in Abraham a figure who epitomizes the frailty that accompanies old age. A viewer could thus be excused for wondering about the father of the nation's sexual prowess, which the biblical narrator simply takes for granted.

---

12. Viewers will, of course, react differently to the scene; a voyeuristic gaze at the naked female body makes different demands upon viewers, depending on what is depicted as taking place, on socialization, on sexual orientation and on numerous other factors; see, further, the discussion in Chapter 6 below.

13. Commentators do not entirely avoid the issue; e.g., although the story never mentions it, Wenham (*Genesis 16–50*, 4) takes it for granted that affection is involved and finds in the story a 'conflict between two women vying for one man's respect and affection'. Westermann (*Genesis 12–36*, 238–39) deals with the question of desire by explaining that Sarah's demand that Abraham have sex with Hagar means that 'Abraham is to turn to Hagar, spend part of his time with her, so that there arises a mutual understanding between them'.

Fig. 4.3. Matthias Stom, *Sarah Presenting Hagar to Abraham*, 1620–1650,
Musée Condé, Chantilly, France

Interestingly, however, elsewhere in the story the narrator appears to let
slip a surprising comment on Abraham's virility by means of Sarah's
response when Isaac's birth is predicted (Abraham is 100 when Isaac is
born, 21.5): 'Now that I am dried up, shall I have pleasure? – and my
husband is old!' (Gen. 18.12). Sarah's words could be taken as suggesting
some doubt about Abraham's ability to please her sexually, given his
advanced years. As if the narrator senses the problem, he removes it by
having the deity paraphrase Sarah's comment in a way that questions only
her ability to have a child: 'Shall I really bear a child now that I am old?'
(v. 13).[14]

   In *Sarah Bringing Hagar to Abraham* (fig. 4.4) Willem van Mieris's
Abraham is old but does not look so frail as he looked in Stom's paintings
above, and his desire for Hagar is unmistakable. Sitting up in bed eagerly,
he gazes expectantly at Hagar, pulling her toward him with his left hand
while making a gesture of invitation with his right. The scene seems
especially designed for the visual pleasure of a heterosexual male viewer,
who has a better view of Hagar's body than Abraham. Hagar lowers her
eyes modestly as she seeks to cover her breast with one hand and grasp
the wrap to cover her genitals with the other in the classic stance of Venus

   14. Exum, *Fragmented Women*, 111–13. rsv and nrsv take Hebrew *balah* (here
translated 'dried up') as a reference to Sarah's age, and reverse the word order
in Sarah's speech: 'After I have grown old, and my husband is old, shall I have
pleasure?' jps, in contrast, renders more precisely: 'Now that I am withered, am I to
have enjoyment – with my husband so old?'

pudica. Her right foot already rests on the side of the bed, as the old, wizened Sarah urges her on and offers her to Abraham with her upturned right hand.

Fig. 4.4. Willem van Mieris, *Sarah Bringing Hagar to Abraham*, 1650,
Private Collection

It is a curious feature of biblical narrative that women who want to have children cannot conceive (Sarah, Rebekah, Rachel, Hannah), whereas women who have sexual intercourse only once in dubious circum-stances conceive immediately (Lot's two daughters, Tamar [Gen. 38], Bathsheba).[15] In Gen. 16.4, 'he went in to her' is followed directly by the

15. This is not always the case; for example, Leah, as a foil to Rachel, has no difficulty conceiving, and the book of Ruth deals with the marriage, intercourse, conception and birth in one verse. But all these cases serve the androcentric politics of conception in biblical literature.

statement 'she conceived'. So the question is, is a reader to assume that Abraham has sexual intercourse with Hagar only this once? The question occupied the rabbis (*Gen. Rab.* 45.4), for, if it was more than once, it could be taken as a sign of Abraham's sexual desire for Hagar, or, as van Mieris depicts it, his lust.

In Genesis 16, Sarah is the one who wants a son, and in marrying Hagar Abraham is simply following her instructions. Since a woman's worth was measured by her ability to give her husband children, especially sons, Sarah is willing to go to extreme lengths to have a son. As in the account of the expulsion, the narrator uses Sarah to make Abraham look better. She gives Hagar to Abraham as a wife, planning to make Hagar's child her own. When, however, Hagar becomes pregnant and apparently has ideas beyond her station (v. 4), Sarah is angry. She complains to Abraham (v. 5), and she 'afflicts' Hagar (v. 6), so that it is her fault that Hagar flees from Abraham's household ('from her presence [face]', as the text puts it). The word used in v. 6 for 'afflict' (the root *'nh* in the *piel*) has a wide range of meanings, including 'humiliate', 'torment' and 'subdue'.[16] Interestingly, in view of the way paintings draw attention to the rape of Hagar, *'nh* in the *piel* also occurs in contexts of what we would call rape (e.g. Gen. 34.2; Deut. 21.14; Judg. 20.5; 2 Sam. 13.12).[17] Figuratively speaking then, Hagar is raped by Sarah in a manner different from, but paralleling, her rape by Abraham.

It might appear that, by marrying Hagar at Sarah's bidding (v. 2) and then leaving the matter of dealing with Hagar in Sarah's hands (v. 6), Abraham is only indirectly involved. Or is he? By making Hagar's marriage to Abraham Sarah's idea, the narrator effectively (which does not mean consciously) projects Abraham's desire onto Sarah. In other words, by making Sarah responsible, the narrator avoids having to deal with

16. It is used, for example, to describe the way Laban does not want Jacob to treat his daughters (Gen. 31.50); in Ps. 105.18 it describes Joseph's feet in fetters, as a slave; it is used of the Egyptians' treatment of their Israelite slaves (Exod. 1.11-12), but also of God's treatment of Israel in the wilderness to prove them (Deut. 8.2-3, 16); in Judg. 16.19, it describes how Delilah treats Samson after cutting his hair, which suggests at least a figurative connection to its meaning 'rape'.

17. Ellen van Wolde examines these and other passages in which *'nh* appears in the *piel* and concludes that it does not describe rape but rather debasement from a social-juridical point of view; 'Does *'innâ* Denote Rape? A Semantic Analysis of a Controversial Word', *Vetus Testamentum* 52 (2002): 528–44. This would seem to reflect what I said at the outset of this chapter about the difference between what a modern reader and the biblical author or his original audience might regard as rape.

Abraham's sexual desire. This is actually more like a displacement, where the subconscious narrative desire takes a distorted form, with Abraham's sexual desire becoming Sarah's desire for a son. The displacement facilitates the narrative's success at distancing Abraham from any suspicion that he might have desired to have sex with a young nubile slave in his household. But as is the case with projection and displacement, the narrator has left a trace of the unacknowledged desire. Whereas in Gen. 21.12 Abraham has to be told by God to heed or 'obey' Sarah when she calls for Hagar and Ishmael's expulsion, here in Genesis 16 he obeys Sarah without demurral.[18] In Genesis 21 Sarah's demand is 'evil' in Abraham's eyes, but in ch. 16 nothing is said about Abraham's reaction.[19] 'Who is ultimately responsible for the rape, Abraham, Sarah, or both?', asks Susanne Scholz.[20] Both, of course; as we saw in Chapter 3, both Abraham and Sarah are aspects of the 'self' that is Israel, the self that will eventually abject Hagar and Ishmael irreversibly.

A third painting of the scene by Matthias Stom captures Abraham's desire for Hagar more dramatically (fig. 4.5). He has grabbed her robe, rather impatiently it appears, and, like Sarah, is pulling it off her, as Sarah, her face set, offers Hagar to him. Again Stom gives us a reluctant Hagar, pictured this time in a Venus pudica pose. Abraham looks at her and she returns his gaze with a pleading look in her eyes. This, in my view, is a look that accuses, as in paintings of the expulsion. Hagar's wide hips and large thighs emphasize her suitability for child-bearing. There is a fourth figure in this painting – an exotically clothed servant holding a tray with a jug on it, who is watching the proceedings and whose presumed gaze at Hagar adds to the titillation of the scene (a spectator, like the viewer of the painting, 'with his clothes still on', to borrow John Berger's phrase).[21] A dog sits placidly by Abraham's bed, completely uninvolved as if nothing unusual were happening, and disrupting, for me at least, the coherence of the gaze. Often a dog symbolizes fidelity or domesticity, but this is certainly not an ordinary domestic scene. Sometimes the presence of a

---

18. Gen. 16.2 reads *wayyishma' 'abram leqol saray*, 'Abram heard the voice of [i.e. obeyed] Sarai'. On *shama leqol*, 'hear the voice', as an idiom for 'obey' see *DCH* 8.461a. The same idiom is used in Gen. 21.12.

19. Pursuing a psychoanalytic literary approach to the narrative further, we might view the appearance of *'nh* ('afflict', 'rape') in 16.6 ('Then Sarah afflicted her and she fled from her') as a displacement of Abraham's violation of Hagar onto Sarah, a sort of pre-Freudian slip that betrays narrative guilt.

20. Scholz, *Sacred Witness*, 59.

21. John Berger, *Ways of Seeing* (London: Penguin Books, 1972), 54.

dog alludes to sexuality, lechery, or promiscuity.[22] The dog here seems to convey both ideas, suggesting that there is something illicit about what is taking place under the curtain of domesticity.

Fig. 4.5. Matthias Stom, *Sarah Brings Hagar to Abraham*, c. 1640,
Gothenburg Museum of Art, Sweden

The fact that Stom painted the scene of Sarah presenting Hagar to Abraham more than once is typical of the way he worked, producing numerous variants on the same theme throughout his career and often employing similar compositions for very different subjects.[23] The three paintings discussed here cannot be dated with precision,[24] but it is interesting to note the different perspectives they offer, especially on Abraham. Figs. 4.1 and 4.3 have more in common in terms of style, and exhibit Stom's penchant for posing his figures close to the picture plane and

22. Compare the two dogs in fig. 6.1 below. In light of contemporary debates about polygamy (see above) and Abraham's eagerness to disrobe Hagar, the painting gives the viewer the opportunity to reflect on the morality of Abraham's domestic arrangements.

23. Verdi, *Matthias Stom*, 13, 38.

24. Ibid., 13. Verdi notes that only one of Stom's works is dated and that conses quently a chronology of his career cannot be determined from documentary evidence alone but relies rather on internal stylistic evidence and the provenance of his pictures.

providing them with a minimal setting.[25] The three protagonists are shown three-quarter length and their direct proximity to the viewer draws the viewer into the proceedings. In both, a brazier, one of the few features in the room, separates Abraham from the two women, but the relationship among the protagonists has changed. In fig. 4.1 Sarah stands between Hagar and a seemingly uncertain Abraham. She offers Hagar's hand to Abraham but no physical contact takes place between Abraham and Hagar. Though Sarah seems detached, her presence obviously has an effect on Abraham, and her position draws attention to the bond that exists between them. In fig. 4.3 Sarah also brings Hagar by the arm to Abraham but here Abraham invites Hagar to his bed by reaching out to touch her hand. In this painting, Hagar quite literally comes between husband and wife.

Figure 4.5 is a very different composition. The figures are full-sized, placing the viewer at a distance from the proceedings and making the scene more of a spectacle than a private moment upon which the viewer seems to intrude. There is a fourth protagonist, not in the biblical story, the servant in the foreground, who, like the dog next to a basket, invites the viewer's interest. The background is lighter and there is a greater sense of opulence: in the blue curtains hanging from above, the ornate bedpost, Hagar's lush bright red robe trimmed in gold, and the servant's fancy dress and plumed hat. Most striking is the different portrayal of Abraham and Hagar, and to a lesser degree Sarah. Abraham is old but muscular and vigorous; he is aggressive as well, propping himself up in bed and tugging at Hagar's wrap. Whereas Sarah, who is always standing by, directing events, offers Hagar to Abraham in figs. 4.1 and 4.3, in fig. 4.5 she is involved in disrobing Hagar, delicately removing her wrap as Abraham pulls at it. Hagar's body, bathed in light, is the centre of attention, exposed to Abraham's, the servant's and the viewer's gaze. In her vain effort to protect herself from the gaze, and with a forlorn expression on her face impossible to disregard, she makes a last bid for Abraham's and the viewer's sympathy.

Louis Jean François Lagrenée also gives us a reluctant Hagar (fig. 4.6). She has a look of youthful innocence about her that emphasizes her helplessness. Her face is turned away from Abraham's and her eyes are cast down modestly. As Sarah pushes her toward their husband, Hagar's hand, pressed against Abraham's chest, suggests both her uncertainty and apprehension, as well as her knowledge that she has no choice. Abraham, old but physically fit, leans forward to embrace Hagar, but it is difficult

---

25. Ibid. In Verdi's view this technique intensifies the boldness and immediacy of Stom's art.

to tell how eager he is to have Hagar in his bed. He seems to be looking at Sarah, as if to confirm that this is the right solution to the problem of their childlessness. Sarah, soon to be excluded, is already in the shadows. Her face is careworn. She does not look at either Abraham or Hagar but seems rather to be looking at Hagar's back just below her own hand, as though she would rather not be a party to the sexual encounter she has orchestrated. Through the ambiguity of their poses Lagrenée manages to draw attention to the predicament of the childless couple, which is what drives the plot in the biblical narrative. But unlike the biblical narrator, the artist focuses attention as well on what will be required of Hagar in order for Sarah to obtain the son she needs. In spite of (and perhaps because of) the seeming reluctance of both Abraham and Hagar, whose partially clad bodies are bathed in light, as a prelude to rape the scene here seems designed to appeal to prurient tastes.

Fig. 4.6. Louis Jean François Lagrenée, *Sarah Presenting Hagar to Abraham*, c. 1781, Museum of Fine Arts, Boston

My final example, Adriaen van der Werff's *Sarah Presenting Hagar to Abraham*, depicts a level of engagement between Sarah and Abraham absent in the paintings discussed above (fig. 4.7). They are looking into each other's eyes, Abraham, it seems to me, with some tenderness and Sarah with anguish. With her hand on her heart she seems to be pleading, desperate to persuade a possibly reluctant Abraham to do what she asks.

Abraham's right hand is raised in what seems to be a gesture of demurral, yet it could be seen as a sign of acquiescence, as though he cannot refuse something that means so much to his wife.

Fig. 4.7. Adriaen van der Werff, *Sarah Presenting Hagar to Abraham*, 1699, Staatsgalerie, Schleissheim

If Hagar were not present, we could be witnessing a tender domestic scene of a couple resolving a difference of opinion. Hagar kneels submissively by the side of the bed. Her face downturned, she covers herself in a modest gesture in relation to the spectator. Abraham's left hand rests on her shoulder. This could be interpreted as a sign of protectiveness; but nevertheless, looking at the painting, especially if you are a woman, you can almost feel the chill it sends through Hagar. Not surprisingly, there is an air of resignation and hopelessness about Hagar.[26]

26. There is another version of the painting, painted in 1696, in the Hermitage, St Petersburg.

A sympathetic attitude to Sarah and Abraham, as in van der Werff's painting, serves as a reminder that the biblical characters Abraham and Sarah are subject to a social system in which having a male heir was essential for both men and women. When the events of Genesis 16 take place both are childless. Abraham complains that the only heir he has is his servant Eliezer (15.2), so one might assume that he needs little persuading to take Hagar as a secondary wife. For her part, Sarah desperately needs a son, since bearing a son to her husband to carry on his lineage is her only means of fulfilling her role as a wife. As Naomi Steinberg points out, 'Sarah's actions not only serve to help the reader appreciate the importance of production and reproduction in the world of the family in Genesis, but introduces them from the point of view of a woman – and barren wife – whose social validation and future in the family are determined by her reproductive capabilities'.[27]

As we look at Sarah's role as procurer in numerous paintings of the scene, it is important to recognize that, when they show this story on the canvas, artists are responding to the role given to Sarah by the biblical narrator – who tells the story in this particular way. He has constructed his narrative so that Sarah's infertility (like that of the matriarchs Rebekah and Rachel) is one of many threats to the promise God makes to Abraham, a promise of numerous descendants to whom God will give the land of Canaan.[28] Sarah's solution to her plight – giving Hagar to Abraham as a wife 'so that *I* may be built up through her' (16.2) – far from solving the problem results in yet another threat to the promise, the birth of Ishmael. As we saw in Chapter 3, Ishmael must be removed as the potential heir to the promise because God has decided that Abraham's line shall be traced through Isaac. After Isaac's birth, Sarah will solve the problem she brought about in the first place by having Ishmael disinherited.

Paintings of Sarah presenting Hagar to Abraham that depict Sarah as little more than a procurer add to the indignities endured by the biblical character, who is made to suffer the stigma of infertility, the necessity of relying on a surrogate, the surrogate's disdainful attitude, and the

---

27. Steinberg, 'The World of the Family in Genesis', 289.

28. Other threats include the advanced ages of both Abraham and Sarah, the potential loss of the patriarch's wife to another in Gen. 12 and 20, the possibility that Lot might choose for himself the land promised to Abraham when the two of them part, the possibility that Abraham's servant Eliezer might become his heir if he has no son (15.2), the possibility that Abraham's son Ishmael might inherit the promise, and the potential loss of Isaac, the child of the promise, when God tests Abraham by commanding him to sacrifice 'your son, your only son Isaac, whom you love' (22.2).

failure of her plan to rectify her situation.[29] It is possible for a modern reader familiar with the cultural background reflected in the story to feel sympathy for all the characters. At the same time we have an obligation to the character Hagar to acknowledge that what happens to her is a rape for which both Sarah and Abraham, as joint representatives of the 'self' that is Israel, are responsible.

The paintings discussed above all expose the rape about to take place, but in the process they repeat it in a frequently salacious and generally demeaning way for all the characters. By showing Hagar in various stages of undress, they make her an object of the gaze who signifies and plays to the desire of a presumed heterosexual male viewer. There are a few paintings of Sarah presenting Hagar to Abraham that show a complicit Hagar, thus rescuing Abraham from the charge of rape.[30] There are also prints and paintings that to varying degrees offer a sympathetic, and thus less judgmental view of Sarah and of Abraham, but their theme is nevertheless what I have been referring to as the rape of Hagar. My intention in examining paintings of the scene has not been to prove that a rape occurred – for rape is notoriously difficult to prove. Rather, I have sought to show how biblical art can affect our perception, and interpretation, of a biblical text. These paintings, in my view, require their viewers to consider what assumptions about women and slaves and their rights to their bodies lie behind the biblical narrator's simple 'he had intercourse with Hagar and she conceived', assumptions biblical commentators too readily ignore.[31] As modern readers approaching ancient texts whose

29. What we might call karma is a common feature in the Genesis stories (especially the stories of Jacob, who is paid back in kind for his deeds). Reversing the relationship of power between Israel and Egypt, in Gen. 12.10-20 Abraham allows Sarah to be taken into Pharaoh's harem, putting her in a similar situation to Hagar's (but with a beneficial solution for Israel).

30. One, a painting of a coy Hagar by Caspar Netscher (*Sarah Leading Hagar to Abraham* [1673]), is reproduced in Sellin, *Fractured Families and Rebel Maidservants*, 82, and also serves as the cover to her book. Another, on copper, Philip van Dijk's *Sarah Presents Hagar to Abraham* (1670s) is discussed by Sellin (85). Cases of rape usually involve two versions, the victim's and the perpetrator's version in which the victim is blamed for encouraging it or having willingly engaged in sexual intercourse.

31. For a reading of the Hagar story that takes seriously the abuse and violence suffered by slaves in the ancient Near East, and the role played by gender, see Kari Latvus, 'Reading Hagar in Contexts: From Exegesis to Inter-Contextual Analysis', in *Genesis*, ed. Athalya Brenner, Archie Chi Chung Lee and Gale A. Yee (Minneapolis, MN: Fortress Press, 2010), 247–74.

worldviews we no longer share, and some of whose ethics we cannot endorse, we cannot afford to ignore such assumptions when explicating these texts. The stakes for women and other exploited groups are too high. Mieke Bal's comments on rape in art and rape and art merit repeating here:

> Art forms repeatedly choose [rape] as their privileged theme; rape must be taken as emblematic for our culture. Too pregnant with relevant and problematic meanings for all members of our culture to be dismissed merely as 'high' culture, as elitist, these representations of rape are central in any definition of culture one can come up with... [A]rbitrary or ideological delimitations of the domains of the visual and the verbal can only serve to obscure the urgency with which these works confront us. In a certain manner a raped woman can stand for every interpreter who can opt to identify with her.

What happens to Hagar after her ill use by Abraham and Sarah is the subject of the next chapter.

The Theophanies to Hagar

In Chapter 3 above we looked at the account of Abraham's abjection of Hagar and Ishmael in Gen. 21.8-14, and in Chapter 4 we considered the abuse of Hagar that leads her to flee from Sarah, in effect abjecting herself from Abraham's household (Gen. 16.1-6). Neither story ends there, however. In both, attention shifts from events in the family of Abraham to the fate of Hagar and her son after the abjection. The attention the narrator gives to Hagar – a woman, a secondary wife, a foreigner and a minor character in the larger story of the patriarch's life – is remarkable, and we shall consider first some possible reasons for this narrative focus before turning to examples from art, where the visual narratives, while foregrounding the role of Hagar, 'tell' a version of events rather different from the verbal narrative.

A theophany is, properly speaking, a visual manifestation of a divine being. I have called this chapter 'The Theophanies to Hagar' because in artistic renditions of Gen. 16.7-16 and 21.15-21 the divine presence is typically represented as an angel (Hebrew *malak*, 'messenger', is often translated as 'angel'). In the biblical story there is only one theophany to Hagar, Gen. 16.7-16, where we are told that the messenger of God 'encountered her by the spring of water in the steppe on the way to Shur' and spoke to her, after which she appears to profess to have seen a god. In Genesis 21, in contrast, the divine messenger does not appear to Hagar, but rather speaks to her 'from heaven' (21.17). Interestingly, however, even in Genesis 16, the biblical narrator does not unambiguously report that God appears to Hagar, but only that the divine messenger 'found her', 'met her' or 'encountered her' (*wayyimtsa'ah*) by the spring (v. 7). The messenger then speaks to her in vv. 8, 9, 10 and 11.

In theophanies there is often no clear distinction between God and the messenger of God, and in 16.13 the narrator identifies Yahweh as the one who spoke to Hagar. Hagar names the speaker El-roi, 'a god of seeing' or 'a god who sees me'. But whether or not she speaks of having seen the one who spoke is not entirely clear due to the difficulty of the Hebrew in v. 13.[1] One might render, 'Truly here I have seen him who sees me'.[2] Hearing and seeing God's messenger or God are both prominent in this account, and, regardless of how we choose to interpret Hagar's words about the god who spoke to her, the fact remains that the biblical narrator makes her the subject of an encounter with the god of Israel, both here in Genesis 16 and also later in ch. 21. Why should this be?

As we have seen, the two versions of the abjection (Gen. 16.1-6 and 21.8-14) illustrate just how difficult abjecting Hagar and Ishmael is for Israel.[3] The only glimpse we get of Hagar's perspective before the dismissal is the narrator's comment that, after she realizes she is pregnant, her mistress becomes 'lowered *in her eyes*' (16.4). Otherwise both versions objectify Hagar and Ishmael in an attempt to distance the reader from them. Only after Hagar flees (ch. 16) or is driven out (ch. 21) does the narrator allow Hagar to become a subject with whom the reader is likely to empathize. In the first version, Hagar's own emerging subjectivity is threatening to Israel's sense of self, and enough to enrage Israel, represented by Sarah – 'since she *saw* that she had conceived, I am lowered *in her eyes*' – whose harsh treatment of Hagar causes her to flee. The narrator thus entertains the possibility of abjecting Ishmael before he is born. But there is another way of interpreting Hagar's flight, one connected to her incipient subjectivity, to which I shall return below.

1. Cf. NJB, 'Did I not go on seeing here, after him who sees me?', and NRSV (with emendation), 'Have I really seen God [or a god] and remained alive after seeing him?'

2. Klaus Koenen ('Wer sieht wen? Zur Textgeschichte von Genesis XVI 13', *Vetus Testamentum* 38 [1988]: 468–74), with one minor emendation of the vocalization of the Masoretic Text, translates: 'Wahrlich hier habe ich auf den gesehen (im Sinne von: hier ist mir der begegnet), der mich ersieht / errettet' [Truly here I have seen him (in the sense of: here is the one who encountered me) who sees / saves me]. On the difficulties of the verse, see Wenham, *Genesis 16–50*, 3; Westermann, *Genesis 12–36*, 247–48. One might wonder if the textual confusion reflects scribal uncertainty about whether or not this is a theophany to a foreign woman.

3. In the case of stories in which the same themes are replayed and the same issues revisited, repetition appears to function as a textual working out of a particular problem or concern, repeated because the problem is not so easy to resolve. Such stories invite consideration from a psychoanalytic perspective; see e.g. Exum, *Fragmented Women*, 148–69, for discussion of Gen. 12, 20 and 26, which, like Gen. 16 and 21, are versions of the 'same' story repeated at different points in the narrative. On repetition within the same story, that of Lot and his daughters in Gen. 19.30-38, see Exum, *Plotted, Shot, and Painted*, 133–59.

Hagar's flight from Abraham's household poses a problem because Abraham does not have another son – yet. It is still possible that the son promised to Abraham (Gen. 15.4-5) will be Ishmael. Hagar will have to return and give birth to Ishmael, and Isaac will have to be born, before Israel can successfully abject Ishmael and his mother. Hagar returns, for the time being, instructed by the divine messenger to submit her 'self' to Israel.

The birth of two sons to Abraham, one by Hagar the Egyptian and the other the divinely promised son by Sarah, creates once again a crisis within the subject (Gen. 21.8-14). There is confusion within the self, seen in the conflict between Sarah and Abraham, both of whom represent Israel. In Chapter 3 above I discussed the narrator's apparent discomfort with the abjection, his effort to minimize the reader's sympathy with Hagar and Ishmael, and his techniques for seeking to justify the abjection. Ishmael will have a future as a great nation, the narrator assures his readers, albeit not the chosen nation (16.10; 21.13, 18). But this promise alone is not quite enough. Something more is needed to ameliorate the trauma experienced by the 'self' that is Israel and to justify the ways of Israel to the reader. Nothing less than a theophany will do, a *deus ex machina* to resolve the problem of the abject.

After Abjection: Hagar's Bid for Subjectivity
(Genesis 16.7-16 and 21.15-21)

Whereas Hagar is by and large objectified in both accounts of the dismissal, in her confrontation with the divine messenger she becomes a narrative subject in her own right, a speaking subject who voices her distress – 'I am fleeing from my mistress Sarai' (16.8) and 'let me not look upon the death of the child' (21.16) – and an object of divine compassion. Furthermore, Hagar, the abject, is accorded the honour of hearing God and perhaps seeing him as well. Few people are granted this privilege in the Bible, and only one is both a woman and a foreigner.[4] Why Hagar? Is God's unprecedented concern for Hagar and Ishmael in Gen. 16.7-14 and 21.15-21 the biblical narrator's way of compensating for the ill treatment Hagar and Ishmael receive at the hands of Israel? Consider what the narrator has achieved. Sarah is blamed for the abjection in both versions. In Genesis 21 Abraham looks better because he opposes it. God shows concern for Hagar in ch. 16 but sends her back to 'submit to harsh

---

4. Another woman who witnesses a theophany is Samson's mother (Judg. 13), and another foreigner who is the recipient of a theophany is Balaam (Num. 22.31-35).

treatment under [Sarah's] hand' (16.9); in 21.12-13 he takes Sarah's part in demanding expulsion but reassures Abraham about Ishmael's future. The portrayal of God up to this point in the narrative is somewhat ambiguous, but now, in 21.15-21, God's image is considerably more positive as he intervenes to ensure Hagar and Ishmael's survival and Ishmael's future.

Both Hagar's flight in ch. 16 and her departure in ch. 21 are the result of rejection by Israel, Israel's refusal to accept Hagar and Ishmael as belonging to its 'self'. Away from Abraham's household, Hagar begins to emerge as a subject. Her point of view is no longer suppressed. But this is not all. *Hagar* at this point becomes a subject in process, seeking to establish *her* subjectivity by abjecting Israel. I mentioned above that the first version of the expulsion, in which Hagar runs away because Sarah maltreats her, is the narrator's first attempt to rid Israel of what he regards as not properly part of Israel's 'self', Hagar and, more importantly, the yet unborn Ishmael. But because Hagar is represented as fleeing of her own volition, her flight can also be interpreted as her attempt to construct herself as an independent subject by abjecting Israel, separating herself from the challenge Israel poses to her autonomy: 'I abject *myself* within the same motion through which "I" claim to establish *myself*'.

As we have seen, however, in ch. 16 Hagar cannot abject Israel because she is bound to Israel by the unborn child, who is Father Abraham/Israel's child. God therefore intervenes to send her back. But before she returns she is permitted a measure of subjectivity. In 16.8, for the first time, Hagar is spoken to, and, for the first time, she speaks. The divine messenger addresses her by name with a question, 'Hagar, servant of Sarai, where have you come from and where are you going?' Ironically her reply, 'from my mistress Sarai', answers both parts of the question: she is fleeing from Israel and she will soon be going back there, for in the next verse the messenger tells her to return and submit to Sarah's harsh treatment.

We are repeatedly told that the messenger speaks to Hagar, which makes it all the more apparent that Hagar does not respond:

> *The messenger of Yahweh said to her*:
>> 'Return to your mistress and be maltreated at her hand'.

> *The messenger of Yahweh said to her*:
>> 'I will so greatly multiply your descendants that they cannot be numbered for multitude'.

> *The messenger of Yahweh said to her*:
>> 'You are with child and will bear a son; you shall call his name Ishmael because Yahweh has given heed to your affliction...'

Hagar's silence all this time is perhaps telling, a sign that she does not want to go back, that she wants to abject Israel. When she speaks again, it is both about and to this numinous being: 'She called the name of Yahweh, who spoke to her, "You are a god of seeing"' (or 'You are a god who sees me').[5] Hagar, the Egyptian, gives Yahweh, Israel's god, a name that acknowledges a connection between herself and this god, a god she will encounter once more after the birth of her son. But for now she must return to her former status as the object of actions of others.

The biblical narrator passes over Hagar's return to Abraham's house in silence. This is a considerable gap in the story that invites speculation. Have Sarah and Abraham even noticed that Hagar had run away? How welcome is she, considering Sarah's cruel treatment of her? What is a reader to imagine her life would be like? Kinder treatment, or, as v. 9 suggests, more abuse? Surely her return is as emotionally laden as her flight, but only in art is attention given to such questions, and this artistic interest can make readers more aware of the biblical narrator's limited interest in Hagar apart from her significance for Israel. In Pietro da Cortona's *The Return of Hagar* (fig. 5.1), for example, Hagar seems to be pleading to be allowed to return or apologizing for having the audacity to leave or both. Abraham welcomes her, but Sarah, from whom she had fled, stands in the background, her eyes cast down, leaving the viewer to ponder her reaction.[6] Despite his grey hair and beard, Abraham does not

5. The meaning of the name is uncertain. The form may be an abstract noun, 'seeing' or 'sight', see BDB 909a, *DCH* 7.364a; or one could read the consonantal text as a participle with a first-person suffix, 'who sees me', which is how the Septuagint and Vulgate understand it. Speiser (*Genesis*, 118) suggests the form may be intentionally ambiguous. See, further, the discussion of Wenham (*Genesis 16–50*, 2–3), who translates, 'You are El, who sees me'.

6. The two figures in the background behind Sarah caught my attention, but who are they? They are adults; the one in front is not elaborately clad as are Hagar, Abraham and (to the extent we can see her) Sarah. He could be a hunter or a wild, coarse man like Ishmael will be (16.12). I am tempted to read these figures as representing the friendship that Ishmael and Isaac will never know, and thus illustrating my point in Chapter 3 about what might have been were it not for the expulsion. That the artist intended this identification is doubtful, since he was a Catholic under the patronage of Pope Urban VIII and Cardinal Francesco Barberini, the papal nephew, and thus unlikely to depict friendship between the representatives of rival religions, Ishmael as Islam and Isaac as Christianity (I am grateful to Yaffa England for this observation). Pietro da Cortona painted another version of Hagar's return in which Abraham brings a penitent Hagar to Sarah; the painting is in the Pushkin Museum; see http://www.italian-art.ru/canvas/17–18_century/p/pietro_da_cortona_pietro_berrettini/the_return_of_hagar/index.php?lang=en.

appear to be extremely old and Sarah looks quite young, so it is difficult to conclude from this painting that old age has prevented them from having children. They soon will have a son, though miraculous intervention is required (Gen. 18.1-15; 21.1-2).

Fig. 5.1. Pietro da Cortona, *The Return of Hagar*, 1637,
Kunsthistorisches Museum, Vienna

Back in the Abrahamic household, after she bears Abraham a son, Hagar as subject recedes from view. Abraham – not Hagar as the messenger had foretold – names 'his son, whom Hagar bore', Ishmael, thereby laying claim to Ishmael as part of Israel's 'self'. Everything changes, of course, with the birth of Isaac, the true Israel. Although, as Abraham's son, Ishmael is the real threat to Israel's proper self – 'the son of this slave shall not inherit with my son, Isaac' – the narrator virtually removes him from the action by making Hagar alone not only the object of the dismissal ('he sent *her* away') but also the subject of the verbs 'go' (*halak*) and 'wander' (*ta'ah*).

> Early next morning Abraham took bread and a skin of water and gave them
> to Hagar. He placed them on her shoulder, with the child, and sent *her* away.
> *She went*, and *she wandered* in the desert of Beersheba (Gen. 21.14).

One can understand why, in an effort to minimize the reader's sympathy
with Ishmael, the narrator would downplay his role in the events leading
up to the expulsion. But why, after the expulsion, is Ishmael still referred
to only as 'the child' (*yeled*) or 'the boy' (*na'ar*)?[7] Hagar never calls him
'my son', nor does God, in his conversation with Hagar, call him 'your
son'.[8] On the one hand, we can see the continued use of this impersonal
language as the narrator's way of distancing the reader from Ishmael. But
since Gen. 21.15-21 also shows us Hagar's point of view, the impersonal
language also reflects Hagar's distancing of herself from the child. For the
second time, Hagar tries to establish her subjectivity by abjecting Israel.
Having left the household of Israel, she abjects what still connects her
to Israel – the child – by casting the child away, abandoning him under
a bush. We might consider how Hagar's situation as a subject in process
(a minor character, a foreigner, a secondary wife, and a mother) is like
and unlike that of Abraham, the major character, the patriarch, the father
of Israel. For Abraham, Ishmael is 'not self' because he is the child of
Hagar the Egyptian. For Hagar, Ishmael is 'not self' because he is Israel's
child. Like Abraham, she needs to abject Ishmael in order to become an
independent 'I', to establish borders for her self. Why should Hagar not do
what Abraham did, and abject the child? Because God instructs Abraham
to abject Ishmael, but he instructs Hagar not to.

---

7. Verses 14–16 refer to Ishmael as a *yeled* and vv. 17–20 as a *na'ar*; both are
general terms for 'child', 'boy' and 'youth', but can be used of a range in age that
makes it impossible to deduce Ishmael's approximate age from them. Naomi Steinberg
discusses both terms in detail and concludes that they refer both to chronological age
and to social age; *The World of the Child in the Hebrew Bible* (Sheffield: Sheffield
Phoenix Press, 2013), 28–41. Ishmael is first a *yeled* to his mother (vv. 15-16), but,
after he attracts God's attention, as a *na'ar* he is distanced from his mother and the
reader (vv. 17-20). Steinberg sees here 'an attempt to disenfranchise Ishmael from the
biological family'; see her discussion of *na'ar*, *yeled* and *ben* in Gen. 21, pp. 86–95.
Verse 20 reports that Ishmael grew up, a further indication that, as far as Gen. 21.8-21
is concerned, Ishmael is a young child when he and his mother are cast out.
8. According to Ellen van Wolde (*Reframing Biblical Studies: When Language
and Text Meet Culture, Cognition, and Context* [Winona Lake, IN: Eisenbrauns,
2009], 126), the word *yeled* never contains a pronominal suffix and is never used to
designate a relationship; thus one would not expect 'your child'. *Yeled* also, she points
out, typically appears in contexts of life and death. The term used of a child in relation
to its parents is *ben*.

Uneasiness about what precisely Hagar does in Gen. 21.15 is reflected in translations:

> When the water in the skin was gone, she *cast* the child under one of the bushes. (New Revised Standard Version)

> When the skin of water was finished, she *abandoned* the child under a bush. (New Jerusalem Bible)

> When the water was gone from the skin, she *left* the child under one of the bushes. (Jewish Publication Society)

> When the water in the skin was finished, she *thrust* the child under a bush. (Revised English Bible)

> When the water in the skin was gone, she *put* the child under one of the bushes. (English Standard Version)[9]

Most commentators have little to say about Hagar's abandoning the child under a bush. Some interpret it as an act of tenderness, a mother's gentle placing of her child where she will not have to witness his death.[10] But

---

9. Cf. also, *inter alios*, Vawter (*On Genesis*, 247), 'she put the child down under a shrub'; Speiser (*Genesis*, 154), 'she left the child under one of the shrubs'; Wenham (*Genesis 16–50*), 'she dumped the child under one of the bushes'; Seebas (*Genesis II*, 173), 'sie warf das Kind unter einen der Sträucher' [she threw the child under one of the bushes].

10. Wenham (*Genesis 16–50*, 77), by translating Gen. 21.16 'Let me not see my child's death' for the Hebrew 'the death of the child', makes Hagar seem more like a caring mother. Bruce K. Waltke (*Genesis: A Commentary* [Grand Rapids, MI: Eerdmans, 2001], 296) prefers the meaning 'abandon' for *hishlik* in v. 15 and considers it 'a notion pertinent to a *loving mother* having to abandon her *beloved* teenager under the shade of a scrawny bush in the scorching desert' (italics mine). J. Gerald Janzen (*Abraham and All the Families of the Earth: A Commentary on the Book of Genesis 12–50* [Grand Rapids, MI: Eerdmans, 1993], 74) describes Hagar as 'shelter[ing] the child in the shade of a bush' and 'take[s] Hagar's words, together with her weeping, as a prayer that Ishmael's life may be spared'. Victor P. Hamilton (*The Book of Genesis: Chapters 18–50* [Grand Rapids, MI: Eerdmans, 1995], 83) explains Hagar's motive differently from the way the character Hagar describes it: she 'leaves Ishmael under the shade of one of the desert shrubs in order to let him die as peacefully and painlessly as possible, or at least to shade him from the harsh sun'. He goes on to say, 'The care Abraham showed in giving provisions to her is matched by her watchful observance of her son'. The parallel between Abraham's and Hagar's actions is apposite but its meaning is the opposite of what Hamilton proposes.

one need only look at the 127 occurrences of the verb used in this verse to recognize that the evidence does not favour this interpretation. The verb *šlk*, which occurs only in the *hiphil*, means 'to throw' or 'to throw away'.[11] When people who are still alive are the object of *hishlik*, they are thrown out or thrown down – in any event, abandoned – to their deaths. Joseph's brothers throw him into a pit; they do not lovingly place him there. Pharaoh commands that every boy born to the Hebrews should be thrown into the Nile – not for a toddler's swimming lesson.[12] Jeremiah is thrown into a cistern. He is let down by ropes, but this is hardly a solicitous action since the intention is that he should die of hunger (38.6-9).[13] Similarly, Hagar casts Ishmael aside, abandoning him under a bush.

Abraham shows no concern about what will happen to Hagar and Ishmael in the steppe when he casts them out with meagre provisions; similarly, Hagar abandons her son to a death she does not want to witness. Like Abraham who abjects Hagar and Ishmael, Hagar abjects Abraham/Israel and seeks to abject her only remaining tie to Israel, Ishmael.

11. Its object is always something thrown, that is, a projectile, whether it is an object (see, *inter alia*, Exod. 4.3; 15.25; 32.19, 24; Lev. 14.30; Num. 19.6; Deut. 9.21; Judg. 9.53; 15.7; 2 Kgs 2.21; 4.41; Isa. 2.20; Ezek. 7.19; 20.7, 8; Nah. 3.6; 2 Chron. 30.14; 33.15) or a person or persons (living or dead) or body part. For example, Joram's body is thrown on the plot of ground belonging to Naboth (2 Kgs 9.25, 26); Sheba's head is thrown down from the wall at Abel (2 Sam. 20.21, 22); the worshippers of Baal are killed and their bodies thrown out of his temple (2 Kgs 10.25); the body of a man is thrown in haste into the grave of Elisha and he comes back to life (2 Kgs 13.21); the body of the king of Babylon is thrown away, and, unlike the bodies of other kings, it is denied burial (Isa. 14.19); the slain are thrown out and their corpses left to rot (Isa. 34.3); bodies are thrown into the streets with no one to bury them (Jer. 14.16); Jeremiah prophesies that Jehoiakim will be buried with the burial of a donkey, his body thrown out beyond the gates of Jerusalem (Jer. 22.19) and also that his dead body will be thrown out to the heat by day and the frost by night (36.30); dead bodies are thrown into a cistern (Jer. 41.9); when God punishes Israel, dead bodies will be indiscriminately thrown out (Amos 8.3). For examples of living persons as the object of *hishlik*, see the discussion above and n. 13 below. The verb is also used of God expelling or banishing his people from his presence or from their land, Deut. 29.28; 2 Kgs 13.23; 17.20; 24.20; Jer. 7.15; 22.28; 52.3; Pss. 51.11; 71.9; 102.10; 2 Chron. 7.20. Throwing away is the opposite of keeping (Eccl. 3.6).

12. The infants should be thrown into or, perhaps better, exposed on the Nile, as proposed by Morton Cogan, 'A Technical Term for Exposure', *Journal for Near Eastern Studies* 27 (1968): 133–35. Cogan argues that *hishlik* does not necessarily include the physical hurling of an object but rather is a technical term for abandoning something with which one cannot or does not want to deal.

13. Other examples include personified Jerusalem, who is thrown out or exposed in the open field because she was abhorred (abject) on the day she was born (Ezek.

Phyllis Trible, following Victor Hamilton, appeals to the use of *šlk* for lowering a dead body into a grave as evidence that Hagar's is a loving act. 'Hagar does not cast away, throw out, or abandon her son; instead, she prepares a deathbed for "the child"', she maintains.[14] Hamilton observes, 'Obviously, carcasses are not hurled into their grave. They are deposited there with dignity.'[15] This may be true for burials in general, but not when bodies are the object of the verb *hishlik*. In these cases, bodies are not treated with dignity.[16] On the contrary, the use of *hishlik* in reference to casting aside a dead body, like its use in reference to throwing the living to their deaths, supports my proposal about Hagar's casting Ishmael away as abjection.

Having thus sought to abject the child, Hagar goes and sits opposite him 'at a distance a bowshot away'. She does not sit near him, watching over him, as Trible, among others, would have it. Trible goes to some length to argue that Hagar is a devoted mother and that '[c]ontrary to translations that place Hagar at a distance from the child, the entire sentence can be rendered, "She went and sat by herself in front of him, about a bowshot away"'.[17] The distance of a bowshot cannot be so easily dismissed, however. How far would a bowshot be? The distance would depend on many factors, such as the type of bow, type of arrow and skill of the archer.[18] Presumably the narrator has an archer with experience in mind, one skilled with the bow like Ishmael (v. 20), since the reference to the bowshot anticipates Ishmael's later association with the bow. Rather than remaining near 'the child', Hagar sits some distance away, where she

16.5); the king of Tyre, who is thrown to the ground by God (Ezek. 28.17); the women of Samaria, who will be thrown into Harmon (Amos 4.3); Jonah, who is thrown by God into the deep (2.3); the Egyptians, thrown by God into the sea like a stone (Neh. 9.11); captives thrown down from the top of a rock and dashed to pieces (2 Chron. 25.12).

14. Trible, 'Ominous Beginnings', 48.

15. Hamilton, *Genesis*, 83.

16. E.g., in Josh. 8.29 the body of the king of Ai is thrown at the entrance of the gate of the city and a heap of stones raised over it; in Josh. 10.27 the bodies of five enemy kings are thrown into a cave and stones placed at the mouth of the cave; in 2 Sam. 18.17, Absalom's body is thrown into a pit and a heap of stones raised over it; in Jer. 26.23 a prophet who offended the king is slain and his body thrown into the burial place of the common people.

17. Trible, 'Ominous Beginnings', 48, following Hamilton, *Genesis*, 76.

18. R. Miller, E. McEwen and C. Bergman, 'Experimental Approaches to Ancient Near Eastern Archery', *World Archaeology* 18 (1986): 178–95. Speiser (*Genesis*, 155) thinks the form is probably dual, 'two bowshots'.

will not have to witness his death ('Let me not look upon the death of the child', v. 16).

I am not proposing that the biblical narrator casts Hagar as a 'bad' mother (a question I doubt occurred to him), but only that her action is a gesture whose meaning can be seen as an attempt to establish her 'self' as an 'I' independent of Abraham/Israel, a connection represented by 'the child'. In this respect, she is no better or worse a mother than Abraham was a father. As we saw with Abraham, it is no easy matter to abject what is perceived as threatening the tenuous boundaries of the self and at the same time as a part of the self. For Hagar too the process is traumatic. She tries to sever her connection to Israel by abjecting Ishmael, but she cannot bear to witness the child's death. According to the Hebrew text, 'she raised her voice and wept' (v. 16), but the narrator leaves it to the reader to decide the reason: grief for her cruel plight, for 'the child', or for both? Whereas the narrator was careful to let readers know that Abraham was distressed because of his son (21.11), he is not so explicit in Hagar's case. And the next verse has God hearing not Hagar's voice but rather the voice of the boy, which has led numerous exegetes and translators to follow the Septuagint in reading 'the child raised his voice and wept' in v. 16. We encounter a further uncertainty when divine intervention supplies the solution to Hagar's predicament. God opens Hagar's eyes so that she sees a well of water. The text does not say that God created a well of water,[19] but rather that Hagar sees a well. Had she not seen it before, perhaps because she had closed her eyes in order not to *see* the death of the child? Or was the well hidden from her until now, and, if so, why?

After Hagar seeks to cast the child off, mother and child are no longer treated as one unit. If we follow the Hebrew text of v. 16, although Hagar weeps, it is the child's voice that God hears.[20] God hears him 'from where he is' (21.17), abjected by his mother, just as he had been abjected by his father. In response, the messenger addresses Hagar with the question, 'What troubles you, Hagar?', assures her that God has heard the boy, instructs her to care for the child and promises to make a nation of him. The narrator does not provide Hagar with a reply to the messenger's question. She simply goes to the well, fills the skin with water and lets 'the boy' drink (v. 19).

---

19. As it does, e.g., for *Israelites* fleeing from *Egypt* (Exod. 17.6; Num. 20.8; cf. also Judg. 15.19, where God miraculously provides water to satisfy Samson's thirst).

20. The divine response in v. 17 would thus point in two directions: 'What troubles you, Hagar?' responds to Hagar; 'God heard the voice of the lad', to the child. The messenger and God are difficult to untangle in vv. 17–18.

As here in vv. 17-20, divine sympathy for Hagar's plight was similarly stressed in 16.11, where the messenger assured her with the words, 'Yahweh has given heed to your maltreatment'. Ishmael's name, meaning 'God has heard', provides a lasting reminder of God's concern. This divine compassion, shown on two different occasions to Hagar, functions as narrative reparation for the cruelty shown to her by Abraham/Israel. Perhaps too divine intervention on Hagar's behalf and the promises Hagar receives help to assuage the guilt that besets the biblical narrator, Abraham/Israel's guilt.[21] In addition to guilt over abjecting a part of the 'self', could there also be a lingering sense of guilt resulting from Israel's treatment of Hagar when Abraham/Israel takes her as a wife in the first place? Both versions of Hagar's abjection resolve Hagar's desperate situation with a promise not unlike that given to Israel (for example, Gen. 12.2; 13.14-16; 17.4-5):

> The messenger of Yahweh also said to her, 'I will so greatly multiply your descendants that they cannot be numbered for multitude' (16.10).

> The messenger of God called to Hagar from heaven and said to her, '…Get up, pick up the lad and hold him fast with your hand, for I will make him a great nation' (21.17-18).

Whatever the motivation, sympathy or guilt or probably both, divine intervention and the promise concerning Ishmael serve as a gesture of recognition, a sign of concern for the 'other'. The account of the decisive dismissal ends in what seems to be a resolution, a sort of muted 'they lived happily ever after', with God showing a greater fatherly interest in Ishmael than Abraham displayed. Although the promise to Ishmael reveals divine care for the outsider (16.10-12; 17.20; 21.18-21), it remains a kind of compensation. Ishmael is an 'also ran', and the promise that he too will be the father of a great nation serves as his consolation prize.

> God was with the boy, and he grew up. He lived in the steppe and became an expert with the bow. He lived in the steppes of Paran. His mother took a wife for him from the land of Egypt (21.21).

21. In each account, there is some confusion in the text at a key moment, the moment when God responds to Hagar's plight. Did Hagar *see* God (Gen. 16)? Whose voice did God hear, Hagar's or Ishmael's (Gen. 21)? The confusion is noteworthy because, like the story of the abjection itself, it occurs twice. Is the narrator intentionally ambiguous? Or has the confusion arisen (or been introduced) in the course of textual transmission?

Readers of the story may find here some comfort, but this is not quite a storybook ending, and Ishmael, after his abjection, does not go away, but hovers at the edges of Israel's consciousness, a reminder of the unstable boundaries of the self that is Israel, and a threat to borders, system and order.

> He shall be a wild ass of a man, his hand against all and the hand of all against him. He shall dwell over against all his kin (16.12).[22]

And what about Hagar? Unlike Ishmael and his descendants the Ishmaelites, Hagar disappears from Israel's ongoing story.[23] This is more like repression than abjection: the repressed (Hagar) is banished to the unconscious, whereas the abject (Ishmael) lingers in the conscious. At the end of the second version of her abjection (21.21), Hagar slips back into obscurity, just as she did at the end of the first version, when Abraham, instead of Hagar, named 'his son'. In the last verse of her 'story', Hagar, whom the narrator and the character God have referred to by name, is no longer 'Hagar' but only 'his [Ishmael's] mother'. In 21.15-21, meanwhile, Ishmael has undergone a transition: at first 'the child', he becomes the subject of the promise, the one from whom God will make a great nation – in contrast to ch. 16, where the promise was made to Hagar ('I will greatly multiply *your* descendants…'). Ultimately Ishmael's future, not Hagar's, is more important to the biblical narrator, because, as 21.11 makes clear, he is *Abraham's* son. Hagar is 'his mother'. Nevertheless, it is no small matter that Hagar becomes a subject in the story, even if only briefly. Indeed, as I have sought to show, what happens in this chapter can be seen as the character Hagar's attempt to assert her subjectivity in a manner more dramatic than commentators have been willing to recognize: by attempting to abject Israel. Moreover, at the end of the story in Genesis 21, Hagar once again asserts her 'self' over against Israel. She does for Ishmael what Abraham does for Isaac: she procures a wife for her son from her own people, Egypt. Hagar's connection with Israel has been severed, and the story of Hagar the Egyptian ends, fittingly, with the word 'Egypt'.[24]

---

22. Although Ishmael returns home to bury his father (Gen. 25.9), he is not reintetgrated into the Abrahamic family.

23. Reference is made to Hagrites, apparently in reference to descendants of Hagar, in Ps. 83.7 and 1 Chron. 5.10, 19, 20; and 27.31 (in the singular) and to the proper name Hagri in 1 Chron. 11.38.

24. Although, unlike Ishmael, Hagar plays no further role in the Hebrew Bible, Israel's dissociation from Egypt is far from final and will receive particular attention in the book of Exodus.

Hagar and the Messenger in Art

Not surprisingly given its narrative power, there are more paintings representing Gen. 21.15-21 than Gen. 16.7-15. In what follows I limit my discussion to depictions of the encounter in Genesis 21, where, as we shall see, by focusing on the moment in the story when the messenger 'appears' to Hagar, the paintings discussed below smooth over problems in the text. In place of the ambiguous portrayal of the deity, who supports expulsion, and the short-lived subjectivity the text allows Hagar to attain, in the story these artworks tell we find divine compassion for Hagar and Ishmael foregrounded and Hagar given an enduring status as a subject.[25] The differences draw attention to the difficulty of the narrator's task: to show divine concern for Hagar and Ishmael while at the same time limiting the reader's identification with them so that their exclusion from the promises to Israel will be less difficult to endorse. Art provides the greater empathy with Hagar and Ishmael that readers want to find in the story, and that biblical commentators often struggle to discover.[26]

---

25. On other themes in wilderness-rescue paintings, see Sellin, *Fractured Families and Rebel Maidservants*, 94–99, 133–47. As in Chapters 3 and 4 above, I use as examples European art from the seventeenth and eighteenth centuries because it so well raises the exegetical issues I want to pursue and because there are many interesting paintings of the wilderness rescue to choose from. Sellin notes their popularity for various reasons, primarily for theological ideas of contrition and redemption (134).

26. In her article on Genesis in the *Women's Bible Commentary*, for example, Niditch entitles her discussion of Gen. 16 and 21 'Hagar: Mothering a Hero' ('Genesis', 34). Recognizing that the story is 'a difficult one in biblical ethics', Niditch finds a 'related people's story of its hero's youth' 'embedded' in the present story. But Ishmael is not a hero in the Bible, and Niditch rather cautiously but reassuringly concludes that in the biblical version 'God is the god of those deserted in the wilderness, of those on the fringes, who are usually in the Hebrew Scriptures not Ishmaelites but Israelites...' Tammi J. Schneider also recognizes the difficulty the story poses for a modern audience, and notes that the story is more concerned about Ishmael than about Hagar. She concludes that the text 'clearly wants to lift up Hagar's pain and critique the actions of Abraham, Sarah, and possibly even Elohim, using the beauty of the prose and the vivid scene of a mother not wanting to oversee the death of her son'; *Sarah: Mother of Nations* (New York: Continuum, 2004), 102. I am more interested in the way the story functions to make the expulsion more palatable for the reader, and the dissonance between the verbal narrative and the visual narrative suggests to me that the narrator, while sympathetic toward Hagar and Ishmael, is not so sympathetic as most commentators would like to think. See also the sources cited in n. 10 above.

A challenge artists face when painting what in art history is commonly referred to as 'Hagar in the Wilderness' or 'The Wilderness Rescue' is that they cannot paint the scene so that it is readily identifiable without putting Hagar and Ishmael in close proximity. As a consequence, the iconographic Hagar becomes a more attentive mother than the biblical mother who sits a bowshot away from her dying child. Like the relationship between mother and child, in many paintings – and all of those discussed below – the relationship between Hagar and God has changed. Whereas the biblical narrator speaks only of a divine voice 'from heaven' (21.17), artists make the divine messenger visible. Decisions about what the angel should look like vary considerably. Representing the angel in bodily form presents an inspiring, dramatic scene that makes the subject of the paintings immediately recognizable rather than one whose theme a viewer would be left to ponder (imagine the scenes below without the angel). Genesis 16, where Hagar speaks of *seeing* the messenger, provides some support for this iconographic tradition.

Fig. 5.2. Pietro da Cortona, *Hagar and the Angel*, 1637–1638, John and Mable Ringling Museum of Art, Sarasota, Florida

In paintings of the wilderness rescue, Hagar and the angel typically share the foreground, while Ishmael's place varies. Sometimes he is in the foreground, as in this painting by Pietro da Cortona (fig. 5.2); at other times in the background. Here Ishmael stands between Hagar and the angel, who is looking at him but gesturing with his right hand toward Hagar, as if summoning her to the source of water outside the frame, to which he points with his left hand. Hagar's attention is focused on the angel rather than Ishmael, as she appeals to the angel with her left hand, which is in line with and mirrors his right (with Ishmael in between). Paintings in which the angel appears in close proximity to Hagar give the impression of a more personal encounter than paintings where he is more removed. And in the angel's facial expression and demeanour artists are able to convey feelings of solicitude, tenderness, or urgency.

The discrepancy in the biblical story regarding Ishmael's age is reflected in art.[27] It makes a difference how old we think Ishmael is, for the older he is, the greater role one might expect him to play in events that concern him decisively, and the younger he is, the more vulnerable and helpless he will seem to us. Whereas paintings of the expulsion usually portray Ishmael as a young child, standing by his mother's side and often crying as Abraham sends them away, Ishmael's age varies considerably in paintings of the theophany. He is often depicted as an infant; in Cortona's painting, however, he looks about the same age as he does in paintings of the expulsion. He has not been cast under a bush and he does not appear in danger of dying any time soon. One could be forgiven for thinking that mother and child have been out for a picnic lunch. Standing here at his mother's side, he participates with her in the encounter with the angel, which makes this painting quite unlike the biblical account. He looks back at the angel somewhat apprehensively, more wary of this sudden apparition than his mother, who is literally rather comfortably 'laid back'.

Not infrequently Ishmael's age appears to correspond to the biblical chronology that makes him an adolescent, as, for example, in Giuseppe Bottani's *Hagar and the Angel* (fig. 5.3). A viewer might wonder why a youth of this age has apparently fainted, and in any event is no help to his mother, while his mother is more animated, especially if one assumes she has been carrying him. The handkerchief in her hand indicates that Hagar has been weeping, but she is not depicted as comforting Ishmael, whom Bottani places some distance away under a bush. Bottani has captured the moment when the angel appears, and Hagar's attention is focused solely on him and not on Ishmael, as it is in some paintings, like fig. 5.4 below, in which Hagar draws the angel's attention to the child.

27. As noted above, according to Gen. 16.16 Abraham is 86 when Ishmael is born, and according to 21.5 he is 100 when Isaac is born. Allowing a few years for Isaac to be weaned would make Ishmael 16 or 17 when Abraham sends him away. In Gen. 21.14-15, on the other hand, he clearly seems to be an infant.

Fig. 5.3. Giuseppe Bottani, *Hagar and the Angel*, c. 1776, Musée du Louvre, Paris

Where artists place Ishmael in relation to his mother has particular relevance for the crucial issues, discussed above, of Hagar's attitude to 'the child' and the distance meant by a bowshot. Where *is* Ishmael when the angel speaks to Hagar? It is here that we find the greatest difference among paintings of the wilderness rescue.

Giambattista Pittoni's *Hagar in the Desert* (fig. 5.4) is fairly typical in placing mother and child in close proximity.

Fig. 5.4. Giambattista Pittoni, *Hagar in the Desert*, 18th century, Santa Maria Gloriosa dei Frari, Venice

Hagar points to the child, who lies at her feet, drawing attention to his plight. The angel is always shown pointing in the direction of the life-giving well of water, which is sometimes beyond the canvas. His pointing gesture recalls Abraham's gesture of dismissal in paintings of the expulsion, again telling Hagar what she must do. Hagar and the angel look into each other's eyes. In this tender scene, the angel's face is close to Hagar's, and his hand almost touches hers. She points to the infant with a pleading look in her eyes.

Similarly, in Gérard de Lairesse's *Hagar in the Desert* (fig. 5.5), Ishmael lies near his mother (whose bared breasts appear to be an eroticizing touch[28]). He is barely visible, just over Hagar's right shoulder. She weeps, and has turned her back to the child in order not to watch him die. The dark background reflects Hagar's desolation. The angel hovers above her and there is no eye contact between them, emphasizing her sense of hopelessness and making this a far less intimate encounter than Pittoni's.

Fig. 5.5. Gérard de Lairesse, *Hagar in the Desert*, 1675–1680, Hermitage Museum, St Petersburg

28. See Sellin, *Fractured Families and Rebel Maidservants*, 44–46.

Whereas the paintings above by Pittoni and de Lairesse would seem to correspond to the scene as Trible describes it – a distraught mother sitting by her child – Pieter Lastman conveys a sense of distance between Hagar and Ishmael in his painting of *Hagar and the Angel* (fig. 5.6). The angel hovers between Hagar and Ishmael, pointing to the well with one hand and to heaven with the other, a forceful recognition of God's concern for the abject.[29] Ishmael is some distance away from Hagar and clearly removed from her engagement with the angel. Hagar makes a gesture of exasperation in his direction and from the position of her body it looks as though she has been watching him, although it is difficult to be sure how well she can see him from her present position.

Fig. 5.6. Pieter Lastman, *Hagar and the Angel*, 1614,
Los Angeles County Museum of Art

One way that an artist could capture the biblical narrative's distance of a bowshot away is by rendering the scene as a landscape painting. Claude Lorrain could have shown Ishmael at a considerable distance from Hagar in his *Hagar and Ishmael in the Desert*, perhaps even a bowshot away from her (fig. 5.7). But instead he follows the painterly tradition of placing

29. According to Sellin (*Fractured Families and Rebel Maidservants*, 136), this gesture appears to be distinctively Dutch. Italian wilderness-rescue scenes do not use it. Note how Hagar's pose in Lastman's painting resembles that of Ishmael and is counterbalanced by the angel's (135).

mother and child together. Hagar, kneeling with hands folded together, seems to have been interrupted by the angel's appearance in answer to her prayer on behalf of her son (who is not an infant in this scene).

Fig. 5.7. Claude Lorrain, *Hagar and Ishmael in the Desert*, 1668,
Alte Pinakothek, Munich

A painting by Alessandro Rosi is somewhat of an exception. Rosi places Ishmael at a distance away from his mother (fig. 5.8). Also, rather atypically, Hagar does not seem remotely interested in 'the child', nor does she seem the least bit distressed about his welfare. She and the angel appear to be engaged in conversation, and she looks pensively and serenely at him, as if spellbound by his countenance as well as his message. Here Hagar becomes a captivating subject in her own right, as she does briefly in the biblical account, inviting the viewer to consider what she might be thinking and feeling at this very moment. The proximity of the figures to the viewer draws the viewer into this close encounter, though the viewer's presence is not acknowledged by the two figures who look so intently, almost erotically, at each other. The angel's pointing finger directs Hagar's, and the viewer's, attention to the child, as if to remind Hagar of his plight while he explains what she needs to do. One assumes that, following convention, there is a nearby well, but it is difficult to see one; there is perhaps a spring behind the ruins of what appears to be a castle, but it is a considerable distance away.

Fig. 5.8. Alessandro Rosi, *Hagar and the Angel*, 17th century, Private Collection

Unlike Rossi, and like biblical readers who assume a strong emotional bond between Hagar and 'the child', artists frequently offer their viewers various visions of motherly devotion and innate concern for Ishmael on Hagar's part. Like much biblical commentary, these visualizations demonstrate the role of cultural constructions of motherhood in influencing interpretation. How, we might ask, do these visions relate to attitudes to children in biblical times? Obviously no parent would want to lose a child, but, as Naomi Steinberg points out, the biblical evidence indicates that children were valued for what they could contribute to the extended family, and not as individuals in their own right.[30] Of the stories in

---

30. Social constructions of childhood in the agrarian society of ancient Israel were based on what a child could do for the parent, not vice versa and not for themselves as they are in the modern West, where attitudes reflect changes that developed with the rise of capitalism; see Steinberg, *The World of the Child in the Hebrew Bible*, 91–97, 122–24 *et passim*.

Genesis in particular, she observes, 'Notwithstanding occasional mention of emotional ties between parents and child, the meaning of childhood was determined by the group interests that controlled all members of the family unit'.[31] From the moment that Ishmael ceases to be 'Abraham's son', he has lost value as far as the biblical narrator is concerned; he will contribute nothing to the building up of Israel ('for through Isaac shall your descendants be named', 21.12). Ishmael's descendants are mentioned later, in Gen. 25.12-18, but it is Israel's lineage that matters, not Ishmael's.

Not surprisingly, in presenting a picture of maternal devotion that is more compatible with the artists', their patrons' and their viewers' culture-bound constructions of motherhood, these paintings 'tell' the story on a more personal level by providing a degree of intimacy lacking in the biblical account – creating a closer bond between Hagar and Ishmael, whom Hagar typically keeps close to her, and between Hagar and God, who appears in the form of an angel to comfort Hagar rather than speaking from heaven.

This romanticizing tendency in art reaches its apogee in paintings that show Hagar holding her flagging child in her arms. Though different in style, these paintings of the wilderness rescue by Giovanni Battista Tiepolo (fig. 5.9) and Benjamin West (fig. 5.10) depict motherly solicitude in the loving way Hagar protects Ishmael by holding him close to her. In both paintings, Hagar is in the centre, between the angel and Ishmael. In Tiepolo's, she looks up at the angel, pleading with him, as is indicated both in her facial expression and her gesture toward the child, while Ishmael appears to have fainted. In West's, where the angel bears an uncanny resemblance to Hagar, both she and Ishmael, who appears to be quite weak at this point, seem reverent as they look up at the angel, who points to the life-giving well in the distance.

31. Steinberg, 'The World of the Family in Genesis', 296, where she also writes, 'A child [that is, a son] is a placeholder in the patrilineage, whose value depends not on individual personality traits but because he is defined by his ability to move the patrilineage forward to the next generation both through reproduction and through economic survival'.

Fig. 5.9. Giovanni Battista Tiepolo, *The Angel Succouring Hagar*, 1732,
Scuola Grande di San Rocco, Venice

Fig. 5.10. Benjamin West, *Hagar and Ishmael*, 1776, reworked 1803,
Courtesy Metropolitan Museum of Art, New York

Hagar and Ismail in the Desert by Andrea Sacchi, in which Ishmael is only a baby, offers a salient example of how art brings the story into greater conformity with artists' more modern ideals of motherhood (fig. 5.11). A solicitous mother hovers tenderly over her child. Her hands are clasped as though she has been praying and has just been interrupted by the angel in answer to her prayer. There is hardly any hint of the utter distress of the situation in the almost pastoral atmosphere. Sacchi's charming interpretation anticipates an easy resolution and a happy ending to Hagar's story.

Fig. 5.11. Andrea Sacchi, *Hagar and Ismail in the Desert*, c. 1630,
National Museum, Wales

As this brief survey of visual renditions of Gen. 21.15-21 indicates, the picture of Hagar as a mother attentive to her child's distress is at odds with the biblical presentation, where Hagar does not sit with the child, watching over him, and the impersonal language used by the narrator ('the child', 'the boy') distances both Hagar and the reader from Ishmael. In addition, these visual narratives involve God on a very personal level, whereas in the verbal narrative distance is created between Hagar and God, whose words are recounted to Hagar by a messenger – a messenger who does not even appear but only speaks – from heaven.

Unlike the expulsion of Hagar and Ishmael, where art exposes the
victim's point of view that the biblical writer cautiously withholds from
readers in order to make the expulsion less troubling, and the rape of
Hagar, where art again reveals the victim's perspective that the verbal
narrative ignores, in the case of the wilderness rescue, the examples
we have looked at in this chapter present an alternative, often exceedingly sentimental version of the story. Given the differences between
the biblical account of Hagar's encounter with the messenger and these
visual representations, does visual criticism in this case contribute to a
better understanding of the text? In my view, yes, by bringing these very
differences into relief. That the biblical narrator's interest in Hagar and
Ishmael is qualified becomes all the more apparent when we compare
the verbal narrative to the visual narrative. Having briefly allowed Hagar
a degree of subjectivity in the wider story, in the end the narrator takes
it away. But he cannot take it back, and Hagar's attempt to abject Israel
by casting Abraham's son under a bush can be construed as the literary
character's claim to her own subjectivity, about which the narrator is
ambivalent.

After he has tackled the problem of the expulsion by showing that
God has not abandoned Hagar and Ishmael, thereby offsetting their harsh
treatment by Israel, Hagar holds no interest for the biblical narrator. What
happens to Hagar afterwards matters to readers, however, and because
readers invariably want to know more about her, Hagar remains a subject
of interest in later tradition.[32] Not without reason she has often served as
an inspiration to oppressed people, especially women, and, in particular,

---

32. See Sherwood, 'Hagar and Ishmael: The Reception of Expulsion'; Thompson,
Writing the Wrongs, 17–99; Carol Bakhos, *Ishmael on the Border: Rabbinic
Portrayals of the First Arab* (Albany: State University of New York, 2006). On
Hagar in Jewish, Christian and Islamic traditions, see Martin Goodman, George H.
van Kooten and Jacques T. A. G. M. van Ruiten, eds., *Abraham, the Nations, and the
Hagarites: Jewish, Christian, and Islamic Perspectives on Kinship with Abraham*
(Leiden: Brill, 2010), which focuses mainly on Jewish and Christian sources; see
also Trible and Russell, eds., *Hagar, Sarah, and Their Children: Jewish, Christian,
and Muslim Perspectives*. Although not mentioned by name in the Quran, Hagar
holds an important position in Islamic tradition; see, especially, Martin O'Kane and
Talha Bhamji, 'Islamic Tradition and the Reception History of the Bible', in *Reading
the Bible in Islamic Context: Qur'anic Conversations*, ed. Daniel J. Crowther et al.
(London: Routledge, 2018), 148–66. See also Fred Leemhuis, 'Hājar in the Qur'ān
and Its Early Commentaries', in Goodman et al., eds., *Abraham, the Nations, and the
Hagarites*, 503–8.

black women whose lives have been influenced by a history of slavery.[33] And, of course, we can find her on the walls of numerous art galleries.

33. See Delores S. Williams, who examines the importance of Hagar for the construction of womanist theology ('Hagar in African American Biblical Appropriation', in Trible and Russell, eds., *Hagar, Sarah, and Their Children*, 171–84). Williams mentions a seminar presentation at Union Theological Seminary by Valerie Ellis, who draws attention to Ishmael, 'abandoned by Abraham' and 'briefly abandoned by Hagar' – precisely the two parallel actions I have been discussing here – as a resource for exploring abandonment as experienced by many African American children (174). See also Nyasha Junior, *Reimagining Hagar: Blackness and Bible* (Oxford: Oxford University Press, 2019); Renita J. Weems, *Just a Sister Away: A Womanist Vision of Woman's Relationships in the Bible* (San Diego, CA: LuraMedia, 1988), 1–19; Janet Gabler-Hover, *Dreaming Black/Writing White: The Hagar Myth in American Cultural History* (Lexington: University Press of Kentucky, 2000).

Part III

From Eve to Mary

EROTIC LOOK AND VOYEURISTIC GAZE:
LOOKING AT THE BODY IN THE BIBLE AND ART

When is looking at the body – the naked or partially clad body – voyeuristic and when is it erotic? Since one person's erotic look may well be another person's voyeuristic gaze and vice versa, can one distinguish between an erotic look and a voyeuristic gaze? Like the erotic itself, the gaze, or look, or glance, is a cultural construct, not a stable or transhistorical 'reality'.[1] In dealing with the topic of looking at the body, the culture-bound and subjective nature of looking needs to be acknowledged, as do the varied social and cultural positions occupied at different times by readers of texts that invoke visuality and by viewers of art. It is not my purpose in this chapter either to propose or to adopt a particular theory of looking.[2] Rather, I want to employ the hypothesis of an erotic look and a voyeuristic gaze heuristically as a way of asking what insights biblical art can give us

---

1. On the gaze, the look and the glance, see Bal, *Reading 'Rembrandt'*, 141–48.

2. In 'Text Appeal: Visual Pleasure and Biblical Studies', in *In Search of the Present: The Bible through Cultural Studies*, ed. Stephen D. Moore (Atlanta, GA: Society of Biblical Literature, 1998), 63–78, Jennifer Glancy questions the 'legitimacy' and 'validity' of relying on discourses of visuality in analysing biblical texts. But who decides what is 'legitimate' or 'valid' in interpretation? Samuel Tongue responds to Glancy's caveats by appealing to Mieke Bal's concept of 'envisioning' as interpretation and W. J. T. Mitchell's work on 'iconicity' 'to *legitimate* the use of visual studies terminology to understand a "biblical visuality"' (italics mine). He cites Mitchell's *Iconology: Image, Text, Ideology* (Chicago: University of Chicago Press, 1986), 155, in observing, 'Not only is it legitimate to draw on an essentially visual category but "transgressions of the text-image boundaries [are...] the rule rather than the exception"' (241); Samuel Tongue, *Between Biblical Criticism and Poetic Rewriting: Interpretative Struggles over Genesis 32:22-32* (Leiden: Brill, 2014), 234–41. It is also, as Mitchell points out, 'something that occurs all the time in practice' (*Iconology*, 154–55). Visual tropes are eminently applicable in analysing

into biblical texts in which looking at the body, usually the female body, is involved.[3] What I want to call erotic looking and voyeuristic gazing are neither strict oppositions nor fixed positions. Readers of texts that appeal to the visual imagination and viewers of paintings may find their perspective shifting, and texts and paintings may offer multiple positions to readers and viewers.

In what follows, I want to address the issue of looking by considering four examples from the Bible in which the following features are all present: (1) the act of looking is represented in the text, (2) the object of the look becomes the object of sexual desire and (3) the desire is acted upon. How artists respond to this textual looking, facilitating the look or resisting it, or even in one case reversing it, may help us 'see' aspects of the texts in a different light. Of course looking that takes place in a text and its rendering in art are not the same, and nowhere will this be more apparent than in my example of the erotic look.[4] Nevertheless, visuality, as Mieke Bal points out, is a specific semiotic mode that can be employed in both visual and verbal media, and thus there are connections to be found between looking in these texts and in their visual representations. As Bal observes, 'The possibility of verbal pornography (based, as pornography is, on the thrill of voyeurism, of detached viewing) is evidence for the visuality of the verbal as much as for the imaginative nature of seeing'.[5]

texts that are concerned with looking; on the gaze as also a useful concept for analysing a text where visuality is implicit rather than explicit, see Caryn Tamber-Rosenau, 'Biblical Bathing Beauties and the Manipulation of the Male Gaze: What Judith Can Tell Us about Bathsheba and Susanna', *Journal of Feminist Studies in Religion* 33 (2017): 55–72. See also Sheaffer, *Envisioning the Book of Judith*, 8–10, 127–33.

3. The female body is the quintessential object of the look in Western art, and equally popular, it would seem, in literature.

4. Perhaps the difficulty of capturing the textual erotic looking that I discuss below in so-called naturalistic painting says something about the look as distinguished from the gaze and raises the question of what counts as 'erotic art'. Although my discussion touches on it, I have not entered the debate on erotic art versus pornography. As Lynda Nead points out, '…art and pornography cannot be seen as isolated regimes of representation, but should be recognized as elements within a cultural continuum that distinguishes good and bad representations of the female body, allowable and forbidden forms of cultural consumption and that defines what can or cannot be seen… "Erotic art" is the term that defines the degree of sexuality that is permissible within the category of the aesthetic' (*The Female Nude: Art, Obscenity and Sexuality* [London: Routledge, 1992], 103). In dealing with the Song of Songs below, I am concerned especially with aesthetics.

5. Bal, *Reading 'Rembrandt'*, 155–56.

In my examples, the obsession with viewing the body is shared by the text and the iconographic tradition.[6]

Bathsheba and Susanna

Let us begin with two classic cases of biblical voyeurism. In the stories of David and Bathsheba in 2 Samuel 11–12 and of Susanna and the elders in the Additions to Daniel,[7] looking at a beautiful woman activates desire:

> ...he *saw* from the roof a woman bathing, and the woman was very beautiful... And David sent messengers and took her (2 Sam. 11.2, 4).

> The two elders used to *observe* her every day, going in and walking around [the garden] and they began to lust after her... They *watched closely* day after day to *see* her... So it was that while they were *watching closely* for a suitable day, she went in as on the previous day and the day before with only two maids, and she wanted to bathe in the garden, for it was very hot. No one was there except the two elders, hidden and *watching her closely* (Sus. 8, 12, 15-16).

The voyeuristic gaze at the female body occurs in both stories when a woman is bathing – or in Susanna's case simply preparing to bathe – and a man or two is watching. In 2 Sam. 11.3, David, it seems, is not the only voyeur. Having seen the bathing beauty, David enquires about her: 'Is this not Bathsheba, the daughter of Eliam, the wife of Uriah the Hittite?' It is not clear who says these words, whether David[8] or an attendant,[9] but, in any event, 'Is this not Bathsheba?' suggests that someone else is looking too. In the story of Susanna, the elders are initially solitary voyeurs,

---

6. This applies also to the case of Joseph and Potiphar's wife, with a telling gender-motivated twist: the subject of the look in the text becomes its object in art; see the discussion below.

7. In the Septuagint and Vulgate Susanna appears as ch. 13 of the book of Daniel. In the longer text of Theodotion, which I follow here with most scholars, it is part of ch. 1 of Daniel. On the differences, see Carey A. Moore, *Daniel, Esther, and Jeremiah: The Additions* (Garden City, NY: Doubleday, 1977), 77–116. For a detailed comparison and analysis of the two versions, see Helmut Engel, *Die Susanna-Erzählung: Einleitung, Übersetzung und Kommentar zum Septuaginta-Text und zur Theodotion-Bearbeitung* (Freiburg Schweiz: Universitätsverlag; Göttingen: Vandenhoeck & Ruprecht, 1985). On the textual history, see also John J. Collins, *Daniel* (Minneapolis, MN: Fortress Press, 1993), 426–28.

8. So, convincingly, Randall C. Bailey, *David in Love and War: The Pursuit of Power in 2 Samuel 10–12* (Sheffield: JSOT Press, 1990), 85.

9. So most commentators and most translations.

'ashamed to disclose their lustful desire' (Sus. 11). Upon discovering that their desire is mutual, however, they jointly wait for a 'suitable day' to accost the unsuspecting object of their fancy.

Although neither text gives any indication of the state of the woman's undress, bathing seems to be an intimate activity (Susanna, in fact, takes pains to do it in private) and carries suggestions of the exposure of (some) flesh.[10] The sight of Bathsheba bathing is clearly sexually provocative because it leads David to act on his lustful desire and to send for her. In Susanna's case, the elders' lust is already aroused before the hot day on which she decides to bathe in the garden, for they have been in the habit of watching her during her daily stroll in her husband's garden (Sus. 7-8). The way the narrative builds up to the bathing scene seems designed to encourage readers to *participate* in the elders' voyeurism. One might ask if the cards are already stacked against the women – if, by representing them bathing or about to bathe, the biblical narrators have set the stage for readers to imagine provocation on the woman's part. Bathsheba's is a case in point, and not a few readers have suggested that she sought the king's attention.[11] Although the story of Susanna precludes any such intention on the woman's part, this has not hindered artists from representing Susanna as well as Bathsheba as rousing the voyeuristic gaze. After all, if you don't want to be the object of a potential voyeur, why bathe in a garden, or where you can be seen by someone standing on a roof – where, as it turns out, there is a very good possibility you could be seen?[12]

10. The topos of a bathing woman arousing male desire also appears in *Jub.* 33.2-9 (in a story with some striking similarities to the story of Joseph and Potiphar's wife) and *T. Reub.* 3, both of which recount Reuben's rape of Bilhah after seeing her bathing (cf. Gen. 35.22, which reports only that Reuben had sexual intercourse with his father's wife Bilhah).

11. H. W. Hertzberg, *I & II Samuel*, trans. J. S. Bowden (Philadelphia, PA: Westminster Press, 1964), 309; George G. Nicol, 'Bathsheba, a Clever Woman?', *Expository Times* 99 (1988): 360; Nicol, 'The Alleged Rape of Bathsheba: Some Observations on Ambiguity in Biblical Narrative', *Journal for the Study of the Old Testament* 73 (1997): 50–52; Bailey, *David in Love and War*, 88–90; Lillian R. Klein, 'Bathsheba Revealed', in *Samuel and Kings: A Feminist Companion to the Bible (Second Series)*, ed. Athalya Brenner (Sheffield: Sheffield Academic Press, 2000), 52–54; cf. Sandra Ladick Collins, *Weapons upon Her Body: The Female Heroic in the Hebrew Bible* (Newcastle upon Tyne: Cambridge Scholars Publishing, 2012), 146–52 *et passim*.

12. As in cases of rape (and we have in Bathsheba's case what could be construed as a rape, and in Susanna's intended repeated rape), the woman is often blamed. Alexander Izuchukwu Abasili argues that what happens between David and Bathsheba does not qualify as rape in terms of the biblical understanding of rape

When we first encounter them, Bathsheba and Susanna are described as 'very beautiful' (2 Sam. 11.2; Sus. 2; see also Sus. 31). The women's beauty is the cause of male desire in these stories. Like bathing or preparing to bathe where they could be seen, beauty makes the women somehow or other responsible for what happens to them.[13] Daniel – who in answer to Susanna's prayer steps in to save the day by revealing the elders' perfidy and Susanna's innocence – says as much when he tells one of the elders that 'beauty has led you astray' (Sus. 56). (The elder, it turns out, is a victim.) The gaze in both stories is voyeuristic – detached looking – and the impression is given that its object is exposed female flesh. The women do not know that they are being observed in an intimate activity (though, as noted above, some commentators speculate that Bathsheba planned to be seen). The men's looking intrudes upon what is seen, as does ours if we assume the position of the voyeurs that the texts invite their readers to assume. The women do not come face to face, as it were, with their voyeurs until the men's desire is made known to them: David sends for Bathsheba; the elders accost Susanna.

Voyeurism gives the one who looks the advantage over the one who is seen. It is frequently aligned with the power of men over women, especially in art, and in these stories of voyeurism as well. David's power as king enables him to act on his lustful desires and send for the wife of another man. The woman is not given a choice. In the story of Susanna, the elders' standing as leaders of the community and judges empowers them to think they can have their way with Susanna and, when that plan fails, to bring a nearly successful charge of adultery against her. Is Susanna given a choice? The elders attempt to coerce her into having sexual intercourse with them, but she refuses. Although the woman is allowed to refuse, refusal has dire consequences and the choice she is given is a choice between two evils: to be raped by the elders or condemned to death for a fictive consensual sexual encounter.[14] At issue

('Was It Rape? The David and Bathsheba Pericope Re-examined', *Vetus Testamentum* 61 [2011]: 1–15). It should come as no surprise that it does not, but, as I observed in the case of Hagar in Chapter 4, that should not prevent a contemporary reader from describing it as rape.

13. Beauty is a liability: the matriarch's beauty leads to her being taken into the harem of a powerful foreign ruler (Gen. 12 and 20) and puts her husband in danger (Gen. 12, 20 and 26, though the danger may be only in the patriarch's mind; see Exum, *Fragmented Women*, 115–33); a woman's beauty puts her in danger of sexual appropriation by and for men (Tamar in 2 Sam. 13; Abishag in 1 Kgs 1 and Esther).

14. The text informs the reader at the outset that Susanna fears God and had been instructed in the law of Moses by her parents (Sus. 2–3). With regard to

in each scenario is adultery, the sin against God that Susanna will not commit.[15]

Although the voyeuristic gaze at the women in these texts is not sanctioned, the biblical narrators have so constructed their accounts that it is possible for them to have their gaze and condemn it too. This narrative strategy allows the reader to take the moral highground – to pass judgment on the voyeurs (which these texts do) and, at the same time, if the reader is so inclined, to enjoy the voyeurs' gaze at the exposed female body.[16] Many factors, not the least of which are sexual identification and sexual orientation, will affect our response. As we shall see, many artists will draw on this strategy.

Susanna's piety, Amy-Jill Levine observes, 'While the repeated notices of Susanna's piety and fidelity reinforce her innocence, the references and the character are both compromised by the elders' desires. For the story to function, their desire must be comprehensible to the reader...'; Amy-Jill Levine, '"Hemmed in on Every Side": Jews and Women in the Book of Susanna', in *A Feminist Companion to Esther, Judith and Susanna*, ed. Athalya Brenner (Sheffield: Sheffield Academic Press, 1995), 313. Levine, who sees Susanna as representing the threatened Jewish community in exile, observes pertinently that 'Susanna's sex and class impede any unambiguous reading of her character as a paradigm of righteousness or her setting as the epitome of patriarchy. Susanna, as a character and as text, carries possibilities for condemnation as well as praise, for the recognition of women's social and religious freedom as well as their confinement, for the discovery of how Judaism survived challenges to its self-definition as well as the compromises it made in this process' (307–8).

15. Susanna's husband Joakim, who would obviously be shamed if the charge against her were true, does nothing to defend her and is absent at her trial (Theodotion mentions Susanna's parents, children and relatives as those present; the Septuagint, her parents and four children). His inconspicuousness is a narrative necessity, for, were he to defend his wife, the story would be about his honour and not hers, and he would become a rival to Daniel as Susanna's champion. Unlike Joakim, Bathsheba's husband Uriah plays a significant role in the account of David's adultery as a foil to David.

16. Interestingly, the bath scene in Sus. 15–18 does not appear in the Septuagint, which leads Moore to conclude it must have been a later addition. 'If so', he writes, 'from a literary point of view it is *a most welcome one*: the bathing scene *not only excites the elders*, thereby enabling them to attempt their dastardly deed, but *it can also fire the imagination of some readers*. Of such considerations are good stories made!' (Moore, *Daniel*, 97, italics mine; as a feminist reader, I would ask for whom and at whose expense the scene makes this a good story). Cf. Collins (*Daniel*, 426), who observes that the bath scene 'serves to heighten the dramatic and erotic interest'.

In both cases the men are condemned not for looking but for its conse-quences, for acting on the lustful impulses provoked by their voyeurism (though we are told at the outset that the elders are evil). Looking leads David first to take another man's wife and then to have the man killed to conceal his crime when the woman becomes pregnant.[17] By setting it up so that what we see through David's eyes becomes part of our judgment against David, the biblical narrator offers readers the moral highground, and thus moral distance from which to enjoy David's gaze at the bather without necessarily feeling guilty or embarrassed or concerned about the potentially damaging portrayal of the woman.

The Susanna story provides the reader with a clear moral stance. The narrator introduces the elders as wicked men, scoundrels who have turned their eyes away from heaven to look at a beautiful woman (Sus. 5, 9). They entertain lustful desires that they are ashamed to admit, and confess to each other only when they discover that they both have the same goal. Their plot to observe Susanna, their attempt to blackmail her into having sex with them and their false witness against her – their 'lawless intention to have Susanna put to death' – are all laid bare as heinous crimes by the narrator.[18] Unlike the voyeur David, whose desire thrusts him into a situation that spirals out of his control, and who has his redeeming qualities, they have none. David's voyeurism was not planned; theirs is. And we are allowed to look *with them* – to visualize the scene if we so choose – as well as to look *at them* and hear their salacious proposition (a sexual fantasy within a sexual fantasy, if you will).

At one point, the narrator drops his guard and adopts their perspective, and focalization coincides with the voyeurism of the elders. This does not take place in the garden, but later, at Susanna's trial for adultery:

> Susanna was very refined and beautiful in appearance. And the scoundrels ordered her to be uncovered, for she was veiled, so that they might feast upon her beauty (vv. 31-32).[19]

---

17. There is no evidence in the biblical story to suggest that David wanted Bathsheba either for his wife or his paramour. On the contrary, the text makes clear that David would prefer to have Uriah assume paternity of the child and, presumably, continue in his marriage to Bathsheba as before. David has Uriah killed and then marries Bathsheba only because his ploy to get Uriah to 'go down to his house' and have sex with his wife fails (2 Sam. 11.11).

18. Daniel, in fact, accuses them of having used their blackmail ploy successfully before, thus adding to the list of their sins (Sus. 57).

19. So Theodotion; the Septuagint makes no mention of a veil.

Bal comments:

> [T]he embedded clause 'so that they may feast their eyes on her beauty' insinuates the focalization of the Elders into the framing 'righteous' perspective. Although the unveiling is condemned, the visual feast is promised by the same token. Perniciously, the moral dimension of the tale absorbs the pornographic one and provides the innocent reader with an excuse to anticipate the pleasure *sanctioned*, rather than countered, by the moral indignation.[20]

One can, of course, read these two biblical stories without visualizing the women as seen through the voyeurs' eyes. And a painting can facilitate or problematize voyeurism or both, with much depending on the viewer's disposition to adopt or resist a voyeuristic stance. We should not be surprised to find that, when artists actualize the visual potential of the narrative, they typically dramatically reinscribe the texts' voyeuristic gaze at the body, using it as both theme and pretext for painting the exposed female body.[21]

Bathsheba

David's voyeurism is but a brief narrative moment, but it is enough to have inspired numerous paintings of Bathsheba's bath.[22] Conventionally, David is pictured in the background behind Bathsheba, on the balcony of his palace roof from where he cannot see or have seen her very well. Sometimes he is not even visible in the distance. Her nakedness is for the spectator's benefit, a spectator assumed in most European oil painting to be male.[23] The viewer is invited to participate in David's voyeurism,

---

20. Bal, *Reading 'Rembrandt'*, 155.

21. Margaret R. Miles (*Carnal Knowing: Female Nakedness and Religious Meaning in the Christian West* [New York: Vintage Books, 1991]) argues that female nudity in the art of the Christian West, whatever else it conveys, carries associations of shame, sin and guilt. 'Women's bodies', she observes, 'are presented as revealing their "nature"' and 'the primary pictorial device by which the problem of "woman" – for men – is signalled is female nakedness' (120).

22. See Exum, *Plotted, Shot, and Painted*, 28–59, where I discuss the biblical story and paintings, as well as film, at greater length, using different examples of paintings from those discussed briefly here.

23. As John Berger observes, 'In the average European oil painting of the nude the principal protagonist is never painted. He is the spectator in front of the picture and he is presumed to be a man. Everything is addressed to him. Everything must appear to be the result of his being there. It is for him that the figures have assumed their

and is, moreover, given the opportunity to see more than David can see. Much more. Bathsheba's exposed body both communicates and explains David's desire.[24]

In the biblical story Bathsheba is not held accountable for any of the events arising from her sexual involvement with David. God, through the mouth of his prophet Nathan, condemns David alone for the crimes of adultery and murder:

> Why have you despised the word of the Lord to do what is evil in his eyes? Uriah the Hittite you have slain with the sword, and his wife you have taken to be your wife, and him you have killed with the sword of the Ammonites. Now therefore the sword shall never depart from your house.

> Because you have despised me and have taken the wife of Uriah the Hittite to be your wife – thus says the Lord – I am raising up evil against you out of your own house, and I will take your wives before your eyes and give them to your neighbour, and he shall lie with your wives in the eyes of this sun. For you did it in secret, but I shall do this thing before all Israel and before the sun (2 Sam. 12.9-12).[25]

David's wrongdoings are crimes against Uriah and against God. But they are not treated as crimes against Bathsheba, who is mentioned only in her role as 'the wife of Uriah the Hittite' or 'his wife'. Having sexual intercourse with Bathsheba is a crime because it violates another man's marital rights. David's punishment for adultery is that *his wives* will be raped; what he did to another man will be done to him, only more so. Neither in Bathsheba's case nor that of David's abused wives is the woman's point of view represented. Paintings of Bathsheba's bath, in contrast, tell a different story, often conveying what the text does not (though its silence encourages reading between the lines): Bathsheba's guilt or exhibitionism or both.

nudity. But he, by definition, is a stranger – with his clothes still on' (*Ways of Seeing*, 54). Viewers may want to resist this position or may take another perspective; see e.g. Deryn Guest, 'Looking Lesbian at the Bathing Bathsheba', *Biblical Interpretation* 16 (2008): 227–62.

24. Miles (*Carnal Knowing*, 123) makes this point with regard to Susanna.

25. Dividing v. 10 with J. P. Fokkelman (*Narrative Art and Poetry in the Books of Samuel*. Vol. 1, *King David* [Assen: van Gorcum, 1981], 83–86), who makes a convincing case against the Masoretic division.

Fig. 6.1. Jan Massys, *David and Bathsheba*, 1562, Musée du Louvre, Paris

There is nothing retiring or modest about Bathsheba in this painting by Jan Massys (fig. 6.1). She seems aware of her power to arouse desire and not the least reluctant to display herself to the messenger David has sent to fetch her, as she listens, apparently with interest, to the proposal he is making on the king's behalf. Typically, David is in the background. He stands on his balcony with two attendants, who are conferring with each other while David watches to see how the woman, who has clearly been bathing out in the open, responds to his messenger. Here it appears that not only has Bathsheba invited the gaze but also that *she* will be the one to decide whether or not to accept the king's proposition. Massys thus reinforces the stereotype of Bathsheba as instigator of the affair. Her attendant in the foreground observes the negotiations with an impish, knowing smile as she dips her fingers in a pan of water. The attendant in the background holds a jug, perhaps containing ointments for the bath. Although she faces the viewer, she does not look at us directly; nevertheless, one gets the impression that she knows we are looking. The black attendant on the left, holding a dog by the collar and acknowledging the viewer's presence with a knowing smile, lends to the opulent setting an atmosphere of the exotic.

Fig. 6.2. Sebastiano Ricci, *Bathsheba at the Bath*, c. 1724,
Museum of Fine Arts, Budapest

Bathsheba is frequently pictured with servants, preparing her to be seen in person and subsequently sexually enjoyed by David. Sebastiano Ricci shows Bathsheba bathing in a colonnaded portico with servants who are busy attending her every need: one holds a tray with ointments for her toilette, one delicately dries her leg, one combs her hair and one holds a mirror in which Bathsheba admires her reflection (fig. 6.2). David looks on from the balcony in the distance. In paintings in which Bathsheba looks at her reflection in a mirror, as here, the mirror not only accuses her of vanity, it also allows her to join her voyeurs in making herself the object of the gaze.[26]

Similarly, in another painting by Jan Massys, Bathsheba colludes with the voyeuristic gaze (fig. 6.3). She has been looking at herself in her mirror, and perhaps in it she has caught sight of David behind her, looking at her, making her both the object and the subject of looking. Her gaze seems to have shifted from the reflection in the mirror to the viewers who stand before the painting, as if, suddenly, we have caught her attention. By acknowledging our presence, she accuses us of participating in David's voyeurism. But she appears unperturbed by our gaze, and in fact plays to it, which allows us, in return, to accuse her of narcissism and exhibitionism.

26. On the mirror in paintings of Bathsheba and Susanna as a symbol of wealth, vanity and culpability, see Katherine Low, 'Sharing a Mirror with Venus: Bathsheba and Susanna with Mirrors in Early Modern Venetian Art', *Biblical Reception* 2 (2013): 57–74.

Fig. 6.3. Jan Massys, *Bathsheba Observed by King David*,
first half of the 16th century, Private Collection

Sometimes Bathsheba is not the only object of the gaze. In this painting
by Jacopo Zucchi, for example, she appears with other naked women in
what looks like a grand public bath (fig. 6.4).

Fig. 6.4. Jacopo Zucchi, *The Toilet of Bathsheba*, after 1573,
Galleria Nazionale d'Arte Antica, Rome

There seem to be two 'stories' here, the familiar one of Bathsheba bathing and another story of women enjoying a pleasant afternoon at the baths. Bathsheba is surrounded by four servants who are assisting at her toilette. The one with exposed breasts who holds a tray of ointments appears to be acknowledging the viewer's gaze with a kind of knowing smile. The black servant next to her, but in the background, looks directly at the viewer, though the viewer is not allowed visual access to her body. Bathsheba looks at the servant who is handing her an urn, but it is difficult to tell whether the servant looks back at her or is looking off in the distance, while the servant standing behind Bathsheba's left shoulder appears to be looking down at her mistress. David, whose desire we assume to be activated by the scene before us, cannot be seen in the distance.

The four women on the left-hand side of the painting, two of whom are looking at each other as if in conversation, show no interest in Bathsheba. They seem to be at ease with their bodies and simply enjoying their bath in the company of other women. Rather than playing exclusively to the male gaze, they destabilize it, offering viewers an opportunity to adopt a female gaze.[27]

In this brief look at paintings of Bathsheba's bath, I have not included works that humanize Bathsheba and might therefore be considered counter-voyeuristic, such as Rembrandt's famous *Bathsheba at Her Bath*, in which the expression on Bathsheba's face suggests an interiority that the viewer cannot penetrate, a private, inner space that is hers alone.[28] Conventionally the iconographic tradition of Bathsheba at her bath goes beyond the text in portraying Bathsheba as exhibitionist, narcissistic and conspiring with the gaze. One might reasonably assume that a representation of viewing in a painting can affect the experience of viewing the painting itself.[29] Paintings that offer Bathsheba freely to the voyeuristic gaze – like paintings of Adam and Eve that place responsibility for the 'Fall' squarely upon the woman – have undoubtedly influenced the view readers form of the woman in 2 Samuel 11.

27. My comments about the representation of these figures, a representation that could be seen as acknowledging female homoeroticism, were stimulated by Linda Nochlin's discussion of Renoir's *The Great Bathers*; Nochlin, *Bathers, Bodies, Beauty: The Visceral Eye* (Cambridge, MA: Harvard University Press, 2006), 1–53. To be sure, the historical periods and cultural circumstances are different; nevertheless, the diverse ways a modern (as well as early) viewer might understand the relationship of figures in a painting, regardless of the painter's intentions, underscores the decisive role played by the viewer in interpretation.

28. For discussion of this painting, see Bal, *Reading 'Rembrandt'*, 219–46; Exum, *Plotted, Shot, and Painted*, 37–40.

29. So Bal surmises, *Reading 'Rembrandt'*, 143.

But what about the text itself? What, if anything, in the text are artists picking up on when they paint a seductive, exhibited if not also exhibitionist – and thus guilty – Bathsheba? Although the biblical narrator does not pass judgment on Bathsheba, he does not remove her altogether from suspicion. In particular, by withholding her point of view, he invites speculation about Bathsheba's complicity in David's voyeurism. Does Bathsheba plan to be seen? Does she know for what purpose she is summoned? Is it against her will that David has sex with her? Could she have resisted?

There is little to be gained in speculating about what a character in a story might have done or felt. In the final analysis, whether this is a story of seduction or of rape is a moot question. The fact that King David's encounter with the beautiful Bathsheba takes place in a narrative context of aggression and violence – war with Ammon during which David stays at home – is perhaps an intimation that force or intimidation is used in David's taking of Bathsheba. The aftermath of this ill-fated sexual encounter also hints of force, for when, as part of his punishment for adultery and murder, David's children re-enact his sins, David's adultery with Bathsheba is replayed as rape, not once but twice. First, Amnon rapes his beautiful sister Tamar (2 Sam. 13) and later, to signal his takeover of his father's kingdom, Absalom rapes ten of David's wives. Nathan had prophesied that God would do to David in the sight of the sun and all Israel what David had done in secret (2 Sam. 12.11-12; 16.21-22). The ten women are raped in a tent on the roof, a location that recalls the place where David was led into sin by spying on Bathsheba's bath.

The way the story of David's sexual encounter with Bathsheba begins also indicates aggression on David's part: he '*sent* messengers and *took* her'. Yet, at the same time, the two actions attributed to Bathsheba – 'she came to him' and 'she returned to her house' – are not what one would expect if resistance were involved. The king sends for a subject and she obeys. The issue of force versus consent, which is crucial for constructing the woman's point of view, is not raised. I have argued elsewhere that it is not the character Bathsheba who should be held accountable for appearing on the scene bathing but rather the biblical narrator who has chosen to portray her this way.[30] Narrative dynamics inform the picture of Bathsheba that has come down to us over the centuries. By withholding Bathsheba's point of view, the narrator has made it easy for artists to exploit Bathsheba's bath not only as an opportunity to paint a naked

30. *Fragmented Women*, 138; *Plotted, Shot, and Painted*, 33. Cf. Rachel E. Adelman, *The Female Ruse: Women's Deception and Divine Sanction in the Hebrew Bible* (Sheffield: Sheffield Phoenix Press, 2015), 169–74.

woman but also to expose Bathsheba as guilty of inciting King David's desire – thereby making him less culpable at her expense.

Susanna

Unlike the story of David and Bathsheba, the story of Susanna deals overtly with voyeurism, looking that intrudes upon the one seen. Events in the garden hinge on the results of being seen and not being seen. So that they can spy on Susanna in the garden, the voyeurs hide in order not to be seen themselves.

> No one was there except the two elders, who had *hidden* themselves and were *watching her closely* (Sus. 16).

Fig. 6.5. Guercino, *Susanna and the Elders*, 1617,
Museo Nacional del Prado, Madrid

Guercino's Susanna is absorbed in her bath (fig. 6.5), unaware of the voyeurs whose close proximity allows the viewer to feel as if he is in collusion with them, especially since the elder on the left, whose face is in the shadows, turns to the viewer with raised finger, warning him to keep silent and thereby inviting the viewer to join in the conspiracy of looking (I say 'he' because it is heterosexual male complicity the painting specifically invites. As a female viewer, I want to scream, 'Run!') As we saw in the case of Bathsheba, Susanna's nakedness both communicates and explains the elders' desire. The biblical tale, in contrast, is not nearly so clear about what the two voyeurs see. Susanna sends her maids to bring oil and ointments and tells them to shut the garden doors so that she can bathe. They shut the doors behind them when they go to fetch the ointments, at which point the elders rush out of their hiding place and accost Susanna:

> They did as she said; they shut the garden doors and went out by the side doors to fetch what they had been commanded. They did not *see* the elders, because they were *hidden*. When the maids had gone out, the two elders got up and ran to her (Sus. 18-19).

The biblical Susanna is not given the opportunity to begin her bath, so for all the reader knows, she is still clothed (an option the text leaves open, but, by not commenting on it, open to speculation about her state of undress). The elders threaten her, and she explains her decision (for their benefit and the reader's). She chooses not to be blackmailed into having sex with them, preferring to 'fall into [their] hands' rather than to sin against God. Then she cries out.

In contrast to Guercino's Susanna, who seems natural and at ease, unaware of the voyeuristic gaze,[31] Tintoretto's Susanna, though also not yet aware of the voyeurs' presence, colludes in the gaze and thereby authorizes it for the viewer (fig. 6.6). As Margaret Miles says of this painting, 'light fetishizes Susanna's body as the viewer is placed in the position of the Elders, spying on her, a voyeur, enjoying her body'.

> The Elders, placed in crepuscular shadows, do not bear the weight of communicating the urgency of their active desire; rather, her body represents that desire. Viewers are directed – trained – by the management of light and shadow and by the central position of Susanna's body to see Susanna as object, *even as cause*, of male desire.[32]

There is a hint of vanity, or at least self-satisfaction, in Susanna's pose, as she indulges herself in leisurely enhancing her beauty at her toilette. Her carefully coiffured hair, the jewellery with which she is adorned and the

---

31. But nevertheless still guilty of bathing where she can be seen; Miles argues that these sixteenth- and seventeenth-century paintings of Susanna belong to 'a visual culture in which it was impossible to paint a naked female body in such a way that it symbolized innocence' (*Carnal Knowing*, 124).

32. Ibid., 123; italics mine.

expensive objects that lie at her right foot – perfume jars, ointment bottles, jewellery, a mirror, a comb and flowers – show her to be a woman of wealth. These objects visually emphasize the beauty ritual, whose sexual implications are heightened by the symbolism of the garden setting.[33]

Fig. 6.6. Jacopo Tintoretto, *Susanna and the Elders*, c. 1555, Kunsthistorisches Museum, Vienna

Another painting of Susanna by Tintoretto is similar to paintings of Bathsheba. As in many paintings in which David is pictured as spying on Bathsheba from his rooftop balcony, the elders are pictured some distance away, in the background, from where they cannot see the full frontal view of the woman's body that the artist offers to the spectator (fig. 6.7). Not only is Susanna already engaged in her bath, but an attendant is also present to help her at her toilette, a feature of many paintings of Bathsheba. Susanna's body is displayed to the viewer bathed in light, like

33. Diane Apostolos-Cappadona, 'Toilet Scenes', in *Encyclopedia of Comparative Iconography: Themes Depicted in Works of Art*, vol. 2, ed. Helene E. Roberts (Chicago, IL: Fitzroy Dearborn Publishers, 1998), 874. In some instances, she adds, 'the presence of a variety of jars and bottles for ointments, cosmetics, and perfumes heightens the sexual symbolism, for these varied fluids will presumably cover the woman's body as she caresses it, an implication of the desire for her lover's touch' (871). The conscious or subconscious recognition of such symbolism would heighten the voyeuristic appeal of this painting.

the artist's Susanna in fig. 6.6, and her elaborately coiffured hair adorned with jewels and the bracelets she wears are reminiscent of the earlier Susanna.

Fig. 6.7. Jacopo Tintoretto, *Susanna*, c. 1575,
Courtesy National Gallery of Art, Washington, DC

The expression on this Susanna's face seems pensive or possibly sad. There is an interiority about her reverie that humanizes the woman whose body is so very vulnerable to the spectator's gaze – a detail that might elicit from some viewers pity for the soon to be assaulted woman. Unlike the voyeurs represented in the background, her servant is not looking at Susanna. Her eyes are downcast, focused on the jar of ointment that Susanna is also looking at. The servant thus makes the viewer aware of the alternative: not looking, looking somewhere else. In tension with these counter-voyeuristic features, the blatant exposure of Susanna's body to the viewer (with the completely transparent cloth, which intensifies the visual effect of her nakedness), her unawareness of being seen and the painting's relative lack of interest in the voyeurs – old men, spectral figures well covered in heavy-looking grey robes – make this painting undeniably voyeuristic. The elders' presence is a crucial feature, for it allows the viewer to accuse them and thus to look and still take the moral highground (fig. 6.8).

Fig. 6.8. Tintoretto, *Susanna*, detail

Equally if not more popular among artists is the moment when the elders accost Susanna. They hope – wrongly – that 'because no one can see us' (Sus. 20), Susanna will be forced to agree to have sexual intercourse with them in order to protect her reputation. Whereas the elders abandon their detached looking in favour of acting on their licentious desires, the viewer of such paintings remains in the position of voyeur, observing scenes that are arguably more titillating because of the elders' sexual aggression and the woman's vulnerability, fear and shame. It is also possible, however, that such paintings might have the opposite effect: to problematize identification with the voyeur position. By drawing attention to the men as contemptible rapists and showing the woman's acute distress – in other words, by exposing the threatened rape for what it is – these paintings can raise viewers' consciousness of our position vis-à-vis the action depicted, making it unmanageable, at best unbearable or at least uncomfortable, for the viewer to enjoy the power of the gaze.[34]

34. On the possibility of antivoyeuristic interpretation, see Bal, *Reading 'Rembrandt'*, 167–69. What I am proposing here is not unlike the 'ridiculous overdressing of the men' in Rembrandt's *Susanna Surprised by the Elders* that Bal discusses as among features supporting an antivoyeuristic interpretation of the painting: 'These elements hamper the viewer's gaze in that they activate the

In the text the threat posed by the elders is verbal: 'Agree and have sex with us. If you refuse we will testify against you that a young man was with you' (Sus. 20-21). So too is Susanna's response:

> I am hemmed in on every side. For if I do this, it will be my death, and if I do not, I cannot escape your hands. I choose not to do it and to fall into your hands rather than to sin in the sight of the Lord (Sus. 22-23).

The textual Susanna chooses death rather than endure the sexual attack to which many paintings will later subject her. In art the elders' cruel and calculated threat frequently becomes an aggressively physical one, and Susanna's rational consideration of her options becomes an image of vulnerability, alarm and distress.

In Pompeo Batoni's *Susanna and the Elders*, Susanna is accosted while bathing in a fountain far from the house, in what only a few moments earlier was an Edenic setting (fig. 6.9). The startled look on her face shows she has been taken entirely by surprise. She clutches at her garment, crossing her legs defensively and barely succeeding at covering her breasts, while one of the elders pulls her clothing from her with one hand and appears to be offering her a sack containing a bribe in the other. The other elder points in the distance, possibly indicting the absence of any witnesses, or perhaps invoking the absent public to which the elders threaten to denounce Susanna if she refuses them. The act of exposing Susanna's body in paintings like this finds its parallel only later in the story, at the trial, when the elders succeed in having her veil removed (or uncovering Susanna, if we read with the Septuagint). At the trial the elders testify that they were unable to apprehend Susanna's paramour because he was too strong for them.[35] The elder leaping over the bench in this painting seems perfectly capable of catching a strong young man, had there been one with Susanna.

---

narrative of abuse of power with which most viewers will not automatically wish to identify' (167–68). In an investigation that reveals how complex looking actually is in the story, Jennie Grillo argues that the text of Theodotion works to dissuade readers from aligning themselves with the elders' voyeuristic viewpoint, 'making the elders' perspective uncomfortable to the reader and discouraging our uptake of their voyeuristic focalization'; 'Showing Seeing in Susanna: The Virtue of the Text', *Prooftexts* 35 (2015): 253–55 (citation from 255).

35. The Septuagint has a different version: 'On approaching them, we recognized her but the young man fled in disguise'.

Fig. 6.9. Pompeo Batoni, *Susanna and the Elders*, 1751,
Civici Musei, Pavia

Artemisia Gentileschi's *Susanna and the Elders* (fig. 6.10) is my only example painted by a woman. The threat of rape is something every woman lives with. I cannot imagine that women (especially women who have been raped) and men look at rape in the same way (unless the man has been raped). Not surprisingly, Gentileschi's *Susanna and the Elders* painted in 1610 is the most powerfully disturbing of all my examples.[36] In this painting, there is nothing to compete with the woman and her attackers for the viewer's attention – no lush or magnificent garden in the background, no oils or ointments or other accoutrements for her bath. The stone bench on which Susanna sits seems cold and uninviting, and the pool in which she has dipped her foot is barely visible. Behind the elders we see only a cloudy sky. Indeed, it is these very features that lead Nanette Salomon to describe the painting as abstract:

36. Gentileschi's rape by her tutor Agostino Tassi, their continued sexual relatione ship based on the prospect of marriage and the ensuing trial that followed are well documented. Her art is often explained in reference to it, in contrast to male artists whose art does not tend to be appraised in terms of one life experience. This painting is often related to the rape (with the men identified as Tassi and Artemisia's father Orazio Gentileschi) even though it is dated a year earlier. Gentileschi later painted other versions of Susanna and the elders; see Salomon ('Judging Artemisia', 38–48), who discusses this painting and the 1622 and 1649 versions.

Specifically, it is abstract in the extreme compression of three-dimensional space, pressing everything forward yet tellingly not out of the pictorial space; abstract in the heightened formal division of a stark, stagelike foreground affected by the stone parapet that stretches relentlessly from one side of the frame to the other, a division that bounds Susanna but does not keep the elders out. It is abstract for its pointed absence of any gardenlike foliage, transposing instead organic, leaflike forms into the stony relief panel just behind Susanna's torso; abstract with only the most minimal indication of water for her bath; abstract in the collusive unity of the form of the two elders as one...abstract in the body language of Susanna whose torqued body and rhetorical gestures neither protect nor defend her.[37]

Fig. 6.10. Artemisia Gentileschi, *Susanna and the Elders*, 1610,
Schloss Weissenstein, Pommersfelden

37. Salomon, 'Judging Artemisia', 38–40. It is, in fact, the starkness of the painting that led me to choose it rather than one of the other versions Gentileschi painted.

Although Susanna's gestures may prove useless to protect or defend her, her posture and facial expression reveal how urgently she is attempting to fend off the elders, while simultaneously recoiling from the proposition that at this very moment they are expounding. Mary Garrard sees the painting 'as a narrative completely mimed in the movements of the six hands clustered at upper center'.

> Through gesture, the elders express male bonding, conspiracy, and silencing, while Susanna's two-handed gesture conveys her intimidation and desire to escape. Yet these hands do more, for while the resisting right hand next to the twisted head conveys Susanna's fear and aversion, her left hand springs upright, relieving the torsion and compression of the head and right hand, and hinting at a resurgence of will and autonomy that the story in fact doesn't allow.[38]

Susanna has turned her head as far away from the elders as possible without getting up and running from the scene, which she cannot do. Huddled together, the elders are clearly in collusion, and collusion is necessary for their plan to succeed.[39] One whispers in the other's ear as if formulating the plan while the other lifts his finger to his lips to counsel Susanna' silence. Susanna's body, on which the light falls, immediately attracts the viewer's attention, and the white cloth across her left leg and upon which she sits offers virtually no protection against the viewer's and the elders' gaze, rendering her all the more vulnerable. The contrast between her white exposed body and the bodies of the elders is glaring; their faces are partially hidden in shadow, while the red and blue clothing of the older man provides the only colourful part of the picture. The starkness of the painting and the confined space of the canvas from which Susanna cannot escape highlight Susanna's lack of choice.[40]

38. Mary D. Garrard, 'Artemisia's Hand', in Bal, ed., *The Artemisia Files*, 6–8. I find it strange that Garrard does not recognise Susanna's expression of her will in the story.

39. That there are two witnesses against Susanna alludes to the biblical laws that call for the evidence of at least two witnesses in order to convict the accused (see Deut. 19.15; 17.6; Num. 35.30; 1 Kgs 21.10-13).

40. A modern version of this painting that reveals the underlying violence is Kathleen Gilje's *Susanna and the Elders, Restored* (1988), discussed by Mieke Bal in 'Grounds of Comparison', in Bal, ed., *The Artemisia Files*, 159–67. Gilje's fictional restoration displays the savagery of the rape in its terrifying actuality and proposes revenge by putting a dagger in Susanna's hand (alluding to Artemisia's defence at the rape trial that she wounded Tassi with a dagger). Gilje has made a video about her 'restoration': https://www.youtube.com/watch?v=jq2bmbPL7rA.

Fig. 6.11. Alessandro Allori, *Susanna and the Elders*, 1561,
Musée Magnin, Dijon

Alessandro Allori offers the spectator the rape scene avoided in the text (fig. 6.11). Here the men are embarking on the rape that they do not accomplish in the story because Susanna cries for help. As in the text, it is not a matter of a proposition but of a very real threat: rape or death.[41] Although there is no touching at all in the story, here the men are vigorously molesting Susanna. One man's hand is already between her legs

41. It is not, as Collins calls it, an 'attempted seduction' (*Daniel*, 431).

and his face pressed against her; the other is pulling her face toward him. Susanna looks at him in fear. Her fingers clutch at his face and at the head of the other man, her body contorted in an effort to fend them off. She is, as she describes herself, 'hemmed in on every side' (Sus. 22).

These paintings of a violation embarked upon, whether or not intended to titillate the viewer or to satisfy the voyeuristic impulses of their patrons and owners, draw attention not only to the true nature of the elders' intentions (rape) in the biblical story but also, significantly, to the victim's point of view. In visualizing Susanna's reaction as one of terror and distress, artists have given viewers a more realistic representation of a woman's point of view than the author of the story of Susanna gives readers. Batoni, Gentileschi and Allori capture on the canvas the physical and mental distress occasioned by the threatened rape more powerfully than Susanna's fatalistic but self-possessed, reasoned response to the elders in the text (Sus. 22-24). As in the case of the paintings of Hagar brought to Abraham's bed by Sarah discussed in Chapter 4, these visual narratives – even if we judge the paintings to be salacious bordering on pornographic – draw attention to problematic aspects of the verbal narrative. Using the visual narrative to interrogate the verbal narrative, in addition to contributing to a more discriminating and nuanced exegesis, raises questions that need to be addressed about the suppressed point of view of women characters such as Hagar, or the narrator-controlled point of view of characters like Susanna.[42] The absence of the woman's point of view in a biblical story, or its manipulation by the story's narrator, makes it easier for commentators on the text to allow biblical attitudes to the sexual exploitation of women by men to go unchallenged. Proving literary rape, like actual cases of rape, depends on taking the woman's word for it.[43] Art can often enable the woman to testify convincingly.

42. I have not used examples where Susanna looks at the viewer, such as Rembrandt's famous *Susanna and the Elders* in the Gemäldegalerie, Berlin, where the look can be interpreted, among other things, as an appeal for help; Bal discusses the complexity of the look in this painting in *Reading 'Rembrandt'*, 156–76.

43. Like many of the paintings discussed in this chapter, these literary rapes perpetuate ways of looking at women that encourage objectification and violence. I am not impressed by the argument that because the concept of rape is anachronistic it should not be used of an ancient text like the Bible, or that we should seek to understand biblical attitudes to rape in its ancient context rather than criticize them from our modern perspective. From what other perspective can we criticize them? For compelling arguments, see Scholz, *Sacred Witness*, 44–51.

Joseph and Potiphar's Wife

If the stories of Susanna and Bathsheba fire the imaginations of artists to reinscribe the voyeuristic gaze at the female body in powerful visual scenes, what happens with a text in which a woman casts her eyes upon a man? In the story of Joseph and Potiphar's wife (Gen. 39.6-20), Joseph, like Bathsheba and Susanna, is the object of looking that gives rise to desire. Indeed, his position resembles that of a biblical woman: he is passive, more an object of the actions of others than a subject. Like Susanna, he is the object of ongoing desire seeking an opportune occasion, and, like her, he is god-fearing, and thus rejects the illicit proposal of sex. His reason for refusing is the same as hers: to yield would be a sin against God (Gen. 39.9; Sus. 23).

Susanna is accosted by the elders while she is alone in the garden, Joseph is accosted by his master's wife while he is with her in the house alone. Susanna calls for help, Joseph flees. Each is the object of a false testimony against them that casts them in the role of the one guilty of illicit sexual behaviour: the elders accuse Susanna of having sexual intercourse in the garden with a young man; Potiphar's wife accuses Joseph of attempted rape.[44] As a result both are wrongly convicted. And neither tells their version of the story.

If it can be asked of Bathsheba and Susanna, did they provoke the gaze, what about Joseph? He too is beautiful – both beautiful in form and beautiful in appearance, or 'well built and handsome', as the New Jerusalem Bible and Jewish Publication Society's translations have it (*yepeh-to'ar vipeh mar'eh*, v. 6, a combination used elsewhere only for Joseph's mother Rachel, Gen. 29.17). Like the women he has been held responsible for attracting the gaze.[45] He is not, however, observed in an

44. She does what Susanna did, cry out, but she, unlike Susanna, is believed. Commentators have speculated, however, whether or not the fact that Potiphar has Joseph thrown in prison rather than executed for his attempted adultery is an indication that he doubts his wife's story; see e.g. Claus Westermann, *Genesis 37–50: A Commentary*, trans. John J. Scullion (Minneapolis, MN: Augsburg, 1986), 67; Jürgen Ebach, *Genesis 37–50* (Freiburg im Breisgau: Herder, 2007), 186; and for a cinematic version in which Potiphar believes Joseph's version of the story and even comes to visit him in prison, see the TV movie *Joseph* (Turner Pictures, 1995), starring Ben Kingsley as Potiphar and Paul Mercurio as Joseph.

45. E.g. *Bereshit Rabbah* (Par 87 on 39.11): 'Free from anxieties, he turned his attention to his external appearance. He painted his eyes, dressed his hair and aimed to be elegant in his walk.' It is for this reason God decides to 'stir up [his] mistress against [him]'.

intimate act such as bathing or planning to bathe. And herein lies a crucial difference between this and the stories of Susanna and Bathsheba: the look here – the woman's look – is not voyeuristic. There is no description of her spying on Joseph unawares. Nor is her looking detached. She sees him and pursues him, but, unlike King David with Bathsheba, she cannot – as a woman – simply take what she wants. She may be the wife of a powerful man – Potiphar is an officer of Pharaoh and the captain of the guard[46] – but Joseph the slave is in charge of the house. '[Potiphar] is not greater in this house than I am', Joseph protests, 'and he has not withheld anything from me except you, because you are his wife'.[47] Like the elders in the book of Susanna, the wife of Potiphar is portrayed negatively by the narrator from the outset.[48] She is represented as bold, adulterous and carnal, not unlike the 'strange' or 'foreign' woman so vividly described in Prov. 7.6-23.

She tries to get Joseph to have sex with her, and she is persistent. She invites him to have sex with her 'day after day' (v. 10) but he remains steadfast in his refusal. One day when he is in the house to work but no one else is there except the woman, she grabs hold of his garment and invites him to have sex with her (as in Susanna's case, no witnesses are present who could testify to the hero's innocence). Although the righteous Joseph escapes her clutches, he leaves behind his garment, which she will

46. Potiphar is described as a *saris* and a *sar hattabbahim* in Gen. 39.1. Most often the word *saris* is used of a high official, but it could refer to a eunuch (Isa. 56.3 and possibly Sir. 30.20). The latter possibility suggests motivation for the woman's behaviour: sexual desire or the desire for a child or both (a possibility that has not gone unnoticed by readers, with the desire for a child typically viewed more positively than female sexual desire). The other term, *sar hattabbahim*, could refer to a chief butcher or to a military official, possibly a bodyguard or chief executioner; see the discussion in Ebach, *Genesis 37–50*, 163–65.

47. Hugh C. White sees the narrator's comment in 39.6 that Potiphar 'had no concern for anything but the food that he ate' as a subtle suggestion that Potiphar did not have sexual relations with his wife; *Narration and Discourse in the Book of Genesis* (Cambridge: Cambridge University Press, 1991), 255.

48. The stories of Potiphar's wife and Susanna are frequently compared and cone trasted in Christian lore; see Joy A. Schroeder (*Dinah's Lament: The Biblical Legacy of Sexual Violence in Christian Interpretation* [Minneapolis, MN: Fortress Press, 2007], 191–220), who observes that, although the two women are opposites (treacherous wife and virtuous matron), their stories are used to make the same point: a woman who speaks about sexual violence cannot be trusted. For a fascinating comparison of Joseph and Esther that engages both the biblical text and rabbinic interpretation, see Adelman, *The Female Ruse*, 198–230.

use to indict him.[49] Like the elders, she seems to have power – Joseph is convicted on her word – but her power is illusory.[50] As if recognizing this, rather than give the woman the power of the gaze, artists turn the voyeuristic gaze upon her.

Fig. 6.12. Guercino, *Joseph and Potiphar's Wife*, 1649,
Courtesy of National Gallery of Art, Washington, DC

49. For a rhetorical analysis that shows the manipulative nature of the speech the narrator places in the woman's mouth, see Sternberg, *The Poetics of Biblical Narrative*, 423–27. In spite of her rhetorical prowess, I fail to see how the woman can be regarded as a trickster figure, as argued by Peter Bekins, 'Tamar and Joseph in Genesis 38 and 39', *Journal for the Study of the Old Testament* 40 (2016): 390.

50. The woman is not accorded the dignity of a name by the biblical writer. After all, the story is not really about her but rather about the principled, god-fearing Joseph, his success in the house of Potiphar and his power to resist the foreign woman. Alice Bach reads for the suppressed or imagined woman's story by resisting the narrator's ideology and drawing on postbiblical retellings of the tale; *Women, Seduction, and Betrayal in Biblical Narrative* (Cambridge: Cambridge University Press, 1997), 34–127. See also Nyasha Junior, 'Powerplay in Potiphar's House: The Interplay of Gender, Ethnicity, and Class in Genesis 39' (PhD diss., Princeton Theological Seminary, 2008).

True to the text, Potiphar's wife casts her longing gaze at the handsome young man in Guercino's *Joseph and Potiphar's Wife* (fig. 6.12). He, refusing her amorous advances, looks up to heaven. But what the artist exposes to the viewer's voyeuristic gaze is not Joseph, the object of desire in the story, but rather the iridescent body of Potiphar's wife. Whereas in the text there is no gaze at the woman, here she becomes an object of desire for the presumably heterosexual male viewer, who in Joseph's position might not be so reluctant, and who is invited to enjoy the nakedness of the woman and the temptation she offers, and to take the moral highground Joseph's refusal represents as well.

How reluctant is Joseph anyway? Artists often do what readers over the centuries have done: entertain the possibility of desire on Joseph's part. In the Babylonian Talmud (*b. Sota* 36b), for example, as well as other rabbinic texts, Joseph is described as not reluctant to have sex with Potiphar's wife.[51] Guercino's Joseph makes a gesture of refusal with his left hand, but his right arm is in a rather awkward position for pushing the woman's outstretched hand away. The woman reclines on a bed or couch, and the artist has made her attractive to heighten the temptation. She gazes at Joseph longingly, almost tenderly, and grasps in her right hand the garment with which she will later accuse him. Since she has propped herself up with her right arm, one might wonder how she has been able so easily to grab hold of Joseph's robe. For a man who would not deign to have sexual intercourse with his master's wife, Joseph has allowed himself to be suspiciously close to the woman. His head is turned away, but he has not yet begun to flee out of the house, as in the biblical story. Such features raise the question whether or not this painting suggests that Joseph is attracted to the woman even while resisting her advances.[52]

51. See, *inter alios*, Isaac Kalimi, 'Joseph between Potiphar and His Wife: The Biblical Text in the Light of a Comparative Study on Early Jewish Exegesis', in *Early Jewish Exegesis and Theological Controversy: Studies in Scriptures in the Shadow of Internal and External Controversies* (Assen: van Gorcum, 2002), 88–97; Joshua Levinson, 'An-Other Woman: Joseph and Potiphar's Wife: Staging the Body Politic', *Jewish Quarterly Review* 87 (1997): 269–301; Ebach, *Genesis 37–50*, 180–82, 187–97; and the sources discussed by Bach, *Women, Seduction, and Betrayal*, and James L. Kugel, *In Potiphar's House: The Interpretive Life of Biblical Texts* (San Francisco, CA: HarperSanFrancisco, 1990).

52. Their struggle is described on the National Gallery website as follows: 'As the temptress reaches for the strong and handsome Joseph, he struggles vigorously to extricate himself. But she holds tight to the vivid blue cloak and sets Joseph spinning like a top out of his garment' (http://www.nga.gov/content/ngaweb/Collection/art-obe ject-page.66776.html). I fail to see his struggle as vigorous, and I don't see how she can set him spinning, though I do like the metaphor.

It is striking that artistic representations of this scene often are situated in the woman's boudoir, which casts doubt on our hero's virtue and is not the situation envisioned in the biblical text. The bedroom provides a plausible occasion for the woman's state of undress, but what is Joseph doing in her private chamber, and so close to her bed? A similar question could be asked of the text: why has he allowed himself to be alone in the house with the woman when he knows how desperate she is to have sex with him?

In contrast to the tenderness expressed by the woman in Guercino's painting above, the woman in Tintoretto's *Joseph and Potiphar's Wife* seems more brazen (fig. 6.13). She does own the gaze here and she does more than look lecherously at Joseph. She pulls on his garment, lifting it from him as though she were peeking under it. But there is no exposed male flesh for *her* to see. Rather, lying on her couch naked except for her jewels (a hint of decadence as well as power and position), she is the one fully exposed to the viewer's voyeuristic gaze. Joseph, who seems younger than the woman here, cannot resist looking either.

Fig. 6.13. Tintoretto, *Joseph and Potiphar's Wife*, c. 1555,
Museo del Prado, Madrid

The reversal of the voyeuristic gaze in these paintings should come as no surprise, given the artistic preference for portraying the naked female body as the object of looking.[53] But what are we to make of Joseph's exposed leg in this painting? The woman is not looking at it, but, thrust forward into the foreground of the painting (and toward the woman), it

53. As Bal (*Reading 'Rembrandt'*, 162) muses: 'Is the female body so often the object of this indiscreet looking, not because it is what "we" want most to look at, but because it is simply the most convincing case for the illegitimacy of looking in general?'

attracts the viewer's gaze. Is it a sign of Joseph's sexual arousal? The prominence of Joseph's suggestively phallic leg and knee in this painting disrupts the coherence of the gaze, shifting it back and forth from the woman to the man. It appears as though Joseph could easily lose his balance, his upright-ness. Might his precarious position, together with the fact that he returns the woman's gaze, be read as indecision on his part?[54] Whatever viewers might think about Joseph's response to her, it is the woman's guilt that these paintings, building on the biblical story, emphasize. Making the woman the object of the viewer's gaze (and in the case of Tintoretto's painting, Joseph's gaze as well), as these artists do, diminishes her threat as the subject of the gaze.[55] The power of the gaze given to the woman in the verbal narrative does not really belong to the woman of the visual narrative but rather to the presumed male viewer to whom these paintings are primarily addressed.[56]

54. For possible answers to this question and discussion of readers' responses to gaps and ambiguities in the story and retellings in literature and art, see Athalya Brenner and John Willem van Henten, 'Madame Potiphar through a Culture Trip, or, Which Side Are You On?', in *Biblical Studies/Cultural Studies: The Third Sheffield Colloquium*, ed. J. Cheryl Exum and Stephen D. Moore (Sheffield: Sheffield Academic Press, 1998), 203–19. Hamilton (*The Book of Genesis: Chapters 18–50*, 465), notes that the word *beged* can refer to an outer or inner garment, and speculates that the narrator's choice of this term 'may be implying something about Joseph's own emotional involvement in this story. He is on the verge of acting faithlessly to his master.'

55. Representations of the female body seen through the male gaze have a social function. In the Western artistic tradition, according to Miles (*Carnal Knowing*, 82), they represent attempts to capture the complexity of woman on canvas; in other words, they serve as a man's way of managing the threat women pose. 'Figuration works to displace threat in that women seem to be understood in advance of any relationship with a real woman'. Similarly, Nead argues that artistic representations of the female nude can 'be understood as a means of containing femininity and female sexuality' (*The Female Nude*, 2). Nead stresses the importance of the image in culture: 'The framed image of a female body, hung on the wall of an art gallery, is shorthand for art more generally; it is an icon of western culture, a symbol of civilization and accomplishment', she writes (1); '...the female nude is a symbol of the transforming effects of high culture. It stands as a paradigm of the aesthetic of the beautiful, a testimony to wholeness and integrity of form. The female nude is precisely matter contained, the female body given form and framed by the conventions of art' (29; see esp. her discussion, 5–33).

56. In this brief discussion of Joseph, I have used only two examples from art but others can easily be adduced, and there are numerous examples in the reception of the story in which Joseph appears as a model of virtue. On the story in art and Thomas

Erotic Looking? The Song of Songs

Over against the voyeuristic gaze, looking that intrudes upon that which is seen, I want to posit the presence in the Bible of another way of look-ing, an erotic look, looking that participates in that which is seen. It can be found in that most unusual of biblical books, the Song of Songs. Of course readers will make their own decisions about the nature of looking or gazing in this love poem – both their own look or gaze at the characters and the characters' look or gaze at each other. In affirming the presence of an erotic look in the Song I am not claiming that looking in the Song is free of voyeuristic undercurrents or tendencies.[57] There are, however, a number of features that lead me to view looking as represented in the Song by the poet as more erotic than voyeuristic.[58] For one thing, looking is not detached. When the man is depicted as looking at the woman and describing her body, he is speaking to her (and ultimately to the poem's readers) – describing her to herself and inviting her to see herself through his eyes.[59]

4.1   Look at you! You are beautiful, my friend!
           Look at you! You are beautiful.
      Your eyes are doves
         behind your veil.
      Your hair, like a flock of goats
         winding down Mount Gilead.

Mann's *Joseph and His Brothers*, see Bal, *Reading 'Rembrandt'*, 94–137; see also her later reflections in *Loving Yusuf: Conceptual Travels from Present to Past* (Chicago: University of Chicago Press, 2008).

57. The discordant nature of the bodily imagery in the Song is demonstrated by Fiona Black (*The Artifice of Love*), whose investigation reveals the complexity of the imagery, and consequently of looking, in the Song. Some commentators think that in Song 6.13–7.9 (7.1-10 in the Hebrew) the woman is dancing, perhaps dancing naked, and that she is the object of an unwelcome, perhaps voyeuristic gaze. Whereas it is possible that the reply, 'How you gaze [or 'Why should you look...', NRSV] upon the Shulammite...' in 6.13 [7.1] is critical of the desire to look, there is little support in the text that the woman is either dancing or dancing naked; see Exum, *Song of Songs*, 230–32.

58. For the view that the gaze in the Song is not voyeuristic, see Elaine T. James, *Landscapes of the Song of Songs: Poetry and Place* (New York: Oxford University Press, 2017), 122–50.

59. The Song consists entirely of dialogue between a man and a woman (and occasionally the women of Jerusalem); voices that seem unmediated are the voices of lovers created by the poet. On the illusion of immediacy that the Song's dialogue format creates, see Exum, *Song of Songs*, 3–6 *et passim*.

2   Your teeth, like a flock of shorn ewes
        that have come up from the wash,
    all of them have twins,
        none has lost a lamb.
3   Like a scarlet thread, your lips,
        and your mouth is lovely.
    Like a slice of pomegranate, your cheek
        behind your veil.
4   Your neck, like David's tower,
        built in courses,
    a thousand shields hung on it,
        all sorts of warriors' bucklers.
5   Your two breasts, like two fawns,
        twins of a gazelle,
        grazing among the lilies.[60]

This is the sense of his 'behold', *hinneh* (v. 1). 'Look at you', he says to her, 'you are beautiful!' He then proceeds to build up a picture of her, part by part, for her benefit but ultimately for the pleasure of the poem's readers.[61] Is being looked at necessarily objectifying? And is the one who looks, the subject of the gaze, automatically in a position of power over the one seen? That does not seem to be the case here. Rather than giving the man a sense of power, looking at his lover makes him feel as though he has lost control. When she looks back, he is vanquished: 'You have captured my heart with one glance of your eyes' (4.9); 'Turn your eyes away from me, for they overwhelm me' (6.5).[62]

The look is voyeuristic and objectifying when the one seen is accessible to a viewer who remains detached and inaccessible. In the Song, the man does not just look; he loses himself in the vision he sees before

60. For the translation and discussion, see ibid., 151–54.

61. We might see the degree to which the inventories of body parts in the Song objectify the loved one as counterbalanced by the extent to which the lover is affected. The totality of the woman overwhelms the man. In order to keep the overpowering feelings she arouses at bay, he distances himself from the whole person through the breakdown of the body into parts – eyes, hair, teeth, lips, mouth, cheeks, neck and breasts – each inchoately anticipating a successful assemblage. This tactic could also be read as fetishizing: he fragments her body and makes it the object of the look, transforming her physical beauty into something satisfying in itself, and thus making her a fantasy object that marks her as reassuring rather than dangerous.

62. Whereas the woman in the Song talks about what *love* does to her, the man speaks to her about what *she* does to him; he thinks in terms of conquest, of power relations; see Exum, *Song of Songs*, 15–17.

him when he surveys the woman's body. If he distances himself from the whole person by perceiving her body in parts, he does not remain distanced but rather puts himself in the picture.[63] He is overwhelmed by her eyes and held captive in her tresses (7.5) – overcome by the very features he contemplates.

Erotic looking in the Song preserves the mystery, the otherness, of the other through figuration. By clothing the body in metaphors, the Song never quite gives access to the body being described.[64] The images may be strongly visual – a flock of goats winding down Mount Gilead, a tower built in courses with shields hung upon it – but they do not create a picture of the woman's body. So we might say that, unlike the narrators of the stories of Bathsheba and Susanna, the poet protects the woman from the voyeuristic gaze, while at the same time representing her as the object of the look (but one who is aware of being looked at). The woman's look at the man functions similarly.[65]

Another feature that makes looking in the Song more erotic than voyeuristic is its mutuality. Each of the lovers looks at the other's body and describes what they see, and both use suggestive, highly charged erotic language. The man describes the woman's body three times. Although she describes his only once, both her gaze at and description of his body are of the utmost significance, for if only the man looked there would be no mutuality in the Song and consequently no erotic look.[66] Whereas the

63. At the end of the description cited above, he professes his intention to be with his lover, to make his way to the mountain of myrrh and the hill of frankincense (4.6). The description reaches a climax in a metaphor of the woman as a pleasure garden, which he enters, at her invitation, to feast upon its exotic fruits (4.12–5.1). Similarly, his metaphoric description of her body in 7.1-5 gives way to a metaphor for his desire when he compares her to a palm tree that he will climb and whose clusters – her breasts – he will take hold of (7.7-9).

64. See Peter Brooks, *Body Work: Objects of Desire in Modern Narrative* (Cambridge, MA: Harvard University Press, 1993), 123. Although Brooks's subject is modern narrative, many of his insights can be applied *mutatis mutandis* to an ancient love poem like the Song. His first chapter sketches an interesting, though brief and highly selective, history of the representation of the body in literature. He also makes a move I consider important: he views the body as both a cultural construct and as its other, something outside language that language struggles to be embodied in. In my view, this struggle captures something of the erotic dynamic of the Song.

65. See Exum, *Song of Songs*, 202–9.

66. There are differences in their ways of looking. She is not pictured as looking at him when she describes his body but rather as having looked. She describes him in answer to a question raised by the women of Jerusalem, who ask, 'What distinguishes

man's imagery is more vivid and picturesque than the woman's, hers is more relational than his.[67] She describes some of the same features he did when he described her (eyes, hair, lips, cheeks, mouth), but her description of his statuesque body of precious materials is less an engrossing visual image than a comment on his value to her:[68]

10	My lover is radiant and ruddy,
	he stands out among ten thousand.
11	His head is gold, pure gold,
	his locks, palm fronds,
	black as a raven.
12	His eyes, like doves
	by watercourses,
	bathing in milk,
	sitting upon brimming pools.
13	His cheeks, like beds of spices,
	pouring forth perfumes.
	His lips, lilies,
	dripping flowing myrrh.
14	His hands, rods of gold,
	inlaid with Tarshish stones.
	His body, an ivory bar,
	adorned with lapis lazuli.
15	His legs, marble pillars
	set on gold pedestals.
	His form, like Lebanon,
	distinguished as the cedars.
16	His mouth is sweet,
	and all of him desirable.

If looking in the Song, for the lovers, is more erotic than voyeuristic, what about the poem's readers? Undeniably voyeurism is involved in being privy to lovers' intimate descriptions of each other's bodies. But just as the narrators of the stories of Bathsheba and Susanna had a strategy for

your lover from other lovers?' His descriptions, in contrast, are represented by the poet as spontaneous outbursts inspired by the sight of her.

67. The man and the woman, as the poet constructs them, have different ways of looking at love; Exum, *Song of Songs*, 14–17.

68. His head, hands and legs do not look like gold in the way that wavy hair resembles goats winding down a mountainside; rather he shares qualities with gold. Like gold he is rare and precious, and dazzling. Whereas he says, 'your mouth is lovely' (4.3), she says, 'his mouth is sweet'. His 'all of you is beautiful' (4.7) is matched by her 'all of him is desirable'.

giving readers the moral highground, the poet responsible for the Song of Songs has a strategy for making the relationship between the lovers less private, less closed, and the Song thereby less voyeuristic. The poet provides an audience within the poem, the women of Jerusalem, whose presence facilitates the reader's entry into the lovers' seemingly private world of erotic intimacy.[69] The lovers do not view the presence of these women as either intrusive or embarrassing, and the woman sometimes invites their participation. These women, who look and whose look the lovers are aware of, function to authorize the reader's look.[70]

The lovers' bodies are created through the way in which each is imagined by the other and in relation to the other. We follow the lovers' gazes downwards or upwards as they enumerate details about each other's body that progressively build up a fuller picture. We see the bodies through images and not in their entirety; they are both available to our gaze and not available, and perhaps this accounts in part for the limited representation of the Song in art compared to the stories discussed above.

Whereas a work of art might readily invite a voyeuristic gaze at the Song's bodies,[71] can art do justice to the Song's erotic look? Rather than

69. The women are sometimes addressed directly (1.5; 2.7; 3.5, 10-11; 5.8, 16; 8.4) and sometimes speak (5.1, 9; 6.1; 8.5; and perhaps 1.8; 6.13 [7.1 Hebrew]). At times their presence is simply assumed. When the woman says, for example, 'Listen! My lover! Look! He's coming!' (2.8) or 'What is this coming up from the wilderness?' (3.6), to whom is she speaking? In the world of the poem, her audience is the women of Jerusalem, but ultimately it is the poem's readers. At other times, readers are reminded of the women's presence when the lovers seem to be enjoying the most intimate pleasures (2.4-7; 3.4-5; 5.1c; 6.1-3; 8.3-4).

70. Alternatively, one might argue that the women function as authorizing a voyeuristic gaze at the lovers' bodies, making it easier for readers to look without feeling guilty about it. But erotic looking and voyeuristic gazing are, after all, points on a continuum and not stable positions. The look that the Song invites strikes me as different in kind from what we find in the other texts discussed in this chapter (as does the overall treatment of the characters by the poet).

71. For example, František Kupka (1871–1957), illustrator, painter, and pioneer of abstract art, produced a series of erotically charged and sexually explicit illustrations of the Song of Songs (there were two bibliophile editions, one in 1905 illustrated with woodcuts and the other in 1931 printed in aquatint); Kupka, *Illustrations to the Song of Songs* (Israel: The Israel Museum, 1980). Ze'ev Raban (1890–1970), a leading member of the Bezalel school art style, whose work includes elements of Symbolism, Art Nouveau and Orientalism, illustrated *The Song of Songs* (Jerusalem, 1930) with erotic images of the female body (the more readily available 1994 edition published by Korén Publishers does not include the scenes in which the naked woman

considering examples of naturalistic painting, for which representing an erotic look seems to me to pose a serious challenge in contrast to more abstract works, I propose to look here at two artists whose work, in my view, captures and conveys to the viewer, in different ways, something of the Song's erotic look. One adopts the Song's metaphoric gaze and the other appeals to the text's poetic features to create a visual equivalent of the Song's sensuous lyricism.

Let us begin with metaphor. The metaphors used to describe the lovers' bodies in the Song are bold and unusual, and they are strongly visual (especially 4.1-5; 5.10-16; 6.4-7; 7.1-9 [2-10 Hebrew]). Since words and images are never simply denotative, and in poetry they are excessively connotative, trying to pin down the meaning of each image in these descriptions is risky – though it is what commentators inevitably end up doing to some extent. There is no scholarly consensus about what principles should be followed in interpreting the Song's metaphors, and the range of interpretations well illustrates the reader's role in making meaning, a role confirmed in artistic re-presentations of the Song's imagery. It is clear that the descriptions are not meant to inform the reader what the female and male protagonists look like, for they do a very poor job of that. Because they are partial and selective and describe parts of the body one at a time in a series of discrete images, with one simile or metaphor used for each body part, we might conclude that each image should be taken on its own and not as part of a larger, total portrait. On the other hand, because the descriptions move down or up the body sequentially, the images seem to be striving for completion, as if to compensate for the dividing up of the body into parts by creating a composite picture.

Behind Your Veil (fig. 6.14), a print by Israeli artist Lika Tov, takes the text literally and combines metaphors the text uses for individual body parts to form a composite picture. It also incorporates words from the text into the image, thus blurring the boundary between text and image. No longer simply text, words become adornment. The text on the veil reads, 'Look at you! You are beautiful, my friend! Look at you! You are beautiful. Your eyes are doves behind your veil; your hair, like a flock of goats winding down Mount Gilead.' The Hebrew of Song 4.1 decorates the woman's veil like rich embroidery, shaping its contours to produce a luxurious flowing veil, balancing the goats that represent the hair.

appears). Though the protagonists are clothed, Abel Pann's pastel, *Let him kiss me with the kisses of his mouth*, makes me uncomfortable. It shows a young woman who looks ill at ease in the king's embrace.

Fig. 6.14. Lika Tov, *Behind Your Veil*, 1992.
Used by kind permission of the artist.

Tov shows us only the woman's face. As in the Song of Songs, the face is animate.[72] The dove-like eyes are not symmetrical and one dove's head is turned back, which makes it seem as though the doves are in motion.[73] The goats seem to be frolicking as they wind their way down to the woman's shoulders. As an allusion to the text's 'winding down Mount Gilead', the goats in motion suggest wavy hair (which is what most commentators think the image represents). Tov has made the lips small and red, representing the text's 'like a scarlet thread, your lips, and your mouth is lovely' (4.3). She does not clutter the image by trying to picture the (evenly paired, white?) teeth as well. The dappled complexion harks

72. On the articulate face as a displacement of the body, see Francis Landy, *Paradoxes of Paradise: Identity and Difference in the Song of Songs*, 2nd ed. (Sheffield: Sheffield Phoenix Press, 2011), 84.

73. Something commentators often point out about the woman's description of the man's eyes as doves in 5.12.

back to an earlier verse in the Song, 'Black am I, and lovely' (1.5).[74] The earthy colours reflect the prominence that the Song gives to nature and its beauty, in which the lovers participate.[75]

The nose is perhaps the most striking feature in this picture, especially because the text likens the woman's nose to the tower of Lebanon in 7.4, but nowhere does it describe it as a tree. We could see it as a pomegranate tree, evoking the description of the woman's cheek (or some other area of her face) as resembling a slice of pomegranate behind her veil in 4.3.[76] I find here an allusion to the palm tree to which the woman is compared at the end of the metaphoric description of her in 7.1-8 [2-9 Hebrew]:

> You are tall like a palm tree,
> 　　and your breasts are like clusters.
> I say I will climb the palm tree,
> 　　I will take hold of its branches.

These verses liken the woman's breasts to clusters of the palm tree that the man intends to climb. The breasts that are not depicted in Tov's print but present in the source text ('your two breasts, like two fawns, twins of a gazelle, grazing among the lilies', 4.5) are suggested, for the viewer familiar with the Song, through an association of images: the tree with the woman, the breasts with the tree. Wider associations of the tree include the apple tree, which is connected with the man in 2.3 and 8.5 (thus in the print we can imagine him symbolically transposed onto his lover's body),[77] the exotic trees and shrubs of the pleasure garden in 4.12–5.1, symbolizing the pleasures the woman's body offers her lover, and,

---

74. Personal communication.

75. The technique used in the print reproduced here is collagraphy (a collage print). The procedure is similar to printing an etching or engraving on an etching press, using moistened paper and etching ink and oil paint. It differs in that the plate from which the image is printed is made from cardboard on which cut-out shapes are glued, as in a collage, and lines are engraved with a pen. About forty to fifty prints of 'Behind Your Veil' were produced from this particular plate, using different colour combinations. Each print is thus an original; this one no doubt appealed to me most because its coloration suggested to me the Song's delight in nature. The three prints discussed here are prints I own; the photographs are mine.

76. The precise meaning of *raqqâ* ('cheek' in many translations) is debated. It occurs in the parallel 6.7 and elsewhere only in Judg. 4.21-22 and 5.26 (of Jael driving a tent peg through Sisera's temple, discussed in Chapter 7 below).

77. For discussion of this phenomenon in the text, see Landy, *Paradoxes of Paradise*, 65–86.

ultimately, through intertextual allusion, the trees in the garden of Eden.[78] The Song itself encourages this kind of association of images through its repetitions, refrains, interlacing patterns and thematic variations that establish echoes among parts of the poem.

Behind Your Veil is literal in the sense that it is faithful in spirit to the poetic metaphor – even to the extent of inscribing the text in the image – and it is beautiful in the way the woman in the Song is beautiful and awesome at the same time (6.4-5, 10). Tov's approach is to preserve the metaphor, even while she interprets it to a certain extent. She has not painted a woman with wavy black hair, lovely eyes with long lashes, and rosy cheeks showing through a translucent veil, and called it *Behind Your Veil*. Instead her visual representation reminds us that metaphor cannot be reduced to something else, be it a pretty picture or a prose paraphrase. To be sure, she has had to ask herself what the metaphors seek to convey, and the way she pictures the goats reveals her understanding of the metaphor in 4.1 as wavy hair. But by incorporating the metaphor into her visual representation, she offers a mode of interpretation that allows the metaphor to stand and provoke in the viewer the variety of responses the text might provoke.

I find Tov's representation of the Song's unusual body imagery in *Behind Your Veil* aesthetically satisfying and captivating. The artist has interpreted the poetic metaphors under the rubric of beauty, 'Look at you! You are beautiful, my friend! Look at you! You are beautiful!', which is how the text presents them (4.1, 7). On the whole, biblical commentators tend to read the imagery used of the body in the Song as flattering.[79] But what happens when, as interpreters of the text, we take the imagery literally?

---

78. On the tree metaphors and their associations with Gen. 2–3, see ibid., 199–211. The tree in Song 2.3 and 8.5 is variously identified as wild apple, apricot and quince, among other suggestions.

79. For some important exceptions, see Athalya Brenner, '"Come Back, Come Back the Shulammite" (Song of Songs 7.1-10): A Parody of the *wasf* Genre', in *A Feminist Companion to the Song of Songs*, ed. Athalya Brenner (Sheffield: Sheffield Academic Press, 1993), 234–57; J. William Whedbee, 'Paradox and Parody in the Song of Solomon', in *The Bible and the Comic Vision* (Minneapolis, MN: Fortress Press, 1998), 263–77; Fiona C. Black, 'Beauty or the Beast? The Grotesque Body in the Song of Songs', *Biblical Interpretation* 8 (2000): 302–23; Black, *The Artifice of Love*, 122–85 *et passim*.

Fig. 6.15. Lika Tov, *The King and Eye (Song of Songs 7.4, 5)*, 2002.
Used by kind permission of the artist.

Fig. 6.16. Lika Tov, *His lips are like lilies, dropping sweet smelling myrrh...*
Solomon's Song 5.12, 13, 2002. Used by kind permission of the artist.

As figs. 6.15 and 6.16 reveal, an overabundance of metaphoric imagery taken literally in one visual representation runs the risk of rendering the picture more grotesque than erotic.[80] What happens when the Song's bodily descriptions are rendered visually, as in these examples, can serve *both* as a caution to biblical critics about reading such descriptions as though they aimed to provide a composite picture *and* as a reminder that there is a genuine element of incongruity in the text's metaphoric presentation of the body. Is metaphorical overload not, in fact, what the text gives us? Overwhelmed with a superfluity of sensory impressions, the reader has difficulty forming a 'picture' of the woman and man in the Song of Songs.[81]

Although in these examples Tov has rendered only the lover's faces, the result would be much the same had she chosen to depict more of their bodies. Artistically, for me, *Behind Your Veil*, with its delicate approach to its subject, captures the text's erotic look, not only by the way it treats the woman's body but also through the associations of images discussed above that bring the natural world into the lovers' ambit. In the Song, the lovers' delight in beholding each other's body spills over into delight in the world around them, described in highly visual terms, and treating the reader to such captivating sights as black tents of Qedar, curtains of Solomon, clusters of henna blossoms in the vineyards of En-gedi, a gazelle or young deer bounding over the mountains, a palanquin made of wood from Lebanon with posts of silver and upholstery of gold and a seat of purple cloth, a pleasure garden filled with exotic plants and fruits, among many others. Erotic looking in the Song includes appreciating the myriad splendid sights the world has to offer lovers, its beauty and bounty.[82]

An artist whose work splendidly communicates the Song's erotic look is Marc Chagall, in his series *Le Cantique des Cantiques*. By rendering visually both the explicit and delicate eroticism of the Song, Chagall offers viewers a vision of love that, like the Song's, is one of mutual pleasure and delight – a vision in which the erotic look embraces not just

80. For an extreme example, see the cartoon illustration of Song of Songs by Den Hart reproduced in Black, *The Artifice of Love*, 10.

81. Should we, for example, combine the three descriptions of the woman's body into one, as Black proposes in *The Artifice of Love*?

82. On the lovers' relation to the world around them, see, especially, James (*Landscapes of the Song of Songs*), who deals at length with the associations between the woman's body and the eroticized landscape. On interrelations between the sensuality of the body, the sensuality of language and the landscape, see also Francis Landy, 'Erotic Words, Sacred Landscapes, Ideal Bodies: Love and Death in the Song of Songs', *The Blackwell Companion to World Literature* (forthcoming).

the body but the world.[83] There are five paintings in the series, and lovers are together in all of them, often represented more than once. In all the paintings we find them in an embrace that is simultaneously an overt and delicate celebration of sexual love. There is some intimate touching and some nudity, but Chagall conveys the depth of their love even when the lovers are fully clothed, or just by their disembodied faces. One of the most striking features of the entire series is Chagall's use of colour to convey sensuality, the warm and hot hues suggesting vitality, vibrancy and the heat of passion. The paintings are all dominated by dazzling shades of pink, rose and red, as if to say that lovers look at each other and at the world through rose-coloured glasses.[84]

Like the biblical poem, the series is non-narrative.[85] Although they are numbered in sequence as *Le Cantique des Cantiques I, II, III, IV* and *V*, the progression is not linear, and in each painting Chagall has used compression to represent different moments in time. The situations he represents do not correspond to any particular scene in the Song or to one scene only. Moreover, he represents more than just the Song's erotic lyricism. In a sense we could say he enters the picture, for we encounter in these paintings the familiar Chagall repertory of images, among them the bride and groom, scenes of the city, angels, donkeys, birds, bouquets of flowers, a figure playing a harp, the acrobat. Though the colours are dramatically different, the series shares a number of features with *To My Wife* (1933/44), Chagall's moving tribute to Bella, especially the reclining woman in *Le Cantique des Cantiques II* and the bride and groom in *Le Cantique des Cantiques III*.

Chagall in each of these paintings creates a visual counterpart to the poetic lyricism of the Song, both its meandering and its habit of repeating themes and images and playing variations on them. He achieves this by representing, as he so often does, many different scenes in a single painting. Like the biblical poet, Chagall blurs distinctions between desire and fulfilment, and between past, present, and future, to create his own version of erotic looking.

83. The series is part of the Message Biblique Marc Chagall, finished in 1966 and installed in 1973 in the Musée National in Nice. Excellent reproductions can be found in Musée National Message Biblique Marc Chagall, *Marc Chagall (1887–1985)* (Paris: Editions de la Réunion des musées nationaux, 1998).

84. Such clichés appear in Chagall's art; e.g. the winged clock signifying 'time flies' in *Time is a River without Banks* (1939), *To My Wife* (1933/44), and *Clock with a Blue Wing* (1949).

85. The only narrative parts of the Song appear in the woman's speeches; see Exum, *Song of Songs*, 14–15 *et passim*.

Fig. 6.17. Marc Chagall, *Le Cantique des Cantiques I*, 1960,
Musée National Message Biblique Marc Chagall, Nice,
Chagall ® / © ADAGP, Paris and DCAS, London 2018

In *Le Cantique des Cantiques I* (fig. 6.17), the lovers in the foreground are in an embrace that could take place at any time in their relationship. The whiteness of the woman's body attracts the gaze, but it is not realistic enough to hold the voyeuristic gaze. The embracing couple floating in the upper right-hand corner represents their marriage (he, wearing a crown, which links him to Solomon, and she, naked except for a bridal veil). Various symbolism from the Song is alluded to, the gazelle for him, the dove for her. On the right side of the painting the man under a tree, playing a musical instrument while sheep graze on the hillside, calls to mind his shepherd guise in the Song. This painting and *Le Cantique des Cantiques II* seem to me the most bucolic of the series (recalling the central role of the countryside in the Song), though the city features in all of them (on the side of the painting, the woman seems to have emerged from the city, a reminder that both city and countryside are sites of erotic encounters).

Fig. 6.18. Marc Chagall, *Le Cantique des Cantiques II*, 1957,
Musée National Message Biblique Marc Chagall, Nice,
Chagall ® / © ADAGP, Paris and DCAS, London 2018

Desire is such stuff as dreams are made on. The floating figures and
dream-like incongruities that distinguish so much of Chagall's art are
particularly at home in a representation of the Song, where they reflect
something of the Song's dream-like quality, its reverie and fantasy. *Le
Cantique des Cantiques II* (fig. 6.18) invites the viewer to contemplate
Song 5.2, 'I was sleeping but my heart was awake', a verse that blurs
distinctions between past and present and between sleep and wakeful-
ness.[86] Here the woman's naked body is displayed in a way that could
invite a voyeuristic gaze, which leads one to wonder if in the temple
of eroticism veiled voyeurism inevitably has its sovran shrine.[87] Other
features of the painting compete with the woman's body for the viewer's

86. Does the painting represent the woman's dream? Does the text? Where in
the text, or in the painting, would the dream end and 'reality' begin? Chagall's
fantasy world suits the flights of imagination characteristic of the lyric poetry of
the Song.

87. In keeping with the predominance of the female body as the object of the
look in art, there is a definite preference for the naked female body in these paintings.

attention, however. The woman seems to be sleeping on a flowery bed atop a tree, floating above the city, and her lover is nearby, represented here by only his face. In the background an angel wearing a crown and playing a harp hovers above a throne, an allusion King David. The woman is represented again in the figure wearing a wedding veil in the bottom right-hand corner, almost as though she is the source of the bucolic vision of herself that dominates the painting.

Fig. 6.19. Marc Chagall, *Le Cantique des Cantiques III*, 1960,
Musée National Message Biblique Marc Chagall, Nice,
Chagall ® / © ADAGP, Paris and DCAS, London 2018

The wedding receives particular attention in *Le Cantique des Cantiques III* (fig. 6.19). The bride in white and the groom of blue stand out against the sensuous pink, red and rose hues that distinguish the entire series. They dominate the left side of the painting and are shown again, stretched out in an embrace, at the bottom of the right side. The scene is one of celebration on the day of the couple's wedding, and the day is one of gladness of heart not just for Solomon (Song 3.11) but for his bride as well. All of creation seems to want to join in. Angels holding a candelabra and blowing a horn seem to be heralding the event, along with an acrobat perched on a rooster and blowing a horn, while two flying figures hold up the bridal canopy. Perhaps we can allow ourselves to identify the group of women playing instruments in the lower left corner with the women of Jerusalem, to whom the lovers of the text appeal to share their intimacy, a feature that, as I suggested above, makes the Song less voyeuristic. Even the artist himself participates (upper left corner). In the centre is the city, both Jerusalem and Chagall's native Vitebsk, whose houses are a constantly recurring motif in his art. The city reminds us not simply that the wedding is a public celebration but also of the fact that the Song of Songs is a celebration of love that invites the participation of its audience.

Is there a discordant note here, hinted at in the upside-down figure of the wandering Jew, a sign of life and love disrupted? If so, this is not unlike the ill-treatment of the woman by the watchmen in Song 5.7. While Chagall's paintings may serve as an example of the erotic look in art, like the Song of Songs itself they cannot be 'read' without recognizing poten-tially disruptive elements that destabilize any overly idealistic reading of its eroticism or its erotic look.

Fig. 6.20. Marc Chagall, *Le Cantique des Cantiques IV*, 1958,
Musée National Message Biblique Marc Chagall, Nice,
Chagall ® / © ADAGP, Paris and DCAS, London 2018

In *Le Cantique des Cantiques IV* the lovers ride on a winged horse, hovering over the city below (fig. 6.20). They stand out dramatically against the dark red background that overwhelms the canvas, as if they are the source of the intense heat that warms the world. As in *Le Cantique des Cantiques III*, she is a bride in white, and he a groom in blue, but this time with a green face and wearing his crown, which like the background is red. The embrace is similar to that in fig. 6.19, but here, instead of being upright, the couple is virtually reclining (and the horse, not the bride, carries the bouquet).[88] The man's left hand is under the woman's head and his right hand embraces her, caressing her breast (cf. Song 2.6; 8.3). They are not looking at each other nor do they acknowledge the viewer by returning the gaze. His eyes appear to be closed (in *Le Cantique des Cantiques III* her eyes are closed); she seems to be looking down, smiling contentedly at the city beneath them. The lovers' heads appear together, just visible in the bottom right-hand corner.

Fig. 6.21. Marc Chagall, *Le Cantique des Cantiques V*, 1965–1966,
Musée National Message Biblique Marc Chagall, Nice,
Chagall ® / © ADAGP, Paris and DCAS, London 2018

It is typical of Chagall to show only the faces of lovers to suggest their intimacy, as he does here in *Le Cantique des Cantiques V* (fig. 6.21; and here also just the man's hand caressing the woman's barely distinguishable breasts). The lovers seem to be represented again in the flying harpist dressed in blue (the groom's colour), serenading a wisp of a bride in white with a blue face (what seems to be a man's face is hovering

88. Cf. the bouquet pictured with lovers as a symbol of love in *The Birthday* (1915), *Bouquet with Flying Lovers* (1934/47), *Still Life of Flowers* (1949), *Blue Landscape* (1949), *The Champ de Mars* (1954–55) and *Le Cantique des Cantiques I*.

just above her). There are naked figures of women in the top right-hand corner, but the painting calls for the viewer's gaze to be divided among many subjects. The prominent levitating figure with a harp recalls the harp-playing crowned angel in *Le Cantique des Cantiques II*, though the figure here is not an angel, and a bird's wing covers part of his head so that he is neither crowned nor not crowned (in *Le Cantique des Cantiques I* a bird was playing the harp). The figure is reminiscent of King David the harpist, who often features in Chagall's work, thus merging the sweet psalmist of Israel with his son Solomon, the legendary composer of the Song of Songs. The city is in the background, and at the bottom in the centre are the women of Jerusalem, playing their musical instruments as in *Le Cantique des Cantiques III*.

The city also features in the right-hand corner of the painting, where in front of it is a tree with sheep beneath it and a shepherd playing a horn, as in *Le Cantique des Cantiques I*. Behind him is another representation of the wedding couple. In superimposing the countryside on the city, Chagall again evokes the country and city settings of the Song and the fluid movement from one to the other.[89] In the Song, the lovers are keenly aware of their surroundings, especially the beauty of nature, even to the extent of imposing their environment on each other's bodies (hair like goats winding down the mountainside, eyes like doves by watercourses, a neck like a tower with shields hung on it, etc.). Chagall reproduces this erotic vision of love in what we might see as an erotic look that brings the world to life even as it rejoices in that world. The heavens are alive with birds, floating figures of women and a bright sun, heralding a new day, like the first day of creation. The couple in the tree in the upper right corner is suggestive of the primordial Edenic couple, of whom the Song of Songs lovers are types.[90]

I have discussed the paintings in this series in some detail because the visual poetry resonates so well with the verbal poetry in terms of their shared ignoring of boundaries in time and space, the access they give to and withhold from the body, their lyricism and their sensuousness. Chagall's *Cantique des Cantiques* series draws attention to the fact that

89. On spatial relations between the countryside and the city, and the sharp division between the garden and the city as an invention of biblical scholarship, see Christopher Meredith, *Journeys in the Songscape: Space and the Song of Songs* (Sheffield: Sheffield Phoenix Press, 2013), 69–109; see also James, *Landscapes of the Song of Songs*, 55–117; Elaine James, 'Battle of the Sexes: Gender and the City in the Song of Songs', *Journal for the Study of the Old Testament* 42 (2017): 93–116.

90. See Landy's discussion of 'Two Versions of Paradise' in *Paradoxes of Paradise*, 172–62.

the erotic look in the Song owes much to its larger context – to all the poetic features that make its vision of mutual desire and satisfaction possible in the first place. If we possessed only the bodily descriptions in Song 4.1-5, 5.10-16, 6.4-7 and 7.1-9, and no other parts of the Song of Songs, it might still be possible to posit an erotic look, but its intensity would be diminished.

Lest the picture I am painting here of the erotic look in the Song seem too rosy, let us consider again the painting of Song 5.7 by Gustave Moreau, discussed above in Chapter 2.

Fig. 6.22. Gustave Moreau, *Scene from the Song of Songs*, 1853,
Musée des Beaux Arts, Dijon

Moreau seizes upon the most difficult scene to explain in the text, in which the woman is struck or beaten by the city guards and her wrap taken from her (fig. 6.22). Like artists who show the elders accosting Susanna, he exploits the voyeuristic potential of this incident, inviting the viewer to imagine the scene as a sexual attack and to watch, from a comfortably safe position, as the drunken and lecherous guards abuse the woman. Has

Moreau *introduced* a voyeuristic gaze into the garden of love? Or are its seeds already there? I observed at the beginning of this chapter that what I have been calling erotic looking and voyeuristic gazing are neither strict oppositions nor fixed positions. Readers and viewers will draw their own conclusions as to whether the body as it is presented in the Song and in the artistic examples discussed above is the object of the voyeuristic gaze or the erotic look or both or something in between or something else altogether. I have sought to indicate what I see as distinctive about looking in the Song as opposed to looking in the other texts discussed above in which voyeurism plays a central role. Whatever we decide about looking in the Song, seeing how artists choose to visualize a text where looking is involved and recognizing what textual clues they might be responding to can sharpen our analysis of features of the text we may have overestimated or underestimated or even overlooked. Biblical art may challenge or it may confirm our interpretation of the biblical text. Either way, it rarely fails to enrich it.

SHARED GLORY:
SALOMON DE BRAY'S
JAEL, DEBORAH AND BARAK

The book of Judges recounts Israel's struggles to occupy the land of Canaan as a series of episodes, most of which deal with the exploits of divinely inspired leaders who deliver their tribes from oppression by their enemies.[1] The only story in Judges in which the judge is a woman is also the only story in Judges in which the judge shares the limelight with other characters (besides God). In Judges 4–5 Deborah shares the glory with not one, but two other human heroes.[2] Israel owes its victory over the militarily superior Canaanites not only to Deborah, who is both a judge and a prophet, but also to Barak, who leads the Israelite troops in battle, and to a Kenite woman, Jael, who, in a surprise twist in the plot, kills the Canaanite general Sisera with a tent peg and a mallet. The unusual situation of role sharing in the text is visibly problematized in a painting of all three characters by the seventeenth-century Dutch master Salomon de Bray (fig. 7.1). In what follows, I offer a further illustration of how visual criticism can contribute to more nuanced biblical

---

1. The so-called 'major judges' for whom Othniel (3.7-11) sets the pattern: Ehud (3.12-30), Deborah (4–5), Gideon (6–8), Jephthah (10.6–12.7), Samson (13–16).

2. God is the only character who appears in all the individual episodes in Judges, and he is credited for the successes of the judges. He is also implicated in their failures; see J. Cheryl Exum, 'The Centre Cannot Hold: Thematic and Textual Instabilities in Judges', *Catholic Biblical Quarterly* 52 (1990): 410–31. Deborah is not, as I observed in that article (415), an unsullied judge. The lack of clear leadership is problematic, her reputation is undermined by the tension hinted at in her relationship with Barak, and one could raise questions about her effectiveness (see below under 'Deborah: Judge, Prophet, Singer, Mother in Israel'). See also Susanne Gillmayr-Bucher, 'Framework and Discourse in the Book of Judges', *Journal of Biblical Literature* 128 (2009): 694–95.

interpretation by staging a dialogue between the text and de Bray's artistic representation. The conversation involves, on the one hand, asking questions of the text such as what sort of heroes are Deborah, Barak and Jael, what is their relationship and how is fame apportioned among them, and, on the other hand, considering how de Bray, as a reader and visualizer of the text, deals with these questions and how he thereby conveys something of the complexity of the biblical account to his viewers.

De Bray's *Jael, Deborah and Barak*, painted in 1635, is not a dramatic painting nor does it represent any scene from the story in Judges 4–5.[3] It would seem therefore to be an unlikely candidate for staging a dialogue between text and image. Interestingly, however, by choosing to represent something that has no textual basis, de Bray foregrounds a striking and significant feature of the biblical story: the strange relationship – or lack of relationship – among the protagonists. As a static composition in which all three of the story's heroes appear as large half-figures against a featureless backdrop, the painting invites the viewer to consider the characters themselves, their respective roles and their relationship to one another.

The remarkable thing about de Bray's painting is that Jael, Deborah and Barak are pictured together, for all three characters never appear together in the biblical story. It is as if, the battle having been won (Judg. 4), and a victory song composed to celebrate it (Judg. 5), the three heroes of the day are now brought together to pose for a group portrait. The painter has asked Jael to bring her trusty hammer and nail with her for effect (or perhaps the idea that they would add a nice touch is hers, since she likes to pose with them). De Bray has arranged the sitters in poses intended to represent for the viewer the roles they played in the victory, as well as in what he sees as the order of their importance. In the foreground, illuminated from the right by a shaft of light that throws into stark relief her white-clad figure and full breasts, he places Jael, holding the hammer and tent peg with which she slew Sisera. In the middle is Deborah, whose pose alludes to her prophetic role, and who is either praying or reciting her victory song. Last, but not least – though partially in shadow – comes the military hero Barak, before whom the entire army of Sisera fell.

---

3. See Athalya Brenner's comments on this painting in 'Afterword', in *A Feminist Companion to Judges*, ed. Athalya Brenner (Sheffield: Sheffield Academic Press, 1993), 233–34.

Jael appears to have dressed up for the portrait, for there is blood on the nail but not on her fine white dress. Barak wears his armour, which identifies him as a warrior. He too may have dressed especially for this occasion. He does not look as though he has just come from the battlefield, though de Bray gives him an expression that suggests his shock at seeing Sisera dead in Jael's tent. Only Deborah seems not to have donned her finest attire for the portrait, indicating to the viewer that, as a woman of God, she would not be concerned with such things.

Fig. 7.1. Salomon de Bray, *Jael, Deborah and Barak*, 1635,
Rijksmuseum Het Catharijneconvent, Utrecht

In the biblical text Israel's god plays a major role, commanding Barak to go to war,[4] routing Sisera and his chariots before Barak's army (4.6-7, 14-15), and even fighting Sisera with the stars of heaven (5.20).[5] Whereas glory ultimately belongs to the deity (4.23), de Bray, in keeping with the widespread preference in the seventeenth century for realistic figures in art, interprets the story on human terms. Only Deborah's hands in prayer allude to the role of providence. De Bray shows all three characters at close range, in direct proximity to the viewer. Two of them look directly at the viewer. Jael seems to rebuff our gaze, whereas Barak stares vacantly at us, as though looking past us, his thoughts elsewhere. Deborah, in contrast, shows no interest in the viewer; her gaze is firmly fixed heavenward. The background consists solely of the folds of a dark curtain, suggesting perhaps Jael's tent, where Sisera met his foreordained end. The absence of any clearly defined setting further serves to focus the viewer's attention on the characters themselves and their roles, symbolized by their poses, physical appearance, dress and, in Jael's case, accoutrements.

Jael is the centre of attention in the painting, while Deborah, in the centre, seems crowded in between Jael and Barak. De Bray has placed Deborah in a position that corresponds to her role in the story, where her narrative importance is encroached upon by Jael and Barak. In spite of the fact that the painting's three subjects form a closely-knit group, they are not touching and no one is looking at anyone else. The absence of contact among them encourages the viewer to ponder the extent of their interaction in the biblical story. Although not a narrative painting, *Jael, Deborah and Barak* draws the viewer into the story of these three subjects, who appear not as types but rather as individuals so realistically portrayed that one wants to know more about them.[6] What kind of woman is Jael? She holds in her hands the domestic tools she would use for pitching a tent. How did she manage to overcome a warrior like

4. Actually, we have only Deborah's word for it; see below.

5. Interpreters generally agree that God appears in Judg. 5 in his role as the divine warrior; see, e.g., Susan Ackerman, *Warrior, Dancer, Seductress, Queen: Women in Judges and Biblical Israel* (New York: Doubleday, 1998), 37–46; cf. Jack M. Sasson, *Judges 1–12* (New Haven, CT: Yale University Press, 2014), 286, 303–4. Danna Nolan Fewell and David M. Gunn ('Controlling Perspectives: Women, Men, and the Authority of Violence in Judges 4 & 5', *Journal of the American Academy of Religion* 58 [1990]: 400–402) draw attention to the counter-theme of human accomplishment in the poem.

6. A painting of all three heroes could be a narrative painting if the artist used compression to represent events unrelated in the narrative.

Sisera with these as weapons? Why did she kill him, and how does she feel about it? Deborah seems less interesting: old, defeminized, pious. Her large hands in prayer are her most distinctive feature. Her deeply religious attitude invites the question, what is her connection to the cold-blooded assassin on one side of her and the soldier with the blood of countless adversaries on his hands on the other? Barak, arrayed for battle, is in third place in the composition, overshadowed by the women. What does this say about his character?

Three Heroes, One Victory, Two Versions

Biblical scholars conventionally distinguish between the prose version of the story in Judges 4 and the poetic version in ch. 5. The poem, the so-called 'Song of Deborah', is widely thought to be older than the prose, which, as a later version of events, is interpreted in the light of the poem. In particular, where discrepancies occur between the two, the poem is privileged over the prose. Although reading the final form of the biblical text is now a widespread practice in biblical criticism, few biblical critics attempt to interpret the prose and poem in the order in which they appear in the Bible, from beginning to end, as parts of a whole.[7]

Neither de Bray nor his intended audience would have thought of the story in terms of two different versions, nor, in fact, will most viewers of the painting or modern readers of the text who are not biblical scholars. Judges 4 and 5 can easily be read as a continuous story in which a battle takes place and then a victory song is composed (on the spot, as it were) to celebrate it – a situation I envisioned above in order to construct a fanciful background for de Bray's group portrait. Thus what we have is, as Danna Fewell and David Gunn observe, an account told from the point of view of an omniscient narrator (Judg. 4), followed by a version of events told from the perspective of the characters Deborah and Barak (Judg. 5).[8] One might therefore expect a reader to privilege the narrator's version in ch. 4 over that of Deborah and Barak in ch. 5, which, as a limited point of view, is less reliable than that of the omniscient narrator. The omniscient narrator sets out to define the characters' roles, something de Bray does also in his painting, and, in particular, to set limits on Deborah's role and to problematize Jael's.

---

7. An important exception is Fewell and Gunn, 'Controlling Perspectives', 389–411.

8. Ibid., 390; cf. Yairah Amit, 'Judges 4: Its Contents and Form', *Journal for the Study of the Old Testament* 39 (1987): 103–4.

In the discussion that follows, I treat Judges 4–5 as a whole. Although questions of historical priority and the development of the tradition are not relevant for my discussion of the way de Bray has visualized the roles and relationships of the characters, some of the differences between the omniscient narrator's account and the characters' version are, and will be dealt with below. In visualizing the text and selecting what to allude to or to foreground and what to downplay or ignore, the artist has privileged certain aspects of the text over others. Like the omniscient narrator of ch. 4, de Bray is interested in the characters, and by the way he presents them he seeks to achieve similar results: to involve the viewer, as the narrator engages the reader, in the undercurrents of the plot. In Judges 5, the characters Deborah and Barak, in contrast, are more concerned with matters relating to the battle.[9]

De Bray's static painting well suits the biblical story, in which the heroes are not well developed characters,[10] and the contact between them is minimal. The two female heroes, Jael and Deborah, act independently of each other; they never meet. Jael enters the narrative in Judg. 4.17, after Deborah disappears from it (v. 14). When the victory is celebrated in song, Deborah and Jael are mentioned together in a stanza that sets the background for the conflict by locating Deborah's rise to prominence as a 'mother in Israel' 'in the days of Shamgar, son of Anat' and 'in the days of Jael' (5.6-7). But nothing is said of any contact between the two women. The fact that Deborah predicts a woman's victory over Sisera (4.9), a victory that turns out to be Jael's, might suggest to some readers a connection between the women, for example, that Deborah knows who Jael is and what she will do,[11] but positing such a connection is simply gap filling, for the text gives us no insight into Deborah's consciousness.

---

9. For a different view, see Fewell and Gunn, 'Controlling Perspectives', 399–402. I would qualify my point above by noting that, although Deborah and Barak are primarily interested in the battle (the conditions leading to it, the participation of the deity, who came, who did not), their song concludes with a narrowed focus on Sisera's death and Sisera's mother's anxiety.

10. There is enough character development to give rise to numerous questions, as I discuss below. Nevertheless, their characters are less well developed than the other important judge-delivers, Ehud, and especially Gideon, Jephthah and Samson. Moreover, their lack of interiority contrasts sharply with the subtle development of Sisera's mother at the end of the account (5.28-30).

11. Gale A. Yee, 'By the Hand of a Woman: The Metaphor of the Woman Warrior in Judges 4', in *Women, War, and Metaphor: Language and Society in the Study of the Hebrew Bible*, ed. Claudia V. Camp and Carole R. Fontaine (Atlanta, GA: Society of Biblical Literature, 1993), 114.

Only two of the story's three heroes act in unison, Deborah and Barak. In fact, Barak will not lead his troops into battle unless Deborah goes too (4.8). Deborah goes with him (4.9, 10), but precisely what role she plays in the battle – and thus the extent of Deborah and Barak's partnership – is not entirely clear. From 4.14-16, it appears that, spurred on by the prophet Deborah, Barak alone leads the Israelite forces in battle. According to 5.15, Deborah and Barak jointly lead the tribe of Issachar to wage war against the Canaanites, but in what capacities? Do they both lead the troops into battle,[12] or, since the troops are described as entering the battle 'at his [Barak's] heels', does Barak alone lead the troops, while Deborah functions as no more *or less* than the prophet who instructs him? Deborah and Barak sing the victory song of ch. 5 in unison, if we accept the reading of the Masoretic Text in 5.1, 'Then sang Deborah and Barak son of Abinoam on that day...' The verb here, however, is third person feminine singular ('she sang'), which leads some interpreters to posit that 'and Barak son of Abinoam' is a later addition and Deborah alone should be considered the singer.[13] The song begins with a declaration, 'to Yahweh I will sing, I will sing praise to Yahweh' (v. 3). Are these the words of one singer or both? In 5.12 Deborah is called upon to utter a song (the song that 5.1 represents her and Barak already in the act of singing?), and Barak to lead away his captives. These are not joint activities.[14]

Whereas the first half of ch. 4 is devoted to Deborah and Barak, in the second half of ch. 4 an encounter takes place between Barak and Jael. Just as she had met Sisera and invited him into her tent for what he assumed was shelter, so now Jael invites Barak to enter her tent to view Sisera's dead body. She seems to know who Barak is and what he is looking for: 'Come, and I will show you the man whom you are seeking' (4.22).

---

12. So Ackerman, *Warrior, Dancer, Seductress, Queen*, 31–32; Susan Niditch, *Judges: A Commentary* (Louisville, KY: Westminster John Knox Press, 2008), 65, 71.

13. There is no textual evidence for omitting Barak, however, and a singular verb can be followed by more than one subject, in which case it often agrees with the first, as the one closest to it (see e.g. Exod. 15.1; Num. 12.1; GKC § 146f-g).

14. But cf. Ackerman (*Warrior, Dancer, Seductress, Queen*, 44–45), who takes 'awake' as a call to battle, like the call to the divine warrior in Pss. 7.6 [Heb. 7.7]; 44.23 [Heb. 44.24]; 59.4-5 [Heb. 59.5-6]; Isa. 51.9-10 (thus pairing Yahweh and Deborah as divine and human equivalents engaged in a 'holy war' against the Canaanites), and the 'song' Deborah is asked to utter here as 'the cry of reveille that will summon the Israelite troops into battle' (31); see also Jo Ann Hackett, 'In the Days of Jael: Reclaiming the History of Women in Ancient Israel', in *Immaculate and Powerful: The Female in Sacred Image and Social Reality*, ed. Clarissa W. Atkinson, Constance H. Buchanan and Margaret R. Miles (Boston: Beacon Press, 1985), 27.

Deborah and Barak do not mention this brief encounter in their song, but rather focus entirely on Jael's deed (perhaps Barak would rather forget the embarrassment of being so obviously upstaged by a woman).

Since Barak is not willing to accept Deborah's commission of him as it stands and imposes a condition, Deborah and Barak cooperate in a somewhat uneasy alliance. First one, then the other, is the subject of narrative attention, and the reader might well wonder who is destined to be the hero of the story.[15] When Deborah prophesies that the glory will not be Barak's but rather 'Yahweh will sell Sisera *into the hand of a woman*' (4.9), one might expect the glory to be Deborah's.[16] Verse 14, where Deborah spurs Barak on with the prophecy, 'this is the day on which Yahweh has given Sisera *into your hand*', complicates matters, but not for long.[17] Jael soon enters the picture and acts independently, with no guidance or support from anyone. By killing Sisera, she steals the glory from both Barak and Deborah. As Meir Sternberg observes of the story's unfolding, 'Having so far divided interest and merit through the seesaw movement between Deborah and Barak, the narrative now diminishes both protagonists by shifting its focus to a third'.[18]

Although he has painted a portrait rather than a narrative scene, de Bray manages to reflect something of this narrative situation. By representing the three heroes together, he reminds the viewer that all three play an important role in the victory. At the same time, their lack of direct contact alludes to their separate spheres of action. Moreover, by placing Jael first, then Deborah, then Barak, de Bray instructs the viewer how to apportion the glory. Jael is the commanding figure in the painting, more fully represented than the others. She appears in radiant white, while the others, dressed in black, seem to blend into the background. De Bray presents her to the viewer in exquisite detail. She wears an elaborate dress, whose

15. See the detailed analyses of Sternberg, *The Poetics of Biblical Narrative*, 270–83; Amit, 'Judges 4', 99–104.

16. Connecting the characters' thoughts with the narrator's design, Amy Kalmanofsky argues that Deborah expects to be the woman and that to prevent Deborah from becoming too powerful the narrator uses the non-Israelite Jael to undermine Deborah's role; *Gender-Play in the Hebrew Bible: The Ways the Bible Challenges Its Gender Norms* (Taylor & Francis, 2016; accessed through ProQuest Ebook Central), n.p.

17. 'Sisera' stands for the Canaanite army as well as the individual, just as the statement that Barak had gone up to Mount Tabor (v. 12) refers to all the Israelite troops. See Sternberg, *The Poetics of Biblical Narrative*, 278–80, on the way this double referencing contributes to the richness and ambiguity of the narrative.

18. Ibid., 280.

silken texture is almost tangible, and her intricately tied turban calls to mind a helmet, perhaps alluding to her contribution to military success (there is a balance between it and Barak's helmet). We see her head, her upper body, with exposed round breasts, her arms and sturdy hands, which look accustomed to wielding the implements she holds, and her lap, with the hand holding the bloody nail resting on her thigh. In contrast, Deborah, caught up in prayer, is mainly face and hands. Barak's face, as attentively rendered as that of the two women, is partially obscured by shadow, and, though he makes a strong impression, arrayed as he is in full military dress, little of his torso can be seen.

Jael: Femme Forte *or* Femme Fatale?

In the history of interpretation Jael has been viewed both as a *femme forte*, God's instrument and faithful servant, and also as a *femme fatale*, a dangerous woman who lured a man to his death.[19] The way the text presents her invites such speculation, and the painting allows both possibilities.

Clearly the text intends us to see Jael as the instrument by which the god of Israel brings about Sisera's death. Deborah predicts that 'Yahweh will sell Sisera into the hand of a woman' (4.9), and this is what comes to pass. Jael kills the unsuspecting Sisera, to whom she has given refuge in her tent, by driving a tent peg into his head (4.21; 5.26-27). For this deed she is praised as 'most blessed of women...of tent-dwelling women most blessed' (5.24). But why does Jael, who belongs to a clan that has made peace with the Canaanite King Jabin (4.17), kill Sisera? Biblical interpreters have proposed various answers to the question. To vindicate her honour.[20] She was a hero who acted not only to defend her person but also to deliver Heber's household from the threat of slavery.[21]

---

19. See David M. Gunn, *Judges* (Oxford: Blackwell, 2005), 61, 71–87; Conway, *Sex and Slaughter in the Tent of Jael*, 43–89. Especially noteworthy are Conway's examples of illustrations where an image and its accompanying text are at odds, in effect undermining each other. See also Colleen M. Conway, 'The Malleability of Jael in the Dutch Renaissance', *Biblical Reception* 2 (2013): 36–56.

20. John Gray, *Joshua, Judges, Ruth* (Grand Rapids, MI: Eerdmans, 1986), 259. Alternatively, says Gray, Jael could have been an older, discarded wife of Heber; see the critique by Mieke Bal, *Death and Dissymmetry: The Politics of Coherence in the Book of Judges* (Chicago: University of Chicago Press, 1988), 211–13.

21. Victor H. Matthews and Don C. Benjamin, *Social World of Ancient Israel 1250–587 BCE* (Peabody, MA: Hendrickson, 1993), 87–95.

She was a loyal Yahwist.[22] The narrator gives her no motive in order to show that God was directing events and Jael was acting according to his plan.[23] She was a cultic functionary whose tent was regarded as a sacred space, and she killed Sisera, in spite of the fact that he came to her tent for sanctuary, because she recognized that it was God's will.[24] It was a tactical move to demonstrate her allegiance to the victorious Israelites.[25] As Jack Sasson concludes, 'her motivation for murdering Sisera can be endlessly debated'.[26] The absence of a suitable explanation for Jael's behaviour and the brutality of the deed raise doubts about Jael's character. Critics frequently disapprove of Jael's blatant violation of hospitality, deceiving Sisera by making him think that he is safe and then brutally murdering him, but one suspects that what most bothers Jael's detractors is the fact that a vulnerable man is a victim of 'ignominious subjection to the effective power of a woman'.[27]

Jael's reputation is further cast into doubt by the sexual overtones in the account, by means of which the biblical narrator seeks to ridicule Sisera, making his humiliating death at the hand of a woman sound

22. Robert G. Boling, *Judges: A New Translation with Introduction and Commentary* (Garden City, NY: Doubleday, 1975), 97, 100, 119.

23. Amit, 'Judges 4', 96–102.

24. Ackerman, *Warrior, Dancer, Seductress, Queen*, 102, following a suggestion by Benjamin Mazar, 'The Sanctuary of Arad and the Family of Hobab the Kenite', *Journal of Near Eastern Studies* 24 (1965): 297–303; see also Ora Brison, 'Jael, *'eshet heber* the Kenite: A Diviner?', in *Joshua and Judges*, ed. Athalya Brenner and Gale A. Yee (Minneapolis, MN: Fortress Press, 2013), 139–60.

25. Fewell and Gunn, 'Controlling Perspectives', 396, 404; cf. Ryan P. Bonfiglio ('Choosing Sides in Judges 4–5: Rethinking Representations of Jael', in Brenner and Yee, eds., *Joshua and Judges*, 161–74), who makes this case for ch. 4 but not ch. 5.

26. Sasson, *Judges 1–12*, 274.

27. D. F. Murray, 'Narrative Structure and Technique in the Deborah–Barak Story (Judges IV.4-22)', in *Studies in the Historical Books of the Old Testament*, ed. J.A. Emerton (Leiden: Brill, 1979), 173. Murray argues that this fate is shared by Barak and Sisera, but cf. the critique of this view, based on concepts of honour and shame, by Geoffrey P. Miller, 'A Riposte Form in the Song of Deborah', in *Gender and Law in the Hebrew Bible and the Ancient Near East*, ed. Victor H. Matthews, Bernard M. Levinson and Tikva Frymer-Kensky (Sheffield: Sheffield Academic Press, 1998), 126 and n. 35. Cf. also Mieke Bal, *Murder and Difference: Gender, Genre, and Scholarship on Sisera's Death* (Bloomington: Indiana University Press, 1988), 124: 'If "Jael's treachery" is unforgivable, the shame of the men becomes forgivable'. We might also compare the condemnation typically heaped upon Delilah for betraying Samson and the discomfort frequently expressed about Judith's assassination of Holofernes.

embarrassingly like a seduction and rape.[28] Jael invites Sisera into her
tent, much as the wanton woman of Proverbs invites the young man to
'turn aside' to her (Prov. 9.16). While he sleeps there, she 'comes to him'
(4.21). The expression 'come to/unto her' is often used of a man having
sexual intercourse with a woman. She penetrates his body at a vulnerable
point – the temple? the cheek? the neck? the mouth? the throat?[29] – with a
phallic tent peg.[30] In a description rife with sexual innuendo, Sisera kneels
over between Jael's legs, falls and lies there despoiled (5.27).[31]

De Bray was apparently familiar with Jael's dual reputation as a
femme forte and a *femme fatale*, and, though he foregrounds the former,

28. For detailed discussion of this symbolism, see Susan Niditch, 'Eroticism and
Death in the Tale of Jael', in *Gender and Difference in Ancient Israel*, ed. Peggy
L. Day (Minneapolis, MN: Fortress Press, 1989), 43–57; Niditch, *Judges*, 81; Bal,
Murder and Difference, 100–134; Robert Alter, *The Art of Biblical Poetry* (New York:
Basic Books, 1985), 43–49; Fewell and Gunn, 'Controlling Perspectives', 392–94.
Some go so far as to suggest that Jael and Sisera had sexual intercourse (Pamela
Tamarkin Reis, 'Uncovering Jael and Sisera: A New Reading', *Scandinavian Journal
of the Old Testament* 19 [2005]: 24–47) or that this was the case in an earlier version
of the story, which was subsequently censored (Yair Zakovitch, 'Sisseras Tod',
Zeitschrift für die alttestamentliche Wissenschaft 93 [1981]: 364–74). Sasson, who
holds that the imagery used of Jael in Judg. 4 is that of a mother, not a seducer (*Judges
1–12*, 275; he seems sceptical about seduction imagery in Judg. 5 as well), comments
on the rabbinic view that Jael and Sisera had sexual intercourse many times but Jael
did not enjoy it (275, 316).

29. All have been proposed; the precise meaning of the word *raqqâ* is uncertain.
It occurs elsewhere only in Song 4.3 and the parallel 6.7, where it could be the
cheek, the temple or the brow. For a review of proposals and argument for the
traditional translation 'temple', see Serge Frolov and Alexander Frolov, 'Sisera
Unfastened: On the Meaning of Judges 4:21 αβ-γ', *Biblische Notizen* 165 (2015):
55–61.

30. Based on a suggestion by Bernard Grossfeld ('A Critical Note on Judg
4.21', *Zeitschrift für die alttestamentliche Wissenschaft* 85 [1973]: 348–51), Frolov
and Frolov take the latter part of Judg. 4.21 to refer to Jael rather than to her
weapon and translate, 'she stuck the tent peg into his temple, and sank/collapsed
to the ground' ('Sisera Unfastened', 59–60). Exactly how Jael dispatches Sisera is
much discussed; see, e.g., Sasson, *Judges 1–12*, 269; Richard D. Nelson, *Judges:
A Critical and Rhetorical Commentary* (London: Bloomsbury T&T Clark, 2017),
89–91.

31. Hebrew *raglayim*, 'legs' or 'feet', can be a euphemism for the genitals. The
verb *kara'* ('to bend, kneel over') can suggest a sexual posture (cf. Job 31.10). The
verb *shakav*, which means 'to lie', can also refer to sexual intercourse. Sisera falls
'violently destroyed' or 'despoiled' (*shadud*), which is suggestive of rape (cf. Jer.
4.30); see Niditch, 'Eroticism and Death', 43–49.

he alludes to the latter.[32] The painting is a pendant, or companion piece, to *Judith with the Head of Holofernes*, which pictures a virtuous Judith holding Holofernes's head, while her maid looks over her shoulder (fig. 7.2).[33]

Fig. 7.2. Salomon de Bray, *Judith with the Head of Holofernes*, 1636, Museo del Prado, Madrid

32. Judith van Gent and Gabriël M. C. Pastoor, 'Die Zeit der Richter', in Tümpel, ed., *Im Lichte Rembrandts*, 66–67.

33. A later owner of the painting had the head painted over to look like an urn; see Jacqueline Boonen, 'Die Geschichte von Israels Exil und Freiheitskampf', in Tümpel, ed., *Im Lichte Rembrandts*, 117. On the confusion of Jael and Judith in art and literature, see Margarita Stocker, *Judith, Sexual Warrior: Women and Power in Western Culture* (New Haven, CT: Yale University Press, 1998), 13–14, 120–72.

Like *Jael, Deborah and Barak, Judith with the Head of Holofernes* is more of a portrait than a depiction of an event in the story, though it could represent, without the gore or the crowd, Judith's showing the head to her people (Jdt. 13.15). She appears without her sword, the counterpart to Jael's domestic tools as weapons. Elaborately dressed and elaborately coiffured, she is serene, a *femme forte*, her eyes turned slightly heavenward, acknowledging the source of her triumph. De Bray's association of Jael with Judith, who delivered her people from an evil oppressor, and his inclusion of Jael in the company of Deborah and Barak, clearly locate her among the heroes of the faith. At the same time, in *Jael, Deborah and Barak*, even as Jael's implements direct the viewer's attention to her act of deliverance, her exposed breasts, on which the light falls, suggest the deadly allure of the *femme fatale*.

Jael, Deborah and Barak shows us a Jael whose expression seems to defy the viewer to ask questions about her motives. Who would venture to cross-examine a woman with a hammer and tent peg, who has only recently used them to dispatch an unwary victim? But just as readers stimulated by tantalizing textual gaps cannot resist filling them, viewers will likely find themselves captivated by Jael's enigmatic expression and unable to resist speculating about what lies behind it. Many meanings could be read into it: defiance, determination, resolution, tension, sensuality. She looks at the viewer in a way that seems to say both 'come hither' and 'don't you dare'. Her brow is wrinkled, her lips pursed. If it were not for the scowl, she could be offering a kiss. De Bray has skilfully captured on canvas the ambiguity surrounding Jael in the text.

The painting implies that the assassination was an on the spot decision, as does the text. The murder weapons, pictured here, are domestic tools, which suggests that the murder was not planned in advance. Jael, after all, could not have known that fate would lead Sisera to her tent, though the reader suspects it from the proleptic statement that Heber had separated from the rest of the Kenites and encamped near Kedesh, the site of the battle (4.11).

Do the fine clothes worn by Jael – the elegant billowy white dress, with full sleeves and décolleté, the flowery sash around her waist and the elaborate headdress – convey to the viewer something about her? Does her ornate attire defy the connection between the woman and the bloody deed? She wears white, which typically symbolizes purity. Is she, as the instrument of Israel's god, above moral reproach, a *femme forte* 'most blessed of women'? Or is this part of the *femme fatale*'s guile? Is she not what she seems, which is precisely what the unsuspecting Sisera discovers about her?

Looking at this Jael, who gazes back unflinchingly, a viewer might well wonder how this woman, determined as she appears, could overpower a warrior like Sisera, even if he were exhausted from battle.[34] In the iconographic tradition she is frequently pictured driving the tent peg through Sisera's temple while he sleeps, as, for example, in Artemisia Gentileschi's painting of the scene, which, like de Bray's painting, uses an indistinct background to draw attention to its protagonists (fig. 7.3).[35]

Fig. 7.3. Artemisia Gentileschi, *Jael and Sisera*, 1620,
Szepmuveszeti Museum, Budapest

Gentileschi's Jael is less complex, less morally equivocal than de Bray's – a *femme forte*, not a *femme fatale*, calm and deliberative, almost

34. That Sisera is exhausted is generally taken to be the sense of the Hebrew *wayya'ap* in 4.21; some, following a suggestion of G. R. Driver ('Problems of Interpretation in the Heptateuch', in *Mélanges bibliques rédigés en l'honneur de André Robert* [Paris: Bloud & Gay, 1957], 74), take it to mean 'he twitched convulsively'. On the difficulties of the verse, see George F. Moore, *A Critical and Exegetical Commentary on Judges* (Edinburgh: T. & T. Clark, 1895), 125–26; C. F. Burney, *The Book of Judges* (New York: Ktav, 1970 [1903]), 93–94; Barnabas Lindars, *Judges 1–5: A New Translation and Commentary* (Edinburgh: T. & T. Clark, 1995), 203–4; Sasson, *Judges 1–12*, 270.

35. There is a column in the background inscribed with the artist's name and date. Both paintings are moderately sized; Gentileschi's is 86 × 125 cm, de Bray's 86 × 71 cm. The absence of a clearly defined setting and the calmness of Jael's pose is in striking contrast to Gentileschi's violent Judiths.

contemplative as she raises her arm to hammer the peg into Sisera's temple while he sleeps.[36] For Babette Bohn, Jael's quiet determination 'reinforc[es] the notion of her moral superiority and divine support'.

> Her downcast eyes, kneeling pose, restrained gesture, and fine but not excessively decorated clothing portray a figure of virtue and refinement who differs markedly from the sexual temptress type favored by most of [Gentileschi's] contemporaries.[37]

Mary Garrard draws attention to the pressure Gentileschi's women exert with their hands, and to their wrists that 'break backward to show the strain of exertion, just as men's wrists do' as signs of both agility and agency.[38] Not only Jael's firm grip on the mallet in this painting but also the space between the mallet and tent peg suggest the power with which the blow will be struck.

By portraying Jael after the murder has been accomplished, rather than in the act of performing it, de Bray hails the deed without indicating the manner in which it was carried out. Viewers who want to know the details are therefore led back to the text, where they will not find a straight-forward answer. Does Jael kill Sisera by driving a tent peg into his temple with her hammer while he is sleeping, as the omniscient narrator's version in Judges 4 has it? Or is he awake and standing when Jael attacks him, since, according to Deborah and Barak's version in Judges 5, he sinks and falls at her feet?[39]

36. For discussion of the artistic tradition of portraying Jael and of this painting as an uncharacteristically positive portrayal, see Babette Bohn, 'Death, Dispassion, and the Female Hero: Artemisia Gentileschi's *Jael and Sisera*', in Bal, ed., *The Artemisia Files*, 107–27; see also the discussion of this painting in Conway, *Sex and Slaughter in the Tent of Jael*, 79–84.

37. 'Death, Dispassion, and the Female Hero', 109.

38. Garrard, 'Artemisia's Hand', 8.

39. Both the differences between the accounts and the details in both accounts are the subject of considerable discussion: Where does the murder take place, in the tent or outside, and under what circumstances? Is Sisera sleeping, or is he standing? Where does Jael strike him and does she use one weapon or two? See, *inter alios*, Moore, *Judges*, 124–26, 163–66; Burney, *Judges*, 79–80, 93–94, 152; Hans Wilhelm Hertzberg, *Die Bücher Josua, Richter, Ruth* (Göttingen: Vandenhoeck & Ruprecht, 1969), 181–82; Lindars, *Judges 1–5*, 200–201; Ellen van Wolde, 'Ya'el in Judges 4', *Zeitschrift für die alttestamentliche Wissenschaft* 107 (1995): 244–45; Baruch Halpern, *The First Historians: The Hebrew Bible and History* (San Francisco, CA: Harper & Row, 1988), 82–84; Jack M. Sasson, '"A Breeder or Two for Each Leader": On Mothers in Judges 4 and 5', in Clines and van Wolde, eds., *A Critical Engagement*, 334–46; Sasson, *Judges 1–12*, 312–18.

Deborah: Judge, Prophet, Singer, Mother in Israel

Deborah, in contrast to Jael who is famous for her one heroic act, holds an impressive number of roles in the text. She is a judge, and, in contrast to other judges who are 'raised up', commissioned or inspired by the Israelite god to deliver Israel in a time of crisis, Deborah is already judging in Israel when the story of Israel's deliverance from oppression at the hand of King Jabin of Canaan begins.[40] As well as being a judge, she is a prophet, and the only person, besides Samuel, to hold both these positions of authority. She is a singer or reciter of tales, called upon to 'utter a song' in 5.12, and one of the singers of the victory song according to 5.1. In addition, she is a 'mother in Israel' (5.7), a phrase that appears elsewhere only in 2 Sam. 20.19 in reference to a city, but which, applied to Deborah, would appear to mean that she ensures the welfare of her people through wise counsel.[41] In view of all her distinctions – judge, prophet, singer, mother in Israel – it is all the more remarkable that Deborah shares the glory with others. Or could it be that her exercise of these roles leaves something to be desired?

Judges 4.3 informs us that Jabin had oppressed Israel for twenty years. If Deborah was judging Israel 'at that time', why had she not acted sooner to deliver her people?[42] Even when she does take action, she does not act independently in leading Israel like other judges. Although she is a prophet, the text does not represent God as speaking directly to her. We (and Barak) have only her word for it when she tells Barak that 'Yahweh, the god of Israel, commands you, "Go, deploy [your troops] at Mount Tabor… I will deploy Sisera, the general of Jabin's army, to meet you by the Wadi Kishon with his chariots and his troops, and I will give him into your hand"' (4.6-7).[43] Sasson argues that Deborah does not summon Barak directly but rather sends her command to him 'likely through

40. Again I refer to the so-called major judges. Othniel and Ehud are 'deliverers' 'raised up' by God (3.9, 15; cf. 2.18); God commissions Gideon to deliver Israel (6.14); Jephthah is appointed leader by the elders of Gilead to deal with a crisis, and inspired by the spirit of Yahweh (11.29); before his birth Samson is destined to 'begin to deliver Israel' (13.5).

41. Claudia V. Camp, 'The Wise Woman of 2 Samuel: A Role Model for Women in Early Israel?', *Catholic Biblical Quarterly* 43 (1981): 14–29; see also Ackerman, *Warrior, Dancer, Seductress, Queen*, 40–43. For a different view, see Sasson, *Judges 1–12*, 290–91.

42. Perhaps the reader is to understand that it was twenty years before the Israelites 'cried out to Yahweh', and only then did their god inspire Deborah to act.

43. Another comparison with the prophet Samuel can serve to illustrate this point. In 1 Sam. 13.8-15 Saul waits for Samuel at Gilgal for seven days, as instructed, and then, because circumstances are desperate, makes a burnt offering. Samuel

messengers',[44] an interpretation that would have Barak receiving the call
to arms at third hand. Like her leadership in the battle, which Deborah
shares with Barak, her role as singer of tales is also a shared one if, as
mentioned above, we follow the MT in 5.1. But, curiously, the text seems
to undermine the singers by casting doubts about their authorship of their
song, for it is odd that, if Deborah and Barak are reciting the song, they
would call on themselves to utter a song and lead away captives (5.12).

Is Deborah's description of herself as 'a mother in Israel' (5.7), a self-
congratulatory boast?[45] As a mother in Israel, Deborah may be responsible
for her people's welfare, but the question remains, what does Deborah
actually accomplish as a leader?[46] Clearly she plays a decisive role in
delivering Israel from oppression; she is the one who sets events in motion
(4.6-7). Whereas other judges lead one tribe or, at the most, a coalition
of two or three tribes against their enemies, Deborah and Barak muster
six tribes to fight together under their leadership (Judg. 5.14-18). But her
relationship with Barak is not a particularly harmonious one, and one
could question the degree of mutual respect they display.

then appears and accuses Saul of not keeping the commandment of God. But in
1 Sam. 10.8 the instructions to go to Gilgal and wait for Samuel are Samuel's, not the
character God's; see, further, Exum, *Tragedy and Biblical Narrative*, 27–30.

44. Sasson, *Judges 1–12*, 257–58.

45. A view found in the Talmud, *b. Pes.* 66a; cf. Fewell and Gunn ('Controlling
Perspectives', 401), who speak of a 'tone of self-congratulation' in the song. The verb
here, *qamti*, is a first person feminine form ('I arose'); most translations, however, take
it as an archaic second person feminine form, 'you arose' (see, e.g., Michael David
Coogan, 'A Structural and Literary Analysis of the Song of Deborah', *Catholic Biblical Quarterly* 40 [1978]: 147). In this case, we would have a situation similar to the one
described above: why does Deborah, the singer, refer to herself as 'you'? On the difficulty of deciding how to translate the verbal form, see Sasson, *Judges 1–12*, 289–90.

46. Unfortunately the text of Judg. 5.7 is difficult and proposals for translating
it vary widely; cf. e.g. Coogan, 'Structural and Literary Analysis', 147: 'Warriors
ceased, in Israel they ceased – until you arose, Deborah...'; Boling, *Judges*, 102:
'The warriors grew plump / In Israel they grew plump again / Because you arose...';
Ackerman, *Warrior, Dancer, Seductress, Queen*, 37: 'Settlements in unwalled hamlets
ceased, In Israel they ceased, Until you arose...'; Renate Jost, *Gender, Sexualität
und Macht in der Anthropologie des Richterbuches* (Stuttgart: Kohlhammer, 2006),
356–57: 'Bewohner des freien Landes (Führende / Bauersleute / Kämpfende) gab
es nicht mehr (Freigiebigkeit / Gastfreundschaft gab es nicht mehr) /in Israel ruhten
sie, bis ich aufstand...' [Inhabitants of the countryside (leaders/farmers [or peasants]/
warriors) were no more (munificence/hospitality were no more) in Israel they ceased,
until I arose...]; Niditch, *Judges*, 67–68: 'Ways of life in the unwalled towns came
to a halt. In Israel they came to a halt until I arose...'; Sasson, *Judges 1–12*, 103–4:
'Hamlets vanish in Israel; simply vanish / Till I, Deborah, arise...'.

Given this surplus of textual information and ambiguity, what does de Bray choose to convey to the viewer about Deborah? For de Bray, Deborah is the religious inspiration for Israel's victory, whereas Barak is the military hero. I have already mentioned the way de Bray pictures Deborah hemmed in by the two figures who encroach upon her leadership role in the text, Barak, with whom she shares the limelight at the beginning of the story, and Jael, who snatches the glory from both of them at the end. In de Bray's painting, Deborah's position, in second place, indicates to viewers that her accomplishment is not so important as Jael's but more important than Barak's. She and Barak are overshadowed by Jael, and, in their dark clothing that blends in with the background, they form a unit that suggests their alliance in the battle against Sisera and his troops. But de Bray offers the viewer no indication that Deborah may have played a vital role in the battle other than influencing the outcome through prayer. Elsewhere in the iconographic tradition, she sometimes appears armed, engaging in the battle, or, more often, inspiring Barak and his army and spurring them on, as in the painting below by Luca Giordano (1632–1705) (fig. 7.4).[47]

This highly dramatic composition offers a marked contrast to de Bray's static portrait, and Giordano's Deborah is nothing like de Bray's. Young and powerful, she directs events from a position of authority above, but not isolated from, the fray. Her role and her attitude mirror God's, and we can trace a clear chain of command from God, at the top of the painting bathed in light, to Deborah, roughly in the centre of the painting and pointing down to Barak on horseback.[48]

The contrast between Deborah and Jael in de Bray's painting is dramatic. Jael is young and sexual, whereas Deborah is aged, wrinkled and not at all feminine. If there is a hint of the *femme fatale* in his Jael, de Bray assures his viewers that there is nothing of the *femme fatale* in

47. Some examples of Deborah going into battle, as well as Giordano's tumultuous battle scene reproduced here, can be found in Herbert Haag, Dorothée Sölle, Joe H. Kirchberger, Anne-Marie Schnieper-Müller and Emil Bührer, *Great Women of the Bible in Art and Literature* (Grand Rapids, MI: Eerdmans, 1994), 115–21; see also Gunn, *Judges*, 66–68.

48. This is the kind of Deborah that Ackerman envisages in Judg. 5, the human counterpart to God above (*Warrior, Dancer, Seductress, Queen*, 29–47). In Ackerman's view, Deborah and God are paired as human and divine equivalents (drawing on Canaanite traditions about Baal and Anat) and Deborah is unambiguously and emphatically 'Israel's chief military commander' with Barak her second in command (31). Possibly ancient listeners to the song would have recognized allusions to the divine warrior Anat in the depiction of Deborah, but, as Ackerman admits, already Judg. 4 presents the reader with a Deborah whose leadership role is diminished.

Fig. 7.4. Luca Giordano, *The Victorious Fight of the Israelites*, Museo del Prado, Madrid

Deborah, only the *femme forte*. Deborah's hands, pressed together in prayer, form a stark contrast to Jael's, which hold her weapons. They are large and illuminated against the dark background, emphasizing her intercessory role. De Bray thus directs the viewer to contemplate the role of Israel's god in guiding these three heroes to victory. The prophet looks up to heaven, her mouth open, perhaps offering thanks, perhaps uttering her song. Possibly in choosing to make Deborah old, de Bray alludes to her role as 'mother'. Who but an aged wise woman could merit such a distinction as 'mother in Israel'?

Barak: Out of the Shadows

When Deborah and Barak describe the battle in the song they sing for the benefit of their audience, all they tell us about Barak is that, together with Deborah, he led the Israelites to victory over the Canaanites. They mention Barak twice, both times in connection with Deborah:

> Rouse yourself, rouse yourself, Deborah!
>   Rouse yourself, rouse yourself, sing a song!
> Rise up, Barak, capture your captives,
>   son of Abinoam (5.12).

> The princes of Issachar were with Deborah,
>   and Issachar loyal to Barak,
>   into the valley they were sent at his heels (5.15).

Have they, like any good politicians after an outcome has been decided, suppressed their former differences and presented themselves as 'uniting in immediate, voluntary response to the cause'?[49] According to the omniscient narrator of Judges 4, they do not work so harmoniously together, though the precise nature of their relationship is not transparent.

Deborah summons Barak to her in order to give him instructions from God:

> Has not Yahweh, the god of Israel, commanded you, 'Go, deploy at Mount Tabor and take with you ten thousand men of Naphtali and Zebulun. I will deploy against you, at the Wadi Kishon, Sisera, the commander of Jabin's army, and his chariots and his troops, and I will give him into your hand' (4.6-7).

49. Fewell and Gunn, 'Controlling Perspectives', 400.

Barak's response to this charge comes as something of a surprise: 'If you will go with me, I will go, but if you will not go with me, I will not go'. Why does he pose this condition? Does he lack confidence? Is his reluctance to do as Deborah commands a sign of cowardice? Most interpreters think so. Sternberg, for example, is particularly harsh in his criticism of Barak: 'Of the two leaders, it is he who plays the woman; and having been called upon to do a man's job, he refuses to act unless the woman who delegated it to him comes along to give him moral courage'.[50] Worse, has Barak been shirking his responsibility? The rhetorical question 'has Yahweh not commanded you' could be seen as providing a hint that Barak should already be aware of what his god expects of him.[51]

Alternatively, could Barak be questioning Deborah's authority, as Fewell and Gunn propose? Does he wonder what a woman, even if she is a judge and prophet, knows about fighting? Can he be sure that what Deborah has commanded him is the word of God?

> Barak is being asked to risk his life as well as the lives of ten thousand men on the strength of this woman's unconfirmable word. Barak's conditional proposal, then, is a test: if Deborah is willing to stake her own life on this word, then he will believe and obey.[52]

If Barak's condition is a test of Deborah's authority, it is hard to see what it would prove. The narrator calls her a prophet (4.4). If Deborah believes that she is speaking on behalf of her god, would she not be willing to stake her life on this word and go with Barak, thus passing his test even if she were wrong about her inspiration? Or do Fewell and Gunn think that Barak thinks that Deborah is deliberately deceiving him, only pretending to be a prophet?

Rather than questioning Deborah's authority, could Barak be overly dependent on it? The Septuagint has a longer reading in 4.8 in which

---

50. Sternberg, *The Poetics of Biblical Narrative*, 274. Sternberg goes so far as to claim that 'the flat character [Barak] gains rotundity with a vengeance as soon as he betrays his lack of self-confidence' (274), but surely this is to overstate the case, for none of the heroes in Judg. 4–5 is very well developed. On Barak as un-manned and shamed by the women in the story, see Yee, 'By the Hand of a Woman', 115–16; Bal, *Murder and Difference*, 115–24. For a different view, see Niditch, *Judges*, 65; Sasson, *Judges 1–12*, 260.

51. Cf. J. Alberto Soggin, *Judges: A Commentary*, trans. John Bowden (Philadelphia, PA: Westminster Press, 1981), 64–65, who acknowledges this as the normal sense of *halo'* but rejects it, primarily on the grounds that the text says nothing about Barak having already received but rejected a divine calling.

52. Fewell and Gunn, 'Controlling Perspectives', 398.

Barak explains his hesitancy in terms of his reliance on prophetic guidance: 'For I do not know on which day the angel of the Lord will give me success'.[53] This justification suggests that he needs Deborah the prophet to go with him to confirm when the time is right to attack, which is, in fact, what happens in v. 14, when she says, 'Up, for *this is the day* on which Yahweh has given Sisera into your hand'. Was her initial commission, then, not sufficient?

Though not especially well developed, the uneasy relationship between Deborah and Barak invites comparison to that between another reluctant leader, Saul, and his nemesis Samuel, who, like Deborah, is both a judge and a prophet. Both Barak and Saul are, initially at least, reluctant commanders. Barak's reliance on Deborah is like Saul's dependence on Samuel, and Deborah's attitude to Barak resembles Samuel's impatience with Saul. Like Samuel, who, in the name of Israel's god, tells Saul what to do, Deborah instructs Barak. Samuel does not take up arms in Saul's military campaigns (another possible parallel with Deborah), but the presence and support of the prophet is important for the hesitant leader (1 Sam. 13.8-12; 15.13, 25-31; 28.15), just as Deborah's support is essential for Barak. Deborah seems to have the same sort of arrogant, or short-tempered, attitude to Barak that Samuel has to Saul. When Barak demurs at his commission, her rejoinder puts him in his place.[54] She takes back the promise she spoke in God's name, 'I will give [Sisera] *into your hand*' (4.7) and declares: 'I will indeed go with you; however, the road on which you are going will not lead to your glory, for Yahweh will sell Sisera *into the hand of a woman*' (4.9). The price Barak will pay for insisting that Deborah accompany him, whether it betrays a lack of manly courage or his over-dependence on the prophet or both, is that a woman will claim the glory that might have been his.

Unexpectedly, the prophet drops out of the story in Judges 4 after v. 14. God throws Sisera and his army into a panic before Barak (4.15), and Barak and his troops pursue them and kill them all except Sisera (4.16-17), who flees the battle on foot.[55] Still in pursuit of Sisera, Barak is met by Jael, who invites him into her tent to see the man he is seeking.

53. LXX reads literally, 'For I do not know on what day the Lord will help the angel on the way with me'. I follow Burney, *Judges*, 89, in assuming a Hebrew Vorlage that the LXX translator misunderstood, reading 'angel' (*mal'ak*) as the object of the verb, thus making *yhwh* the subject, and taking the accusative 'me' (*'ty*) as the preposition 'with me'.

54. Cf. Samuel's harsh rebukes of Saul, 1 Sam. 13.13-14; 15.17.

55. Judg. 5.12 mentions captives. Since, according to 4.16, Sisera's entire army was wiped out, the captives would be women, children and old men (Fewell and

Does Barak know who Jael is, and, more importantly, does he know about the alliance between the clan of Heber the Kenite and Jabin (4.17)? Why does he enter Jael's tent as trustingly as Sisera had done? It is necessary that Barak see for himself, with his own eyes, that God delivered Sisera into the hand of a woman, as Deborah foretold – and thus to get his comeuppance for responding the way he did to Deborah's instructions.[56]

In de Bray's painting, Barak's is a commanding presence, but he is overshadowed by the women, as he is in the text. De Bray celebrates Barak as a military hero. If, in the text, Barak sounds like a little boy who needs his mother, Deborah, the 'mother in Israel' ('if you will go with me, I will go, but, if you will not go with me, I will not go'), there is nothing childish about the man with the moustache in the painting. Like the meaning of Barak's unexpected reply to his commission by Deborah in the text, the expression on Barak's face in the painting is open to interpretation. I read it as a look of shock, a shock of recognition, and thus as de Bray's way of conveying to the viewer what he imagined to be Barak's reaction at seeing Sisera dead in Jael's tent, dispatched by a woman's hand. The hands in the painting tell a story. Deborah's hands, pressed together in prayer, form a stark contrast to Jael's, which hold the murder weapons. Barak's hands, in contrast, are not visible. Thus de Bray reinforces the idea that the god of Israel gave Sisera 'into the hand of a woman'.

Barak may be somewhat in the background here, but tradition brings him out of the shadows. In 1 Sam. 12.11 Jerubbaal, Barak,[57] Jephthah and Samuel are named as deliverers in the time of the judges, and Heb. 11.32 lists Barak along with the judges Gideon, Samson, Jephthah and Samuel as heroes who through faith conquered kingdoms. The judge Deborah is absent from both lists. Biblical commentators, too, bring Barak into the limelight. Soggin, for example, in his commentary, entitles the section on

Gunn, 'Controlling Perspectives', 408). Alternatively, we could allow Deborah and Barak's version of events to cast doubt on the reliability of the omniscient narrator of ch. 4.

56. Although I am inclined to attribute Barak's insistence that Deborah accompany him to battle to over-dependence on the prophet rather than outright cowardice (much like Saul's reliance on Samuel to enquire of God on his behalf), I agree with Bal that the result is his narrative punishment, 'the shame of seeing his enemy killed by a woman – the shame of the other's shame' (*Murder and Difference*, 63).

57. It is an overstatement to say the tradition in 1 Sam. 12.9–11 brings him out of the shadows. The Hebrew reads 'Bedan', but since Bedan is unknown to us and 1 Sam. 12.9 mentions both Sisera and Jabin as enemies from whom Israel was delivered, most commentators emend 'Bedan' to 'Barak'. The textual confusion, however, is a further diminution of Barak's role.

Judges 4–5 'Deborah and Barak as Judges' and speaks of 'the judgeship of Deborah and Barak'.[58] Boling gives his discussion of Judges 4 the title 'Deborah and Baraq', and inexplicably demotes Deborah to an 'honorary judge'.[59] Barry Webb, in a literary reading, deals with Judges 4–5 under the title 'Barak', and considers Barak to be the intended 'deliverer', though admitting that the term *moshia'*, used for other deliverer figures in Judges, is not applied to him.[60] Others use the title 'Deborah and Barak', letting Deborah and Barak share the glory, though not necessarily the same responsibilities.[61]

Visualizing Textual Oppositions

Jael, Deborah and Barak not only leads the viewer to contemplate the heroes as individuals and the roles they play, it also draws contrasts between them that resonate remarkably well with textual oppositions, demonstrating what a keen visual exegete de Bray is. An obvious opposition in both painting and text is that between male and female (though the opposition is destabilized by the text's portrayal of Jael, which does not conform to the two-sex, two-gender binary of male/female).[62] Who is the deliverer, the real hero of the story, the female judge and

58. Soggin, *Judges*, 60.

59. Boling, *Judges*, 94.

60. Barry G. Webb, *The Book of the Judges: An Integrated Reading* (Sheffield: JSOT Press, 1987), 133–34. In *The Book of Judges* (Grand Rapids, MI: Eerdmans, 2012), 34, Webb lists Barak as one of the twelve judges and considers chs. 4 and 5 to be 'essentially about Barak', even though, as he points out, 'Deborah is even said to have judged Israel'.

61. See e.g. Moore, *Judges*, 107 (who uses a longer title for Judg. 4, 'Deborah and Barak deliver Israel from the Canaanites; the defeat and death of Sisera'); Burney, *Judges*, 78; Hertzberg, *Josua, Richter, Ruth*, 169; Gray, *Joshua, Judges, Ruth*, 253; Lindars, *Judges 1–5*, 164. More recent commentaries reflect a shift: Niditch uses the title 'Tales of Deborah and Jael, Warrior Women' for Judg. 4 (*Judges*, 59; I fail to see how either woman qualifies as a warrior or Jael a 'guerrilla warrior', 67, 76); Sasson uses 'Deborah' for both 4 and 5 (*Judges 1–12*, 250).

62. Admittedly, oppositions are never clear-cut. In an important critique of commentary on Judg. 4–5, Deryn Guest calls into question the assumed stable gender of Jael; 'From Gender Reversal to Genderfuck: Reading Jael through a Lesbian Lens', in *Bible Trouble: Queer Reading at the Boundaries of Biblical Scholarship*, ed. Teresa J. Hornsby and Ken Stone (Atlanta, GA: Society of Biblical Literature, 2011), 9–43: 'Jael is not a *woman* warrior and equally Jael is not a *male* rapist… Jael is a figure who unsettles and destabilises, whose performativity provides one of those unintelligible genders that give the lie to ideas of sex as abiding substance' (26).

prophet Deborah or the male military leader Barak, who, commissioned by her, destroys Sisera's entire army? Or is it Jael, the woman who kills Sisera? Is it a coincidence that the only female judge in the book of Judges shares the spotlight with others? Or is this surplus of heroes, vying, with divine assistance, for the glory, the biblical narrator's way of avoiding giving too much power to a woman?[63] A male leader is essential, since a woman could not lead an army in a major military campaign (and one need only recall how dubious Deborah's military role is).[64] Nor is the biblical narrator content for the glory to be shared between a woman and a man; a second woman is introduced to compete for the woman's portion of the glory.[65] Ironically Jael's victory not only detracts from Barak's glory, as Deborah had prophesied, but also from Deborah's, since 'the hand of a woman' that delivers Israel turns out to be not Deborah's but Jael's. Deborah, as prophet and judge, plays a crucial leadership role, but Jael's victory over Sisera, the climactic event in both the omniscient narrator's and the characters' accounts, is not a military victory.[66]

63. If the victory over Sisera had been Deborah's alone, she might appear too powerful and threatening. Imagine, for example, if she, and not Jael, had slain Sisera, much as Samuel slaughtered Agag when Saul did not complete his mission to kill all the Amalekites (1 Sam. 15.32-33). Alternatively, if Deborah had overcome Sisera through deception like Jael's, replete with sexual innuendo, she would no longer be the non-sexual and thus untarnished mother figure she is. Perhaps any role in Sisera's death would have tarnished her reputation (a woman who kills – even Judith, for example – does not escape reproach).

64. But cf. Yee ('By the Hand of a Woman', 110–17), who attributes to Deborah a military role, and argues that the representation of both Deborah and Jael as women warriors in Judg. 4 is the author's attempt 'to cope with the tension between the normative maleness of the military and the apparent involvement of women in war in pre-state Israel' (114); see also Hackett, 'In the Days of Jael', 27; Ackerman, *Warrior, Dancer, Seductress, Queen*, 31–45, 71; Jost, *Gender, Sexualität und Macht*, 126–37; Niditch, *Judges*, 64–67, 76–79.

65. Or, as Bal puts it, the two women function as 'a single *category* in which each has her predetermined place' (*Murder and Difference*, 215); cf. Murray, 'Narrative Structure', 173. On the splitting of woman's roles as a technique for diminishing a woman's power, see Exum, *Plotted, Shot, and Painted*, 96–97; Athalya Brenner, *The Israelite Woman: Social Role and Literary Type in Biblical Narrative*, 2nd ed. (London: Bloomsbury, 2015), 100.

66. For arguments that Jael, like Deborah, should be considered a military hero, see Hackett, 'In the Days of Jael', 28; Yee, 'By the Hand of a Woman', 110–17; Ackerman, *Warrior, Dancer, Seductress, Queen*, 59–72. Niditch calls Jael a 'woman warrior' (*Judges*, 67, 82) and 'guerrilla warrior' (67, 76) and Jael and Deborah 'warrior women' (59, 76).

As Sternberg puts it, '[S]he disarmed Sisera with a woman's weapons: soft words and strong drink'.[67]

The most visually arresting opposition the painting sets up is that between Jael and Deborah. I mentioned above the contrast between the non-sexual, hoary prophet Deborah and the sexual young assassin Jael. De Bray's portrayal of the two women virtually compels the viewer to compare them, to see them as vastly different and to overlook any similarities, similarities often overlooked in biblical commentary as well. The biblical text says nothing about Deborah's age, or anyone else's for that matter. It does, however, draw attention to Jael's sexuality in using language suggestive of seduction and rape to describe her murder of Sisera, language that might lead a reader to imagine Jael as young and coquettish. I suggested above that, for de Bray, making Deborah old and nonsexual may be a way of affirming her role as an otherworldly servant of God, as well as alluding to her role as a wizened 'mother in Israel'. That, in the text, the erotic imagery applied to Jael does not extend to Deborah may reflect patriarchy's attempt to deny the mother's sexuality, especially in the case of a good 'mother', like Deborah.[68]

Interestingly, neither Deborah nor Jael is unambiguously identified as a wife. Deborah's epithet, *'eshet lappidot*, in some translations 'wife of Lappidot', could be translated 'fiery woman'.[69] Jael's epithet, 'wife of Heber the Kenite' (*'eshet heber haqqeni*) might be rendered 'a woman of the Kenite group'.[70] Whereas 'fiery woman' describes Deborah very well, in Jael's case 'wife of Heber' seems more likely, especially in 4.21, where Jael is described a second time simply as *'eshet heber*. It would not be unusual to find both women identified in terms of their husbands, just as Barak, son of Abinoam, is identified in relation to his father. Neither Lappidot nor Heber nor Abinoam plays a role in the story. Both women

---

67. Sternberg, *The Poetics of Biblical Narrative*, 282. Sternberg's patriarchal reading brings to the surface the patriarchal ideology implicit in the text.

68. One can see this clearly in the denial of the mother's sexuality in the story of another judge, Samson; see Exum, *Fragmented Women*, 45–46.

69. So Niditch, *Judges*, 60: 'a woman of fire'; Sasson, '"A Breeder or Two for Each Leader"', 342, and *Judges 1–12*, 250: 'a wielder of flames' (possibly divination using flames, see *Judges 1–12*, 255–56); see also Ackerman, *Warrior, Dancer, Seductress, Queen*, 38. Hebrew *lappid* is a masculine noun meaning 'torch'; *lappidot*, which looks like a feminine plural form, does not appear elsewhere. Van Wolde, reading 'woman of torches', suggests the feminine form appears because of the association with a woman ('Ya'el in Judges 4', 240 and n. 4).

70. Soggin, *Judges*, 62, 65–66. The basic meaning of Hebrew *heber* is 'group', and in Soggin's view it refers here to an ethnic unit.

act independently of husbands or other male authority figures. But both are, symbolically at least, mothers.

Deborah is the good mother. She 'arose as a mother in Israel' (5.7) to deliver her children from danger and make their lives secure. She is the life-giving mother. Jael, on the other hand, is the death-dealing mother. Vying with the sexual imagery in the account of Jael and Sisera is maternal imagery.[71] Jael behaves in a motherly fashion, offering Sisera security ('turn aside to me') and assurance ('have no fear', 4.18). The picture the text paints of her covering him and giving him milk to drink suggests a mother putting her son to bed. She even watches over him while he sleeps to protect him from harm ('Stand at the opening of the tent, and if any man comes and asks you, "Is there a man here?", say "There is not"', 4.20).[72] The maternal aspect of Jael is an important feature in the text that de Bray does not appear to represent at all in his visual exegesis of the story, unless Jael's full breasts allude to the nurturing mother of the text who gives Sisera milk to drink when he asks for water.[73]

As the biblical story shows, the nurturing, protective mother can suddenly, unexpectedly, turn deadly. She may attack her son in his sleep, when he is utterly defenceless (4.21). Or she may turn on him in the maternal act of feeding him (5.25-27). In Mieke Bal's reading of Judg. 5.27, Sisera drops between Jael's legs like an aborted foetus.[74] Thus it

71. For discussion of the mixture of sexual and maternal imagery, see Bal, *Death and Dissymmetry*, 211–17, 227–29; Bal, *Murder and Difference*, 102–9, 121–34; Alter, *Art of Biblical Poetry*, 43–49; Fewell and Gunn, 'Controlling Perspectives', 392–94. Guest, in contrast, illustrates how 'Jael's acts of seduction or maternal womanly attributes are equally performative of a sex that has no abiding substance' ('From Gender Reversal to Genderfuck', 37).

72. There is only a little boy, ironically about to become, as Johanna W. H. Bos observes, 'a dead man, "not there"'; 'Out of the Shadows: Genesis 38; Judges 4:17–22; Ruth 3', in *Reasoning with the Foxes: Female Wit in a World of Male Power*, ed. J. Cheryl Exum and Johanna W. H. Bos (Atlanta, GA: Scholars Press, 1988), 54. Cf. Bal, *Death and Dissymmetry*: 'he also anticipates that his manliness may be questioned' (213), 'his destruction is unmanning' (214).

73. Cf. the rabbinic tradition that the milk Jael gave Sisera came from her breasts (e.g. *b. Nid.* 55b); on rabbinic treatments of Jael and Deborah, see Leila Leah Bronner, 'Valorized or Vilified? The Women of Judges in Midrashic Sources', in Brenner, ed., *A Feminist Companion to Judges*, 78–91. Bronner observes that, whereas Jael receives a mixed reception, the rabbis consistently sought to diminish Deborah's role as judge and leader. Apparently Deborah posed more of a problem for rabbinic interpreters than Jael because the text did not already provide sufficient support for undermining her role.

74. Bal, *Murder and Difference*, 131.

turns out that the nurturing mother and the dangerous mother are one and the same, a characteristic of the mother well established in psychoanalytic theory, according to which the mother has a dual aspect as a source of security and protection but also of anxiety and frustration.[75] Although at first glance it may seem that Deborah is the good mother and Jael the terrifying one, the text in fact reveals that it is not possible to experience only one side of the mother and not the other.[76] Jael is both nurturing and deadly. Deborah is not only concerned for her people's security but also sends her 'sons' off to war, where many of them will die. So, to answer a question I posed at the beginning of this chapter, it would indeed seem that Deborah belongs, as de Bray presents her to us, in the company of a brutal assassin and a military hero who has shed much blood.

There is another opposition in the text, so fundamental that it is rarely discussed: the opposition between 'us' and 'them', between those on the 'right' side, those with God on their side – the heroes, Jael, Deborah, Barak and the Israelites – and those on the 'wrong' side, the oppressors, the enemy – the Canaanites, Jabin, Sisera and Sisera's mother. De Bray is interested only in the victors and, like the text, in commemorating their glorious victory. But, looking at this painting, a viewer might wonder about the defeated enemy, absent but hinted at in the bloody nail and the heroes' poses. The text, in contrast, draws attention to the forces opposing the Israelites at many points, but none so forceful as the final stanzas of Deborah and Barak's victory song. Here the focus is on two individuals as representative of the enemy: their leader Sisera, who, not unexpectedly, dies ignominiously (5.24-27), and, in an unanticipated *tour de force* of *Schadenfreude*, his mother, who grows increasingly apprehensive at his delay (vv. 28-30). The contrast between Sisera's mother and Deborah 'could not be greater', declares Judith McKinlay.

> [Sisera's] is the mother at home, uninvolved in what is happening outside the world of the women's room, only awaiting news of her son, merely dreaming of the spoils of victory, with that chilling 'a girl or two for every

75. Furthermore, according to psychoanalytic theory, the infant's desire for the mother's body has a sexual aspect, which helps explain the mixture of erotic imagery and maternal imagery in the account of Sisera's encounter with Jael.

76. The situation is thus more complex than that described by Fokkelien van Dijk-Hemmes, 'Mothers and a Mediator in the Song of Deborah', in Brenner, ed., *A Feminist Companion to Judges*, 110–14. My discussion of the mother above draws on J. Cheryl Exum, 'Feminist Criticism: Whose Interests Are Being Served?', in *Judges and Method: New Approaches in Biblical Studies*, ed. Gale A. Yee, 2nd ed. (Minneapolis, MN: Fortress Press, 2007), 71–74.

man'. Deborah's child, however, is none other than Israel itself, but an Israel
that she drives into battle.[77]

'So perish all your enemies, Yahweh!', exclaim the singers at the
story's end (v. 31). *Schadenfreude*, however, is double-edged. The singers'
delight in the enemy's false perceptions – Sisera's belief that he is secure
in Jael's tent, his mother's faltering assurance that finding and dividing
the spoil has caused his delay – make it possible for the reader to consider
the events from the perspective of those defeated.[78] Gabriel Josipovici
observes that this is the only time in the book of Judges when one
character, Deborah as singer, displays an awareness of what it feels like to
be another; the poet, he notes, 'has given us a sense of the silent victims
as well as of the exultant victors'.[79] Sisera's mother is given greater interiority than any other character in the story, and the finely crafted portrait
of her is both moving and chilling. Readers are likely both to sympathize
with her anxiety and to be appalled by the vision of rape and pillage,
realities of war, that she relies on to allay her fears.[80] In the portrayal of
Sisera's mother peering through the window, hoping against hope that she
will soon spy her son returning triumphantly, the text opens a window for
its readers to look through the other's eyes, and to catch a glimpse of the
inescapable horrors of war.[81]

77. Judith E. McKinlay, *Troubling Women and Land: Reading Biblical Texts in
Aotearoa New Zealand* (Sheffield: Sheffield Phoenix Press, 2014), 81–82. She goes
on to point out that, if Deborah is the singer, there is a 'trinity of violence' here: 'Jael
is being praised by Deborah for killing the son that Sisera's mother is awaiting, while
dreaming of the rape of Israelite women' (83).
78. Witness the sympathy, albeit qualified, for Sisera and his mother in the
commentaries.
79. Gabriel Josipovici, *The Book of God: A Response to the Bible* (New Haven,
CT: Yale University Press, 1988), 130.
80. See further, Fewell and Gunn, 'Controlling Perspectives', 406–9; Exum,
'Feminist Criticism', 73–74. The text does not mention Israelite casualties, though it
reports the whole-scale slaughter of Sisera's army.
81. McKinlay shows how stories like this one reinforce the position of the
dominant culture by depending for their effect upon a colonizing-imperialist ideology.
In her chapter entitled 'Conversations with Deborah', McKinlay interrogates the
text in such a patient and respectful way that, in the end, Deborah, her conversation
partner, is left speechless (*Troubling Women and Land*, 72–98).

Notorious Biblical Women in Manchester: Spencer Stanhope's Eve and Frederick Pickersgill's Delilah

What do people typically think of when they hear the name 'Eve'? The woman who brought sin and death into the world? The woman responsible for the loss of paradise? The woman who tempted Adam with the 'apple', and the rest is history? And what about the name 'Delilah'? Her name is synonymous with treachery and deceit – a temptress, a scheming woman, a *femme fatale* who betrays Samson by cutting his hair, leaving him weak and helpless, and who thus dramatically illustrates the danger women pose to men. I would venture to say that Eve and Delilah are, in popular culture, the two best known – most notorious – women from the Hebrew Bible. Of course there are differences: Delilah intentionally deceives Samson, whereas Eve is tempted by the serpent, and, so the old argument goes, she is too weak or too gullible to resist. Delilah is tempted also – by money: the Philistine rulers offer her a bribe and she accepts it ('Entice him, and see by what means his strength is great, and by what means we may overpower him and bind him in order to humiliate him, and we will each give you eleven hundred pieces of silver', Judg. 16.5). But whereas Delilah knows what she is doing, Eve, like Samson, is deceived, for the serpent does not tell her the whole truth about the effects of eating the forbidden fruit ('You will not die, for God knows that when you eat of it your eyes will be opened and you will be like gods [or 'God'], knowing good and evil', Gen. 3.4-5).[1] She does not betray or deceive Adam, who knows as much as she does, since he is present during the discussion between Eve and the serpent, an important detail often overlooked in popular versions of the story.

1. To what extent the serpent is lying is open to question. They do not die *on the day* they eat the fruit, as God had said (Gen. 2.17), but, indeed, they will die, since they will be expelled from the garden to prevent them from eating fruit from the tree of life (3.22-23). Their eyes are opened (3.7), and God acknowledges that eating the fruit has made them 'like one of us, knowing good and evil' (3.22). But they also know that they are naked (3.7), knowledge that they did not have before, and they are punished for their disobedience.

Although it would be unfair to describe Eve as a treacherous woman like Delilah, these two biblical figures have more in common than one might initially suppose. Two works of art from the Manchester Art Gallery, both from the second half of the nineteenth century, can help us see this. Frederick Richard R. A. Pickersgill's *Samson Betrayed* was painted in 1850 (fig. 8.1), and J. R. Spencer Stanhope's *Eve Tempted* not long after, c. 1877 (fig. 8.2). These paintings, whose subjects are immediately recognizable, reinscribe the bad reputation Delilah and Eve have acquired over centuries, and one of the questions I want to consider is, To what extent is this reputation deserved? When artists depict women like Eve and Delilah as, say, devious, untrustworthy, seductive or threatening, are they picking up on clues in the biblical story, or are they reading their own culturally conditioned stereotypes into the story? They do both, of course. In neither *Samson Betrayed* nor *Eve Tempted*, for instance, is the stereotype challenged. Neither woman is nurturing, and neither is cast as a hero of the faith, like, for example, Jael, discussed above in Chapter 7, or Judith.[2]

Fig. 8.1. Frederick Richard R.A. Pickersgill, *Samson Betrayed*,
1850, Manchester Art Gallery

2. Jael and Judith, both *femmes fortes* in the artistic tradition, are unable to escape the reputation as *femmes fatales*; on Jael, see Chapter 7; on Judith, see Stocker, *Judith, Sexual Warrior*; Nutu, 'Framing Judith'.

Fig. 8.2. John Roddam Spencer Stanhope, *Eve Tempted*, 1877,
Manchester Art Gallery

Samson Betrayed, Eve Tempted. The titles of these paintings are interestingly similar: the name of a biblical character – Samson, Eve – and
a passive verb: betrayed, tempted. These titles not unexpectedly reflect
my point about the differences between the women: *Samson Betrayed*
casts Delilah as the betrayer; *Eve Tempted* suggests that Eve is the
victim, though she seems to me a rather complicit victim in Stanhope's
version of the story. There is a more striking similarity than the titles of
these paintings, however: the two women look very much alike; they are

sisters in crime, so to speak. They both have the same red hair, parted in the middle, similar facial features, and the same body type. Not inconsequentially, both are naked, apart from Eve's long hair that oddly but conveniently twists around from behind her back to cover her genitals, and the similar role played by the brocade fabric around Delilah's legs. Although we expect Eve to be naked in paintings of the garden of Eden before the couple's expulsion (when God clothes them in animal skins), should we expect Delilah to appear without her clothes on?[3] The text says only that Delilah cut Samson's hair while he was sleeping 'upon her knees' (Judg. 16.19).[4] Nothing is said about Samson falling asleep because he is exhausted from lovemaking but neither is anything said to discourage readers from drawing such a conclusion. Artists typically portray the scene as one in which it appears that passionate lovemaking has taken place, with Delilah provocatively attired, partially clad or dishevelled, and Pickersgill is no exception. The promise of exposed flesh in Delilah's case is more titillating than simple nakedness like Eve's. Eve's nakedness may suggest innocence, but Delilah's hints at wantonness.

But even in Eve's case, how innocent is nakedness? It is, is it not, a fairly common view that Eve was a temptress, and the forbidden fruit she offered Adam was sex? Whatever its other associations, female nudity in the art of the Christian West, as Margaret Miles argues, inevitably carries associations of sexual lust, shame, sin and guilt.

> Only when gender is engaged as a category of analysis do we begin to see that our impression of the positivity of religious nakedness must be revised to account for female nakedness presented as symbol of sin, sexual lust, and dangerous evil. In depictions of the naked female body, interest in active religious engagement, exercise, and struggle is often subordinated to, or in tension with, the female body as spectacle. Insofar as women and their bodies were assimilated to religious meanings, they 'became male'. But the female body ultimately and visibly resisted becoming male, and thus represented the fall of the human race into sin, sexual lust, acquisitiveness, and hunger for power. In short, although religious nakedness generally contradicted social meanings of nakedness, in the case of the naked female body, social meanings were reinforced.[5]

---

3. As Miles (*Carnal Knowing*, 121) notes, 'Scriptural women, some of them minor figures whose recurring appearance in paintings is puzzling, are also [like Eve] repeatedly depicted as naked'.

4. One Septuagint reading (Codex Alexandrinus) is 'between (*ana meson*) her knees', which is more suggestive of a sexual encounter.

5. Miles, *Carnal Knowing*, 81–82.

'Depictions of the Fall', Miles observes, 'focus visual interest on Eve and on her initiative in sin'.[6] This is certainly the case in Stanhope's painting, where Adam is not even present.

Both women serve important narrative agendas. Eve is instrumental in getting the primordial couple out of Eden, thus enabling humanity to enter (biblical) history. Delilah enables Samson to achieve his preordained task: to 'begin to deliver Israel from the hand of the Philistines' (Judg. 13.5). Each of our artists has chosen to represent the decisive moment in the story, the moment that seals the *man's* fate (even though it is only in *Samson Betrayed* that the male victim is depicted). Pickersgill shows Samson's hair being shorn. The canvas is unusually large (243.8 × 306 cm) and dominates the room in which it is exhibited. It overwhelms the viewer with the spectacle of the scene, and, although we might get the impression that we could easily step into the frame, we would remain spectators distanced from the action, for none of the figures communicates with the viewer. Samson is asleep, as yet unaware that his strength and his god have left him. Most viewers know what will happen next: the Philistine soldiers will seize him, gouge out his eyes and take him to Gaza as a slave to grind in the mill.[7] For the time being, Samson is the only one in the painting unaware that something momentous is taking place. The tension is palpable, with everyone watching Samson expectantly, terrified that he might wake up before his haircut has robbed him of his strength.

When the painting was exhibited at the Royal Academy, Pickersgill was praised for his figures and his colouring, and also for his restraint: 'It is a subject so liable to coarseness and violence that we congratulate Mr Pickersgill on his complete freedom from these defects. Etty could not have been trusted with it'. (William Etty was the leading figure painter of the time, who exercised a major influence on Pickersgill.)[8]

In Pickersgill's version of the story, a man warily cuts Samson's hair, while his companion watches. Presumably they are Philistine soldiers, perhaps ambushers Delilah had waiting in an inner chamber (16.9, 12), who often appear in paintings of the scene, for the man cautiously doing the shearing wears a coat of mail and holds a dagger by the hilt in his left hand. If one follows the Hebrew text, it is Delilah who cuts Samson's hair, just as she carries out the earlier procedures Samson describes for

6. Ibid., 121.

7. Most viewers also know what will happen later: when he is brought to their temple for the Philistines' entertainment, Samson prays to his god, his strength returns and he pulls down the temple, killing all the Philistines there and himself as well.

8. http://www.manchestergalleries.org/the-collections/search-the-collection.

subduing him (binding him with fresh bowstrings, binding him with new ropes and weaving his hair into the web on her loom). The matter is not entirely straightforward, however. The text reads, 'She made him sleep upon her knees; then she called to the man and she shaved off the seven locks of his head' (16.19). Who is 'the man' and what is he doing here? It may be that the man is Samson himself, and Delilah calls to him to make sure he is deeply asleep.[9] Still, one must admit that the Hebrew is awkward. In what appears to be an attempt to make sense of it, some ancient versions make the man a barber and have him shave Samson.[10] This is the reading reflected in the King James Version, the translation Pickersgill would have been familiar with, where we read: 'And she made him sleep upon her knees; and she called for a man, and she caused him to shave off the seven locks of his head'. Thus we have two important and influential textual traditions, one that has Delilah cut Samson's hair and the other that has a barber do the cutting, both of which are firmly established in art.

In a famous painting by Rubens, for example, a barber deftly snips off Samson's hair while Delilah watches (fig. 8.3). An old madam looks over Delilah's shoulder and holds a candle for him, its light illuminating the figures in the foreground as well as a statue of Venus and Cupid in an alcove. Dressed in red, with her voluminous breasts exposed, Delilah appears as a prostitute in this rather tawdry, dimly lit brothel. Samson has fallen asleep with his head in her lap, apparently exhausted after spending his passion in fervid lovemaking. The intensity of their lovemaking is suggested by the position of Samson's body, the dishevelled carpet and bedclothes, and Delilah's state of undress. Philistine soldiers wait somewhat apprehensively at the door.

---

9. Jack M. Sasson, 'Who Cut Samson's Hair? (and Other Trifling Issues Raised by Judges 16)', *Prooftexts* 8 (1988): 336–38; or, perhaps 'the man' is an ambusher lying in wait in the inner chamber (16.9, 12), although this does not relieve the awkwardness of the verse either.

10. One major Septuagint manuscript (Codex Alexandrinus) and the Vulgate specify a barber; another major Septuagint manuscript (Codex Vaticanus) has the 'man' do the shaving.

Fig. 8.3. Peter Paul Rubens, *Samson and Delilah*, 1609–1610,
The National Gallery, London

Another painting by Rubens, representing a slightly later moment in
the story, depicts Delilah as the one who cuts Samson's hair. She still
holds the scissors in her hand (fig. 8.4). Here, too, Delilah is depicted as a
prostitute with an old madam looking over her shoulder. It seems apparent
from the positions of Delilah and Samson on the bed and their state of
undress that they have recently made love. Instead of anxiety lest Samson
should wake up, so palpable in Pickersgill's painting, we experience the
violence, as Samson, his hair shorn, is set upon by Philistine soldiers, who
are actively gripping and pulling in their effort to subdue him.

Fig. 8.4. Peter Paul Rubens, *The Capture of Samson*, 1614–1620,
Alte Pinakothek, Munich

Rembrandt too, in *The Blinding of Samson*, discussed above in Chapter 2, accuses Delilah. The painting has all the brutal violence that Pickersgill was praised for avoiding (fig. 8.5). A man in oriental garb brandishes a spear and two soldiers hold Samson down, while a third gouges out Samson's right eye. A dimly lit figure at the far right looks on, mouth agape, with an expression of horror on his face. Delilah flees, still holding Samson's shorn locks in one hand and the scissors in the other. Unlike Pickersgill's Delilah and the partially clad Delilah of many paintings, Rembrandt's Delilah is elaborately dressed.[11]

11. See also paintings of Delilah as a courtesan, as e.g. in Gustave Moreau's paintings *Delilah* (Museo de Arte de Ponce, Puerto Rico) and *Samson and Delilah* (Musée Gustave Moreau, Paris), both of which capture on canvas attributes of the *femme fatale*, whose image Moreau's paintings helped to shape (among his favourite subjects were Salome, Semele and the Sphinx): sensuality, excessiveness, temptation, shamelessness and excitement tinged with danger.

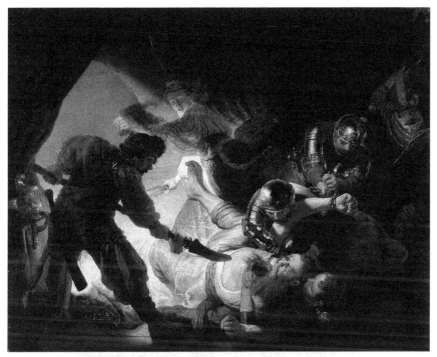

Fig. 8.5. Rembrandt van Rijn, *The Blinding of Samson*, 1636,
Städelsches Kunstinstitut, Frankfurt-am-Main

Having Delilah not only betray Samson to his enemies but cut his
hair as well makes her more culpable than introducing a barber to share
the blame. Distancing Delilah from the evil deed in *Samson and Delilah*
(fig. 8.3) allows Rubens, for example, to humanize Delilah, to give her a
measure of interiority. She looks at Samson perhaps with regret, perhaps
with fondness, and her hand rests almost tenderly on his back. It should
be noted, however, that culpability is not automatically decided by who
does the cutting, but depends on other factors of the pose as well. Two
paintings of this subject by Anthony van Dyck (1599—1641) also follow
the double tradition regarding who cut Samson's hair, but with Delilah's
attitude seemingly the reverse of that in the Rubens paintings. In one, in
the Dulwich Picture Gallery, Delilah, with her hand raised in front of her
bare breasts as if cautioning quietness, looks on as a barber cuts Samson's
hair. The procurer and another figure look over her shoulder, while soldiers
wait in the background. In the other painting, in the Kunsthistorisches
Museum, Vienna, Samson's hair has just been cut and soldiers are seizing
him, wrenching him as it were out of Delilah's arms. She holds out her
arm as if reaching for him and their mutual looks of anguish suggest their

attachment. But the scissors lie on the floor by the bed, where they appear to have fallen out of her hand – or perhaps she threw them aside.[12] These variations show something of the wide range of feelings artists attributed to Delilah even when they depicted the same elements of the story.

In Pickersgill's painting, even though someone else does the cutting, it is easy to hold Delilah accountable. In her eyes there is fear, fear that Samson could wake up, not pity such as we might imagine in the case of Rubens's Delilah in fig. 8.3. She is pinned in, imprisoned by Samson's body on the edge of the couch beside her, and she raises her arms in what seems to be the act of recoiling from him. Interpreting facial expressions is always a matter of individual judgment, and a look can have more than one meaning. As the focal point of the painting, Delilah immediately captures the viewer's attention, and, because she is such a point of interest, her expression invites other interpretations: disdain, scorn, hatred, perhaps tinged with desire or, possibly, something approaching regret or anguish ('What have I done?') (fig. 8.6).[13]

Fig. 8.6. Pickersgill, *Samson Betrayed*, detail

12. Reproductions of both paintings can be found in Haag *et al.*, *Great Women of the Bible in Art and Literature*, 144, 146–47.

13. When I viewed the painting with participants at a symposium on the Bible and Painting at the Manchester Art Gallery (22 September 2007), at which a version of the present chapter was presented, we had a lively discussion about the significance of the look on Delilah's face. I have tried to indicate something of the variety of views here, and I take this opportunity to thank again those present for their contributions.

From the biblical story we know why Samson told Delilah the secret of his strength: he loved her (16.4). In Pickersgill's painting, as elsewhere in the painterly tradition, Delilah appears as a temptress who has aroused Samson's lust and used it to trick him into revealing his secret. Like Susanna's nakedness and that of Bathsheba discussed above in Chapter 6, her nakedness both communicates and explains Samson's desire. In the biblical story, her ultimate weapon is not sex but *love*: 'How can you say, "I love you", when your heart is not with me?', she accuses him. Samson gives in to her and reveals to her the secret of his strength because she harasses him 'with her words', 'day after day', until he cannot stand it any longer.

> She said to him, 'How can you say, "I love you", when your heart is not with me? These three times you have mocked me and not told me by what means your strength is great.' When she harassed him with her words day after day, and urged him, he was vexed to death. So he told her all his heart, and said to her, 'A razor has never come upon my head, for I have been a Nazirite to God from my mother's womb. If I be shaved, my strength will leave me, and I shall become weak and be like any other man' (Judg. 16.15-17).

Delilah does not betray Samson so much as he betrays himself. He does not have to tell her that the secret of his superhuman strength lies in his uncut hair. Moreover, he should have learned from the three previous occasions when he lied to her about the source of his strength that this time too she would do to him exactly what he told her would weaken him (Judg. 16.8, 12, 14).[14]

Why does Delilah betray Samson? Greed, pure and simple? The acceptance of a bribe, which is all the biblical account reports, has proved insufficient to clarify her motives to the satisfaction of readers over the centuries, and those eager to explain her behaviour further have put forward numerous reasons, among them avarice, patriotism, religious zeal, jealousy and revenge.[15] Obviously Delilah does not love Samson enough

---

14. For discussion of Samson's need to reveal his secret to Delilah and what I call the 'Samson Complex', the man's wish to surrender himself to the woman, see Exum, *Fragmented Women*, Chapter 3, 'Samson's Women', esp. 58–60; Exum, *Plotted, Shot, and Painted*, 250–56.

15. On Delilah's motivation, see Exum, *Plotted, Shot, and Painted*, 231–43; Caroline Blyth, *Reimagining Delilah's Afterlives as Femme Fatale: The Lost Seduction* (London: Bloomsbury T&T Clark, 2017), 79–81 *et passim*. An elaborate exploration of Delilah's motives is offered by Cecil B. DeMille's film *Samson and Delilah*; see the discussions in Exum, *Plotted, Shot, and Painted*, 236–43, 258–66, and Blyth, *Reimagining Delilah's Afterlives as Femme Fatale*, 121–38.

to refuse to betray him at any price, but it does not necessarily follow that she feels no affection toward him. After all, capturing Samson is not her idea. She does not approach the Philistine rulers with a plan for subduing Samson and an offer to help them. Nevertheless, when they come to her with a tempting offer, she does not hesitate to accept. Most readers assume that Delilah is a Philistine, who cooperates with her compatriots to defeat an enemy of her people, 'the ravager of our country, who has slain many of us', as they put it (16.24).[16] Another common assumption is that Delilah is a prostitute. This is how many artists portray her, and Pickersgill seems to be following suit.

Rubens, as we have seen, has an old madam looking over her shoulder, and the setting of his paintings is a bordello. Although the biblical text does not identify Delilah either as a Philistine or as a prostitute, it never-theless subtly encourages these assumptions.[17] We might ask, What is achieved by construing Delilah as a Philistine prostitute? Among other things, identifying her as a Philistine would explain why she betrays Samson, for surely no Israelite woman would betray him, would she? Not even for a large sum of money? Moreover, if we take Delilah to be a prostitute as well, we are likely to assume from the start that she is morally reprehensible and thus to have less respect for her. A prostitute can be bought for betrayal as well as for sex; her nature is to dissemble. If we have less respect for Delilah, we can more comfortably place all the blame for Samson's downfall on her.[18] In Pickersgill's painting, Delilah wears a snake bracelet on her left arm. Is this an allusion to Eve and her association with the serpent, a reminder that woman is a source of trouble?

The biblical story does not specify the setting in which Samson's decisive betrayal takes place. Presumably in a room in Delilah's house, for twice when she tries to subdue Samson by using the means he falsely claimed would weaken him, she has a man waiting in an inner chamber to ambush him.[19] Pickersgill supplies a sparse but exotic outdoor

16. On Samson as a terrorist, see Exum, 'The Many Faces of Samson', 17–20.

17. Exum, *Plotted, Shot and Painted*, 217–21. On the way the text encourages readers to think the worst of Delilah and 'foreign' women in general, see Exum, *Fragmented Women*, 47–50 *et passim*.

18. Not only does Samson betray himself, as I observed above, he is also betrayed by his god, as I indicate in my discussion of Corinth's *Blinded Samson* in Chapter 2. It is not surprising that readers find it easier to blame the woman.

19. Delilah is not identified, as biblical women typically are, in relation to a man, usually their father or husband, and we are not told how it is that she has a house. Is she a foreign woman of independent means? A prostitute, like Rahab? A wealthy widow with property, like Judith?

backdrop, suggestive of the mystery and decadence of the Orient, as well as of the mystery and decadence of woman. There are mountains in the background, and the betrayal takes place in a portico, with heavy curtains draped over a beam supported by huge columns. The two columns prefigure the two columns that Samson will later grasp in order to pull down the Philistine temple, another popular subject in art. Samson lies on an ornate couch covered in what looks like red velvet. His head and upper body rest, as the text has it, 'upon her [Delilah's] knees', around which an elegant brocade fabric is loosely wrapped. Flowers lie discarded on the floor, a token of Samson's love, or flowers that have fallen out of Delilah's hair during ardent lovemaking. The latter possibility is suggested by the similar hairstyles of Delilah and the other woman in the painting, who has flowers woven into her hair.

In a significant departure from the biblical text, Pickersgill provides an unconventional audience. Two pale figures clutch each other, mesmerized by the scene unfolding before them. They balance the two dark-skinned soldiers on the left side of the painting. But who are they and what are they doing here? Their presence in this unusual boudoir, like that of the dusky soldier-cum-barber, contributes to the oriental atmosphere, and we may assume they serve Delilah or the Philistines whom Delilah herself serves. They appear to be entertainers; a tambourine lies before them on the floor. The description on the Manchester Art Gallery website identifies them as 'two women [who] look back over their shoulders towards the action; one of these women is almost naked'.[20] One is clearly a woman, but the other, in my view, is a man, or, at the very least, the figure is androgynous. His physique does not look like a woman's; he seems to be supporting the other figure, who clings to him, grasping his shirt in her right hand, while he clutches her wrap with his left; and, most important, unlike the women in the painting, he is clothed. Assuming the figure is a man, Pickersgill has created a contrast between (protective) male and (dissembling) female behaviour. A man seeks to shield a woman from danger, while the *femme fatale* Delilah hands Samson over to his enemies.

This man, his eyes wide open in fear (though we see only one eye), clasps the head of his companion in a protective gesture, but, though she is hanging on to him for dear life, she cannot help looking too. Although Pickersgill does not show us her face, he gives the viewer a tantalizing view of the white flesh of her back, buttocks and right breast. She thus provides a counterpart to Samson, whose face is also hidden from view and whose scantily clad muscular torso is exposed from the back. In

---

20. http://manchesterartgallery.org/collections/search/collection.

addition, she balances the frontal view Pickersgill gives us of Delilah, the focal point in the painting, on whom the light falls and whose white skin looks iridescent.

The nakedness of both women in this painting, and especially of Delilah, is for the pleasure of the male viewer in particular. This is also, and even more evidently the case in Stanhope's painting of *Eve Tempted* (fig. 8.2). Painted for a decorous Victorian spectatorship, *Eve Tempted* could be described as *The Male Viewer Tempted*, with the viewer enticed by Eve as the forbidden fruit. Whether to resist or not, individual viewers will decide for themselves. It is not, however, a fateful decision, for the safety of spectatorship allows the viewer to give in to temptation without suffering the consequences.[21]

One might see Eve's nakedness as a sign of innocence, of her prelapsarian state, but Stanhope draws attention to the shame that results from eating the forbidden fruit by covering Eve's genitals with her hair. The artful way Eve's hair wraps around her body from behind in a serpentine way draws attention to the artificiality of her innocence and links her with the cunning serpent coiled around the tree. Because Stanhope's Eve is passive, her nakedness appears less threatening than the unsettling, potentially intimidating nakedness of the larger-than-life Delilah, with dramatically exposed breasts, who virtually overwhelms the viewer of Pickersgill's painting.

Whereas Pickersgill adds characters to the story – the entertainers – Stanhope leaves out a character, and an important character at that. Unlike Samson, who is so glaringly undone by Delilah, the male victim of Eve's 'wiles' is conspicuous in his absence (which makes him even less to blame for the outcome than the hapless Samson). If we ask, What part of the story does this painting represent?, the answer is, No part of the story at all. Instead, *Eve Tempted* reinforces a popular misconception about the story: the notion that Eve gives in to temptation, takes the forbidden fruit and then wanders around the garden in search of Adam in order to offer it to him. In Stanhope's painting Adam is absent at the critical moment of the temptation.[22] This is not, however, the way the text presents the scene. Here is the King James Version translation that Stanhope would have known:

21. On the Victorian nude, see the exhibition catalogue, *Exposed: The Victorian Nude*, ed. Alison Smith, with contributions by Robert Upstone, Michael Hatt, Martin Myrone, Virginia Dodier and Tim Batchelor (London: Tate Publishing, 2001).

22. Perhaps we are meant to think of Adam as just outside the frame in *Eve Tempted*, but I doubt it.

And when the woman saw that the tree was good for food, and that it was pleasant to the eyes, and a tree to be desired to make one wise, she took of the fruit thereof, and did eat, and gave also unto her husband with her; and he did eat (Gen. 3.6).

Eve shares the fruit with Adam, 'who was with her'. For the biblical writer, Adam's presence during the temptation is important in order to show that the man and woman are equally guilty of failing God's test of their obedience.[23] Adam could have intervened to prevent Eve from eating. He could have told the serpent to mind its own business, or counselled Eve not to listen to perspicacious snakes, or defended God against the serpent's insinuation that jealousy is God's motive for not wanting humans to have knowledge that would make them, too, like gods (which appears, in fact, to be the case, Gen. 3.22-23). Adam passively disobeys the divine command 'you shall not eat' (he simply takes the fruit from Eve and eats it), whereas Eve considers the possibilities and chooses to disobey, and this too is important for the biblical writer, for it serves to justify the punishment that makes the active sinner subordinate to the passive sinner, and that places all women after Eve under the control of their husbands.

As Stanhope pictures her, Eve does not put up any resistance to the serpent's improper advance. Is she considering the possibilities: the enticingly edible fruit, its beauty and, not least, the god-like wisdom it promises? She has the vacant expression, the pensive stance, typical of Pre-Raphaelite women (one can clearly see the influence of Stanhope's friend Burne-Jones). Though not its inspiration, Burne-Jones's *Sibylla Delphica*, painted later than *Eve Tempted* (c. 1886), makes a suitable companion piece to it in the Manchester Art Gallery, where it hangs on the far right end of the wall balancing *Eve Tempted* on the left (fig. 8.8). As Mieke Bal has demonstrated, the placement of paintings in exhibitions exerts an influence on interpretation.[24] Here biblical and classical mythology meet to provoke associations between 'Fall' and redemption,

---

23. For a compelling interpretation of the command not to eat as a test, see Tryggve N. D. Mettinger, *The Eden Narrative: A Literary and Religio-historical Study of Genesis 2–3* (Winona Lake, IN: Eisenbrauns, 2007), 49–64 *et passim*.

24. Mieke Bal, *Double Exposures: The Subject of Cultural Analysis* (New York: Routledge, 1996). In fact, as Bal observes, '...the subject matter of images can be totally subordinated to the visual effect of their combination' (117). For an analysis of the influence of context on the interpretation of biblical art, see O'Kane's discussion of 'Biblical Landscapes in the Israel Museum', in *Painting the Text*, 160–95.

for the Sibyl was said to have foretold the coming of Christ.[25] The women look in each other's direction, one naked, untamed as it were, one clothed, properly socialized;[26] one reaching for the fatal fruit, the other, holding up the laurel leaves on which her prophecies were written.

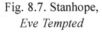

Fig. 8.7. Stanhope,   Fig. 8.8. Edward Burne-Jones,
Eve Tempted   *Sibylla Delphica*

The setting of *Eve Tempted* is a garden, but with a Tuscan wall and well-manicured grounds in the background. Eve stands on a carpet of colourful flowers, beneath the tree of the knowledge of good and evil, whose boughs are weighed down by an abundance of lush fruit amid luxuriant leaves. She leans languorously against the bank behind her, as she takes a piece of fruit from the tree almost absent-mindedly. The

25. Because they foretold the coming of Christ, sibyls were depicted in churches. Burne-Jones's painting began as a church window design.

26. Miles (*Carnal Knowing*, 144) argues that 'the unambiguously good woman is a clothed woman, a fully socialized woman'.

fruit does not look like an apple to me – which is a nice touch, since it is not an apple in the biblical text.[27] Its colour is orange, the same colour as Eve's hair. The serpent, whose unusually long, blue body is coiled intricately around the tree, has a human head. Giving the snake a human face is not an innovation on Stanhope's part. Often in art the serpent has a human face, and sometimes a human-like torso. Often, too, the face of the serpent resembles Eve's, creating associations between the serpent and the woman as source of temptation.

In this early fresco by Masolino (fig. 8.9), for example, the serpent's head and Eve's look very much alike. Unlike Stanhope's snake, however, this serpent's face is young and fair, like Eve's, deceptively non-menacing.

Fig. 8.9. Masolino, *The Temptation*, c. 1427, Cappella Brancacci, Santa Maria del Carmine, Florence

27. In the biblical account it is called simply 'fruit'. Since it no longer exists (otherwise it would still be available to humankind), the Bible does not identify it. The similarity in Latin of the words for 'apple' (*malum* with a short a) and 'evil' (*malum* with a long a) is sometimes appealed to as the source of the identification of the fruit as an apple, but apples have a long history as love fruits in the ancient world. The Manchester Art Gallery website identifies it as an apple, probably under the influence of centuries of tradition; http://manchesterartgallery.org/collections/search/collection.

Eve is not alone here, Adam is with her. With its head poised delicately above Adam and Eve, the serpent looks down almost peacefully on the pair, who have not yet tasted the forbidden fruit, and thus make no attempt to hide their nakedness. Each holds a piece of fruit, a fig, in their right hand, as they look into each other's eyes. Masolino captures the moment just before they eat. Perhaps Adam waits for Eve to taste first, but both are poised to sample the fruit and acquire the knowledge eating it will give them.

Fig. 8.10. Hugo van der Goes, *The Fall*, 1467–1468,
Kunsthistorisches Museum, Vienna

In Hugo van der Goes's version of the temptation scene (fig. 8.10), the serpent is aligned with Eve, who stands in the centre, between it and Adam, creating a chain of guilt from the snake through Eve to Adam. Eve takes a piece of fruit for Adam in her left hand and holds in her right hand a piece of fruit from which she has taken a bite. Here the serpent, whose face resembles Eve's and whose pose is similar to hers, is, like Stanhope's serpent, a disquieting, menacing figure. Not yet cursed by God to crawl on its belly, it boasts bizarre arms, legs and a tail. Adam and Eve, in contrast, already bear witness to the consequences of their disobedience, for they are naked and ashamed. Adam's genitals are covered by his hand, while Eve's are hidden from view by a blue iris (symbol of Mary, the second Eve, who will redeem humankind). She has the rounded belly typical of women in fifteenth-century art, and it hints of the many and painful pregnancies that will be woman's lot ('I will greatly multiply your pain and your childbearing', Gen. 3.16).

Michelangelo's fresco in the Sistine Chapel depicts what seems to be a female serpent with flowing red hair like Eve's and a woman's breasts, underscoring the connection between female sexuality and sin (fig. 8.11).[28]

Fig. 8.11. Michelangelo, *The Fall from Grace*, 1509–1510,
Sistine Chapel, Rome

Grasping the tree of knowledge and supporting itself with its massive tail wound suffocatingly around it, the serpent reaches out to Eve, who takes a piece of fruit, their hands almost touching. At the same time Adam

28. Michelangelo used male models; Eve's body is rather masculine looking, especially in the companion scene of the expulsion from the garden.

reaches for a piece of fruit from the tree.[29] In the examples above, Adam clearly shares Eve's guilt, but there is also a tradition in art where he is an unwilling or resisting accomplice.[30]

Why does the serpent approach the woman and not the man? Like the question why Delilah betrayed Samson, this, too, has long been a subject of fascination and speculation. Traditional answers have focused on female weakness, curiosity, gullibility and inferiority. A modern counterargument is that the woman is more appealing than the man, more intelligent (since she, not the man, considers the advantages of eating the fruit), and thus more of a challenge to the serpent as a theological debating partner.[31] It is not fortuitous that the biblical author chose to have the serpent address the woman and not 'her husband who was with her' (Gen. 3.6). By showing that disastrous consequences follow when a woman makes a momentous decision on her own, the biblical writer is simply affirming the necessity of the subordinate position of women to men that was taken for granted in biblical times. The story teaches its readers that a woman who is not subject to male authority is dangerous and not to be tolerated, an encoded message the first-century CE author of 1 Timothy recognized:

> I permit no woman to teach or to have authority over men; she is to keep silent, for Adam was formed first, then Eve, and Adam was not deceived, but the woman was deceived and became a transgressor (1 Tim. 2.12-14).

Is the snake in Stanhope's *Eve Tempted* male, and thus this is a *seduction* of Eve, who will later seduce Adam into eating the forbidden fruit? Is it female, to stress the close connection between Eve and the serpent, woman and evil, female sexuality and sin? Or is its sex indeterminate, a matter for the viewer to decide? The face is hard, worn, sinister, the hair long and similar in colour to Eve's but darker, the eyes blue like Eve's. So strong is the similarity to Eve that one might wonder if the serpent is Eve's alter ego, and if Stanhope is depicting here the two

29. There are also strong similarities between Adam and the serpent. For discussion of Michelangelo's subversion of conventional images of the temptation and an interpretation of the larger context of the scene, see Gary A. Anderson, *The Genesis of Perfection: Adam and Eve in Jewish and Christian Imagination* (Louisville, KY: Westminster John Knox Press, 2001), 2–8, 111–14.

30. For example, among others, Tintoretto's *The Original Sin*, 1550–53, Gallerie dell'Accademia, Venice; Titian, *Adam and Eve*, c. 1550, Museo del Prado, Madrid; Rubens, *Adam and Eve*, 1597–1600, Rubenshuis, Antwerp, Belgium.

31. Phyllis Trible, 'Depatriarchalizing in Biblical Interpretation', *Journal of the American Academy of Religion* 41 (1973): 40; Trible, *God and the Rhetoric of Sexuality* (Philadelphia, PA: Fortress Press, 1978), 110–13.

sides of woman's nature, beautiful and lethal. The serpent's face seems to prefigure what Eve will become as a result of eating the fruit – wizened by the onerous consequences of knowing good and evil, aged and hardened by the toil of tilling the soil and the pain of bearing children.

The serpent's words, whispered in Eve's ear,[32] are represented in tangible form as a mist, a malignant mist, so to speak, while the closeness of its head to Eve's, its lips to her ear, has a kind of unholy intimacy about it that seems to strengthen the connections between female sexuality and sin (fig. 8.12).

Fig. 8.12. *Eve Tempted*, detail

Julian Treuherz, in a catalogue of Pre-Raphaelite paintings from Manchester City Art Galleries, describes the entire composition as 'slightly unnerving'.[33] The serpent is an unsettling figure, and by drawing attention to its guilt, *Eve Tempted*, like the biblical account, renders Eve less culpable.[34] Nevertheless, since Adam does not appear in Stanhope's

32. So even if we imagine Adam to be outside the frame, he could not hear the serpent's tempting words.

33. Julian Treuherz, *Pre-Raphaelite Paintings from Manchester City Art Galleries* (Manchester: Manchester City Art Gallery, 1993), 119.

34. The presence of the serpent, 'the wisest of all creatures the Lord God had made' (Gen. 3.1), who challenges God's command, enables the narrator to

painting of the temptation scene and we know he will eat the forbidden fruit, we can only assume that it is Eve, pictured here as sexually alluring temptress, who will lead Adam astray. Eve's nakedness, like Delilah's, is a signifier of male desire; it represents the temptation of female sexuality and carries with it a warning to men that giving in to temptation can be fatal.

In choosing Eve and Delilah as their subjects, Stanhope and Pickersgill have not only taken advantage of the opportunity to paint a naked woman, they also convey a visual message both about these women, whose nakedness accuses them of arousing male lust, and also, by association, about women in general. In blaming Eve for the 'Fall' and Delilah for Samson's downfall, Stanhope's *Eve Tempted* and Pickersgill's *Samson Betrayed* perpetuate the notion that women are weak, flawed, suscep-tible to error and temptation, like Eve, and even deliberately malign, like Delilah. Are these reputations deserved? Samson, as I observed earlier, did not have to tell Delilah his secret and was a fool to do so. Adam could have intervened to defend the Law of the Father and prevent Eve from eating. This is not, of course, what happens in the Bible, where the women bear the brunt of the blame. Delilah betrays Samson for money, with no further information given about her motivation. When questioned by God, Adam's defence is, 'The woman you gave to be with me, she gave me fruit from the tree and I ate' (3.12).[35] God, in turn, chastises him for following her lead: 'Because you listened to the voice of your wife and ate from the tree…the ground is cursed…' (3.17). The biblical writers see the subordination of women to men as necessary and natural, and they explain it, and justify it, as a consequence of woman's fickle, weak or devious nature.

Visual criticism can help us both recognize more clearly and challenge more effectively the roots of the reputations these two notorious women bring with them from the pages of the Bible to Manchester. It also, and importantly, highlights the extent to which their bad reputations have been embellished and firmly established in centuries of cultural interpretation

distance the woman and the man from direct responsibility while still holding them accountable for disobedience.

35. In addition to shifting responsibility to the woman, Adam blames God, whose idea it was to create the woman in the first place (Gen. 2.18). For a discerning discussion of Michelangelo's *The Creation of Eve* in the Sistine Chapel by way of Karl Barth's *The Epistle to the Romans*, see Susanne Hennecke, 'A Different Perspective: Karl Barth and Luce Irigaray Looking at Michelangelo's *The Creation of Eve*', in *Out of Paradise: Eve and Adam and Their Interpreters*, ed. Bob Becking and Susanne Hennecke (Sheffield: Sheffield Phoenix Press, 2011), 124–39.

of the Bible.[36] Eve and Delilah not only have a history that Stanhope's and Pickersgill's compositions do not contest. *Eve Tempted* and *Samson Betrayed* embody as well the artists' own prejudices about women and those of the Victorian society in which they lived.[37] As works of fine art displayed on the walls of a major metropolitan gallery, they represent and reproduce these prejudices for contemporary viewers.[38] And what are contemporary viewers to make of them? Are these stereotypes not still with us?

Like the biblical stories, which, it is fair to say, were written by men for men, Stanhope's and Pickersgill's paintings align viewers with a male subject position, not only that of the implied male heterosexual viewer of paintings of the nude,[39] but also that of the man who is 'undone' by a woman. To the extent that female viewers assume the perspective these representations invite us to adopt, we are forced to read against our own interests and to accept a view of woman as a source of temptation that can bring about a man's downfall. Even if we do not identify with Eve and

36. On Eve, see Miles, *Carnal Knowing*, 85–116; Jane Dillenberger, *Image and Spirit in Sacred and Secular Art* (New York: Crossroad, 1990), 15–27; Paul Morris and Deborah Sawyer, eds., *A Walk in the Garden: Biblical, Iconographical and Literary Images of Eden* (Sheffield: Sheffield Academic Press, 1992); Pamela Norris, *Eve: A Biography* (New York: New York University Press, 1998); Bob Becking and Susanne Hennecke, eds., *Out of Paradise: Eve and Adam and Their Interpreters* (Sheffield: Sheffield Phoenix Press, 2011); on Delilah, see Exum, *Plotted, Shot, and Painted*, 209–75; Blyth, *Reimagining Delilah's Afterlives as Femme Fatale*; Gunn, *Judges*, 211–20; and the following articles in Eynikel and Nicklas, eds., *Samson: Hero or Fool?*: Kees Wisse, 'Samson in Music', 161–76; Susanne Gillmayr-Bucher, 'A Hero Ensnared in Otherness? Literary Images of Samson', 33–51; Karin Schöpflin, 'Samson in European Literature: Some Examples from English, French and German Poetry', 177–96; Reinhold Zwick, 'Obsessive Love: Samson and Delilah Go to the Movies', 211–35.

37. Laws regulating obscenity in the visual arts were Victorian creations; see Martin Myrone, 'Prudery, Pornography and the Victorian Nude (Or, what do we think the butler saw?)', in Smith, ed., *Exposed: The Victorian Nude*, 25, with reference to M. J. D. Roberts, 'Morals, Art, and the Law: The Passing of the Obscene Publications Act, 1857', *Victorian Studies* 28 (1985): 609–29 (Myrone gives the page numbers as 606–20).

38. As Miles (*Carnal Knowing*, 10) notes, 'The social function of representa-tions…is to stabilize assumptions and expectations relating to the objects or persons represented'. Moreover, '…representations do not merely *reflect* social practices and attitudes…[t]hey also re-present, reinforce, perpetuate, produce, and reproduce them' (11).

39. Berger, *Ways of Seeing*, 54–57.

Delilah in these paintings – if we read the paintings differently or subversively or perversely – it is not easy for female viewers to escape feeling implicated in the indictment of womankind that they represent.[40]

To be sure, works of fine art in museums and galleries may not have much influence on contemporary society, but visual and other cultural representations of these two notorious biblical women persist and are still used to convey messages about women and woman's nature. An image showing a woman with an apple or a snake or both, or a woman with a knife or scissors cutting the hair of a man stretched out over her lap, is readily recognized, and rare is the viewer of such images, in the West at least, who does not have preconceived notions about these characters formed on the basis of their well-established dubious reputations.[41] Eve, in particular, as a symbol of temptation has become an icon in advertising to sell everything from perfume, underwear, handbags, chocolates and crockery to sports cars and, yes, apples, as well as to promote superstars, television series and department stores, to give but some examples of her marketing value.[42] For her part, Delilah has been a reliable popular subject of film[43] and has starred in advertisements for Weetabix and Fruit of the

40. As I have observed earlier, many factors, including sexual orientation and sensibilities to difference (sexual, racial, class, etc.), will influence the way individual viewers and readers respond to works of art and texts. Nanette Salomon's observation about competing interpretations cited above in Chapter 1 shows how even viewers with similar backgrounds and training in art history can read works of art differently and reminds us, as she puts it, 'how personal vision is' (Salomon, 'Judging Artemisia', 45).

41. Sometimes these two notorious biblical women are conflated, as e.g. on the book cover of *Delilah's Revenge* by S. James Guitard (Washington, DC: Literally Speaking Publishing House, 2007), which shows a woman's torso with an apple in one hand and a large knife in the other; the subtitle is 'There is nothing more dangerous for a man than a woman with a plan'.

42. Edwards, *Admen and Eve*; for some other cultural 'uses', see Linda S. Schearing and Valarie H. Ziegler, *Enticed by Eden: How Western Culture Uses, Confuses, (and Sometimes Abuses) Adam and Eve* (Waco, TX: Baylor University Press, 2013).

43. See the discussion of films both of the biblical story and of Saint-Saëns opera *Samson et Dalila* in J. Cheryl Exum, 'Samson and Delilah in Film', in *The Bible in Motion: A Handbook of the Bible and Its Reception in Film*, Part 1, ed. Rhonda Burnette-Bletsch (Berlin: W. de Gruyter, 2016), 83–100. On film as well as other cultural representations of Delilah, see Blyth, *Reimagining Delilah's Afterlives as Femme Fatale*, 112–78.

Loom,[44] in addition to lending her name to numerous clubs and bars and providing a brand name for makeup[45] and designer lingerie.[46]

Most likely Eve and Delilah will never escape the bad reputations they have acquired. But as consumers – consciously or unconsciously, willingly or unwillingly – of visual images like the paintings discussed above, as well as of other representations of these notorious women in literature, the arts and popular culture, we would do well to ask ourselves what encoded messages about sexual identities, gender roles and expectations these images give us and whether or not we wish to resist them.

44.   E.g. https://www.youtube.com/watch?v=JG0W-aYBIG0 and https://www.youtube.com/watch?v=BNikWHyG5tY. During the promotion for Cecil B. DeMille's film *Samson and Delilah*, Hedy Lamarr appeared in her Delilah costumes in commercials for soaps and cigarettes.

45.   British cosmetics brand Delilah features lipstick with names such as 'Foxy', 'Flirt' and 'Floozy'.

46.   Warner's underwear has marketed girdles and brassieres called 'Delilah', with copy such as 'Warner's Delilah gently eases you into the shape of the temptress…'; 'Delilah must have felt the way you'll feel in it. (How else could she have managed so well?)'. Sigvaris sells Samson and Delilah tights. I owe these examples to Katie Edwards, whose extensive database of biblical characters in advertising shows how alive and well they are in popular culture.

ECCE MULIER:
THE LEVITE'S WIFE, THE MOTHER OF JESUS AND
THE SACRIFICIAL FEMALE BODY

Behold (*idou*) the slave of the Lord.
Behold (*hinneh*) the woman, his wife, collapsed at the door of the house.

The Annunciation

The Annunciation is a frequent subject of representation in art, and the vast majority of paintings of the scene share a reverence for their subject and a conventional way of rendering it. The Virgin is typically depicted as praying or reading at a prie-dieu when the angel Gabriel appears to her.[1] Her posture is traditionally that of submission and reverence, sometimes reverent surprise.[2] Gabriel usually holds a lily, denoting purity and a traditional symbol of Mary, and a dove represents the Holy Spirit.

The depiction of the annunciation I want to consider here, Dante Gabriel Rossetti's *Ecce Ancilla Domini*, represents a radical break from tradition (fig. 9.1).

---

1. The book she reads is typically open at the prophecy in Isa. 7: *Ecce virgo concipiet et pariet filium et vocabitur nomen eius Emmanuel.* Following other ancient traditions, some paintings show her standing by a well or spinning; see Hornik and Parsons, *Illuminating Luke: The Infancy Narrative*, 47.

2. On the various reactions depicted in fifteenth-century Italian painting (*conturbatio* [disquiet], *cogitatio* [reflection], *interrogatio* [enquiry] and *humiliatio* [submission]), see Michael Baxandall, *Painting and Experience in Fifteenth-Century Italy: A Primer in the Social History of Pictorial Style*, 2nd ed. (Oxford: Oxford University Press, 1988), discussed in Hornik and Parsons, *Illuminating Luke: The Infancy Narrative*, 48–51.

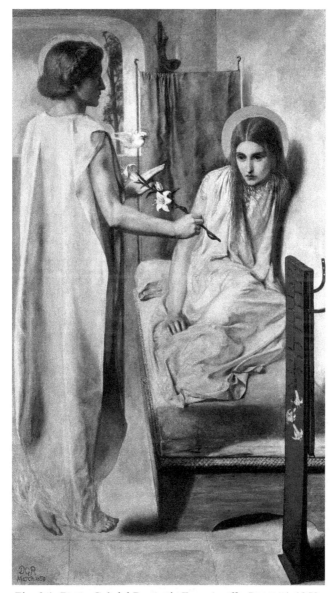

Fig. 9.1. Dante Gabriel Rossetti, *Ecce Ancilla Domini!*, 1850,
Tate Gallery, London

There is a refreshing simplicity – as well as realism – about this painting.
Rossetti has used a primary colour scheme: white for purity; blue, the
colour associated with Mary; red symbolizing the blood of Christ and
yellow/gold for holiness. The scene takes place in the close, intimate
space of Mary's bedroom (the tall, narrow shape of the painting is

probably due to the fact that it was intended as part of a diptych, with the companion piece showing the Virgin's death).[3] Mary is on her bed, rather than reading or in a contemplative pose, and she looks as though she has just been awakened by the appearance of the angel. She is dressed not in the more usual red with a blue robe, but rather, like the angel, in white, a symbol of virginity.[4] She looks dishevelled. Gabriel is unconventional too. He does not have wings but rather, in a more Classical mode, fiery feet; his appearance is arguably androgynous;[5] and his exposed flesh can be seen through the folds of his robe.[6]

The painting is rather unsettling. What is most noteworthy about it, in my view, is the tension between the title, 'Behold the servant of the Lord', and the painting itself. Rossetti's Mary shrinks back against the wall with a look of apprehension, if not outright fear and revulsion, on her face – extremely wary of the phallic lily that Gabriel points at her womb.[7] This does not look to me like a submissive servant, nor one who is at all reverent, but more like an unwilling recipient of unwelcome news.

3. The annunciation typically takes place in Mary's room, where she is reading; sometimes the scene is split between Gabriel, who is outside and Mary who is inside (as e.g. in Leonardo da Vinci's *Annunciation*, 1472–75, in the Galleria degli Uffizi, Florence, where we see a landscape). They are often separated by a portico, marking off their different spaces.

4. The red and blue typically used for Mary's robe are present in the painting in the blue cloth in the background (as well as the blue sky, evoking heaven) and a red embroidery with white lilies in the foreground. *Ecce Ancilla Domini* was painted in 1849–50. In Rossetti's *The Girlhood of Mary Virgin*, painted in 1848–49, Mary is depicted working on this embroidery.

5. This is not so unusual; Gabriel is feminized in numerous paintings.

6. Are there suggestions of a relationship between Mary and Gabriel? Jacqueline Olson Padgett observes that some scholars and artists read some representations of the annunciation as suggestive of courtship; 'Ekphrasis, Lorenzo Lotto's *Annunciation*, and the Hermeneutics of Suspicion', *Religion and the Arts* 10 (2006): 201–2. A sexual dimension would not be unexpected in a painting by Rossetti, whose women subjects always project something of his (and shared Pre-Raphaelite) ideas about and ideals of female desire and desirability; for a fascinating analysis of the function of 'woman' in Pre-Raphaelite art, see Griselda Pollock and Deborah Cherry, 'Woman as Sign in Pre-Raphaelite Literature: The Representation of Elizabeth Siddall', in Griselda Pollock, *Vision and Difference: Femininity, Feminism and the Histories of Art* (London: Routledge, 1988), 91–114.

7. In some paintings the dove is close to her womb, e.g. Filippo Lippi's *Annunciation*, where the dove emits a spray of golden particles from its beak that meets a corresponding golden spray from Mary's womb that flows through a tiny

Elizabeth Prettejohn remarks that 'the ungainly way in which the Virgin folds her legs cannot quite be dismissed as technically inept' and finds the entire scene expressive of Mary's unease.[8] In the light of Rossetti's depiction of the event, I propose to take a closer look at Luke's birth account from a feminist critical perspective, enquiring into the nature of the response given by the Mary constructed for us by Luke, and asking, Whose interest does it serve?

Rossetti shows us a degree of resistance not usually associated with the biblical Mary. He is not the first or only artist to depict a Mary who does not receive the news of her conception with sang-froid. In a study of Lorenzo Lotto's *Annunciation* that draws on modern literature as well as art, Jacqueline Olson Padgett draws attention to Mary's 'startled and pleading gaze' and proposes that Lotto, visualizing the biblical text 'with some suspicion and even amusement', has given us a resistant Mary (fig. 9.2).[9] In support she cites the response of another viewer, poet Wensday Carlton, who, in a poem entitled 'Madonna and Child', with the epigraph 'after seeing Lotto's *Annunciation*', writes:

> Proof for what I've suspected: she didn't want
> this divine child, she's afraid, even angry
> that she has no choice.[10]

slit in her robe; see John Drury, *Painting the Word: Christian Pictures and Their Meanings* (New Haven, CT: Yale University Press, in association with National Gallery Publications, London, 1999), 52.

8. Elizabeth Prettejohn, *The Art of the Pre-Raphaelites* (London: Tate Publishing, 2007), 51. She goes on to say that the painting 'represents the moment of a paradoxical deflowering that excludes the sexual'; in my view sexuality is suggested by the state of Gabriel's undress, the position of the lily and Mary's dishevelled appearance. See n. 6 above.

9. Padgett, 'Ekphrasis, Lorenzo Lotto's *Annunciation*, and the Hermeneutics of Suspicion', 191–218. Just as texts can give rise to more meanings than their authors intended, a painting can show more than the artist intended. The more one looks for resistance in paintings of the annunciation, the more one is likely to recognize at least the possibility of resistance in both older and more recent paintings; e.g. Carlo di Giovanni Braccesco, *Annunciation*, 1490s, Louvre, Paris; Henry Ossawa Tanner, *The Annunciation*, 1898, Philadelphia Museum of Art.

10. Wensday Carlton, 'Madonna and Child', *TriQuarterly* 110/111 (2001): 490.

Fig. 9.2. Lorenzo Lotto, *Annunciation*, 1534–1535,
Pinacoteca Civica, Recanati

Padgett finds this same 'posture of startled response' in another painting,
Lorenzo di Credi's *Annunciation* (fig. 9.3). She proceeds to show how this
painting has been parodied, and the Lucan text dismantled, in a modern
painting of the annunciation by Mary Ellen Croteau (fig. 9.4), in which
'Mary points an angry finger at Gabriel, seemingly ordering him to get out
and take his message with him'.[11]

11. Padgett, 'Ekphrasis, Lorenzo Lotto's *Annunciation*, and the Hermeneutics
of Suspicion', 203. Croteau's painting is part of a series of paintings from a
feminist perspective, Musée de Nouvelle Renaissance 1995–2001 (http://www.
maryellencroteau.net/musee-de-nouvelle-renaissance). Croteau identifies the angel
as 'anti-abortion fanatic Randall Terry (fetus in hand)'. Her painting underscores the
issue at stake in the text: choice.

Fig. 9.3. Lorenzo di Credi, *The Annunciation*, 1480–1485,
Galleria degli Uffizi, Florence

Fig. 9.4. Mary Ellen Croteau, *Annunciation*, 1997.
Used by kind permission of the artist.

Though Rossetti's version does not oppose the experience Luke presents as blatantly as these modern counter-readings, it does challenge it much more dramatically than most paintings of the annunciation. It encourages the viewer to consider the text critically and resistantly and to raise questions about the appropriation of the woman's body in the service of the author's androcentric ideology – or, if you prefer, of Luke's theology.[12] I should stress that I am not talking about a historical Mary; it is the narrative and its agenda that interests me. I see women in the biblical literature as the creations of (probably) male authors, or, in any event, authors who are writing within, and whose writings thus reflect, a patriarchal context. (This is not to say that challenges to patriarchal ideology cannot be found in these texts; it is, after all, a property of texts that they are open to deconstruction.) But women characters in these texts nevertheless reflect androcentric ideas about women and they serve androcentric interests. As Esther Fuchs observed years ago about biblical mothers – and Mary is surely the biblical mother *par excellence* – they 'reveal more about the wishful thinking, fears, aspirations, and prejudices of their male creators than about women's authentic lives'.[13]

Luke's text is far from straightforward, as the pages of commentary devoted to it witness. Not surprisingly, it is a subject of controversy. As Jane Schaberg observes:

> Feminist interpretations of gospel infancy narratives touch a nerve in Christian and scholarly psyches. They challenge the theories of the 'incarnation' and 'divinity' of Jesus, of the activity of the spirit, of the role of women in the process of 'redemption', of women's sexuality, and of a 'Virgin Mother'.[14]

---

12. As Joseph Vlcek Kozar ('Rereading the Opening Chapter of Luke from a Feminist Perspective', in *Escaping Eden: New Feminist Perspectives on the Bible*, ed. Harold C. Washington, Susan Lochrie Graham and Pamela Thimmes [Sheffield: Sheffield Academic Press, 1998], 53–68) observes, 'Patriarchal structure dominates the chapter' (55) and '...male imagery predominates. A male child will be given the throne of David his father and rule over the house of Jacob, establishing an everlasting kingdom' (63). He concludes that, 'Despite its seeming potential for affirmative feminist reading, [Luke 1]...in the end, reimposes patriarchal perspectives upon the unwary reader' (67).

13. Esther Fuchs, 'The Literary Characterization of Mothers and Sexual Politics in the Hebrew Bible', in *Feminist Perspectives on Biblical Scholarship*, ed. Adela Yarbro Collins (Chico, CA: Scholars Press, 1985), 18.

14. Jane Schaberg, 'Feminist Interpretations of the Infancy Narrative of Matthew', in Schaberg, *The Illegitimacy of Jesus: A Feminist Theological Interpretation of the*

The story can be and has been interpreted as having both positive and negative meaning for women. Is Mary an independent, strong woman or simply a tool, a victim? What are the implications of a virginal mother of God for women's self-understanding? For some Mary has provided a role model, for others a stumbling block. It is not my intention to enter into debates about Mary's significance or about how Luke intends his readers to understand the conception of Jesus and what his larger polemical purpose or theological agenda might be. Nor am I suggesting that art can help us solve these questions. My intention, rather, is to make a point about visual criticism and the role it can play in biblical criticism. As I observed in Chapter 1, in addition to sometimes posing a challenge to conventional interpretations, artistic representations of the biblical text can also provide an effective critical model for resistant readers who would take issue with the biblical ideology. A resistant interpretation is what I offer here in dialogue with Rossetti's painting *Ecce Ancilla Domini*.[15]

I shall focus on the aspect of the text that Rossetti visualizes for us, Mary's response and the related issues of consent and of the appropriation of a woman's body for the male author's ideology. In Luke chapter 1, Mary's first reported reaction is disturbance or bewilderment (*dietarachthē*) at Gabriel's message or 'word' (*logos*) to her. Is it his greeting (*aspasmos*) that arouses fear? – for she is assured in the formula typical of theophanies, 'Do not be afraid'. Or could she be frightened by the appearance of the angel as well?[16] The messenger and his message are difficult to separate, and some artistic representations of the annunciation seek to capture this through ekphrasis, drawing attention to the message by representing it visually, as in paintings by Fra Angelico and Melchior Broederlam (figs. 9.5 and 9.6).[17]

Infancy Narratives, Expanded Twentieth Anniversary Edition, with contributions by David T. Landry and Frank Reilly (Sheffield: Sheffield Phoenix Press, 2006), 231.

15. Artistic representations that intentionally expose and critique biblical ideologies, such as Mary Ellen Croteau's above, offer resources for resistant reading; see also David Tollerton, 'Divine Violence Caught on Camera: Negotiating Text and Photography in Broomberg and Chanarin's *Holy Bible*', *Biblical Reception* 3 (2014): 146–60.

16. In v. 29 the Septuagint manuscript Codex Alexandrinus adds 'when she saw him'. Or fear could be the reaction of a virgin to the presence of a strange man; see Mary F. Foskett, *A Virgin Conceived: Mary and Classical Representations of Virginity* (Bloomington: Indiana University Press, 2002), 117–18.

17. In fig. 9.5 (Fra Angelico) the words are: *Gabriel*: Hail full of grace the Lord be with you; *Mary*: Behold the slave of the Lord; *Gabriel*: The power of the Almighty will overshadow you. In fig. 9.6 (Broederlam): Ave gratia plena dominus tecum.

Fig. 9.5. Fra Angelico, *Annunciation* (detail), 1433–1434,
Museo Diocesano, Cortona

Luke 1.27 establishes that Mary is a virgin and that she is betrothed. The annunciation of Jesus' birth reflects the birth announcement type-scene found in the Hebrew Bible, where the birth of a son (always a son, never a daughter) to an infertile woman is foretold (Sarah, Samson's mother, Hannah and others).[18] Although in Luke 1.26-38 the announcement is to a virgin, we might find nothing particularly unusual about an angel prophesying the birth of a son to a woman soon to be married. But Mary finds

18. For discussion of these and other examples, see Robert Alter, 'How Convene tion Helps Us Read: The Case of the Bible's Annunciation Type-Scene', *Prooftexts* 3 (1983): 115–30. The pattern is also present in the birth announcement to Elizabeth (Zechariah) in Luke 1.5-25; scholars regularly point out the parallels between the birth announcements of John and Jesus in Luke; cf. also Matt. 1.20-25.

Fig. 9.6. Melchior Broederlam, *The Annunciation* (detail), 1393–1399, Musée des Beaux-Arts, Dijon

it unusual, and her response indicates that she (which is to say, Luke) understands the prophecy to mean that the conception will take place immediately.[19] Her question, 'How will this be, since I do not have sexual relations with a man' (or 'husband', *andra ou ginōskō*)?, points to a

19. Ambiguity is created by the fact that Luke never explicitly states that this is a virginal conception, and thus the meaning of Mary's response in v. 34 is a topic of considerable debate; see e.g. the detailed analysis of Raymond E. Brown, *The Birth of the Messiah: A Commentary on the Infancy Narratives in Matthew and Luke*, 2nd ed. (London: Goeffrey Chapman, 1993), 303–9. That Mary understands the conception as something that will take place in the immediate future is compellingly argued on the basis of the narrative logic by David T. Landry, 'Narrative Logic in the Annunciation to Mary (Luke 1:26-38)', *Journal of Biblical Literature* 114 (1995): 65–79. The verbs

problem with the plan, and can be compared to the objection frequently found in commissioning stories.[20] The answer she receives is that nothing is impossible with God. Mary acquiesces: 'I am [or 'behold', *idou*] the slave [*doulē*, or as it is frequently translated 'servant'] of the Lord'. As Beverly Gaventa observes, 'there can be no doubt that what the word means is "slave"… To translate "servant" is to misconstrue Mary's role as that of one who has *chosen* to serve rather than one who has *been chosen*'.[21] 'Let it be to me according to your word', says Mary. Is this consent, or simply resignation?[22] It is not the way one responds to good news.[23] It can be compared to Jesus' words in the garden of Gethsemane, 'Not my will but yours be done'. The will of a slave is of no account. In the Graeco-Roman world it was not uncommon for female slaves to be sexually exploited by their masters.[24]

in v. 35 are future. Further ambiguity is created by Gabriel's words in v. 36, 'Elizabeth your relative, she *also* has conceived a son', which could be taken to mean that Mary has just now conceived, but it makes sense for conception to occur (just) after her acceptance of the fact.

20. E.g. Moses (Exod. 3.10–4.17), Gideon (Judg. 6.12-24), Jeremiah (Jer. 1.5-10).

21. Beverly Gaventa, *Mary: Glimpses of the Mother of Jesus* (Minneapolis, MN: Fortress Press, 1999), 54; italics hers. The term *doulē*, she notes, is used of those who serve God and understand God's authority in their lives (Acts 2.18; 4.29; 16.17).

22. Cf. Gaventa: 'Mary has not chosen this task for herself any more than the apostles will later choose their own roles, but she does consent to it' (*Mary*, 54).

23. Cf. Alfred Plummer, *The Gospel according to S. Luke*, 4th ed. (Edinburgh: T. & T. Clark, 1913), 26: 'This is neither a prayer that what has been foretold may take place, nor an expression of joy at the prospect. Rather it is an expression of *submission*…' (italics his), a point Brown, among others, takes issue with, calling it an 'enthusiastic' and 'total and joyful acceptance' (*The Birth of the Messiah*, 319). As Barbara E. Reid ('Prophetic Voices of Elizabeth, Mary, and Anna in Luke 1–2', in *New Perspectives on the Nativity*, ed. Jeremy Corley [London: T&T Clark, 2009], 37–46) notes, 'While many envision the annunciation scene as wrapped in an aura of joy and delight, there is an undercurrent of terror, upheaval, and scandal in the story' (39). And, drawing on understandings of virginity in antiquity, Foskett observes: 'The situation in which Luke presents Mary can conjure images of seduction, lust, and violence that both human and divine figures perpetrate against *parthenoi*' (*A Virgin Conceived*, 118).

24. See e.g. Jennifer A. Glancy, *Slavery in Early Christianity* (Oxford: Oxford University Press, 2002), 10–14, 51–54 *et passim*; Sandra R. Joshel, *Slavery in the Roman World* (Cambridge: Cambridge University Press, 2010), 40, 72, 192 *et passim*. James N. Hoke ('"Behold, the Lord's Whore"? Slavery, Prostitution, and Luke 1:38', *Biblical Interpretation* 26 [2018]: 45) observes, 'Though Luke's Mary appears to submit voluntarily to God, her master (κυρίος), some early hearers of Luke's story

Like Rossetti's painting *Ecce Ancilla Domini*, I want to problematize this response. A literary device in a birth account created after the fact, Mary's acquiescence to the divine will is a necessary feature of the story. Is she free to say 'no'? Then there would be no story.[25] What we have is a story in which the subject is denied subjectivity, for as Ellen Rooney observes, '[a] feminine subject who can act only to consent or refuse to consent is in fact denied subjectivity'.[26] In having Mary surrender her will to God's – however we evaluate that submission – Luke has co-opted the woman's voice for his purpose: to provide a mother for the son of God, one who is willing to accept this role – one who, as Luke has her kinswoman Elizabeth proclaim, is most blessed of all women because she believed the angel's message (Luke 1.42, 45). He has Mary too call herself blessed, but not because of her faith or any attributes of her own: 'all generations will call me blessed', she says, 'for the Almighty has done great things to me' (*epoiēsen moi megala*, Luke 1.48-49).

These words, from the Magnificat, are placed in Mary's mouth as her response to the earth-shattering event in which she is caught up.[27] But whose ideology is this? A thoroughgoing male ideology, argues David Clines. In the Magnificat, he observes, God is praised for his strength and power, male qualities of a male-identified deity, while the 'low estate' that

surely would have pictured this submission in conformity to the slave conditions with which they were familiar. In this case, Mary's portrayal as the Lord's slave means that her master-God has full access and rights over her body, which extended fully into the domain of sex in the Mediterranean world.' See also Michael Pope, 'Gabriel's Entrance and Biblical Violence in Luke's Annunciation Narrative', *Journal of Biblical Literature* 137 (2018): 701–10.

25. We might imagine a story in which first one, then a second virgin *rejects* the role as mother of the son of the Most High, but on the charmed third occasion, the woman accepts it – but Luke's version is less like a fairy tale.

26. Ellen Rooney, '"A Little More than Persuading": Tess and the Subject of Sexual Violence', in *Rape and Representation*, ed. Lynn A. Higgins and Brenda R. Silver (New York: Columbia University Press, 1991), 92. Foskett argues that Mary is portrayed as an acting subject: 'In ancient literature virgins are required to navigate carefully their moral and ethical development. Virgins are figures whose honor and purity are tested...and proven by the choices and actions they welcome or resist...' (*A Virgin Conceived*, 119, 123–24; citation from 119). This is a highly circumscribed agency. It reflects the same androcentric ideology according to which women's bodies are the property of men that underlies my next example, the Levite's wife in Judg. 19.

27. The canticle is modelled on the Song of Hannah, 1 Sam. 2.1-10; here, as in the birth account, Luke draws on material from the Hebrew Bible.

Mary claims for herself can refer only to the fact that she is a woman.[28] As in the annunciation, Mary is a *doulē*, a slave subject to the will of her master, in this case one who accepts the power structures of oppressor and oppressed and wants only to see them reversed, and who declares her master's greatness for making her a mother.

In the Magnificat, Luke appropriates Mary's voice in the service of an androcentric ideology that proclaims a new world order, but actually only reverses the old one. In the birth announcement, Luke appropriates not only her voice – 'let it be to me according to your word' – but also, more intimately and invasively, her body, to serve his purpose of providing a mother for the son of the Most High.[29] With or without a man Mary fulfils the primary female role in a patriarchal system: to give birth to a son.[30] As Rossetti's painting suggests, the role of mother of God is not sought by the woman in this story, not anticipated or prepared for or longed for. Indeed, it is presented as decided already – '*you* will conceive in your womb and bear a son...and he will be called the son of the Most High' (1.31-32). The woman in this text has no real control over her own body; her only decision is to accept her divinely ordained function. The character Mary is a victim of literary violation, whether one sees it as sexual – as Jane Schaberg argues[31] – or asexual – as most commentators describe the conception. Violation by the Holy Spirit?, as one might wonder, looking

28. David J. A. Clines, 'Gendering the Magnificat', in *Let the Reader Understand: Studies in Honor of Elizabeth Struthers Malbon*, ed. Edwin K. Broadhead (London: T&T Clark, 2018), 175–82.

29. Does 'he will be called the son of the Most High' in v. 32 imply that Jesus is not the son of Joseph? Cf. Luke 3.23. Luke will have had both theological and apologetic reasons for his version of the birth account; e.g. to show God's concern for the poor and downtrodden, to counter charges of illegitimacy by claiming miraculous origin for Jesus. For a reading of the infancy narrative in the context of apologetic discourse in the first three centuries CE, see Loveday Alexander, 'The Four among Pagans', in *The Written Gospel*, ed. Markus Bockmuehl and Donald A. Hagner (Cambridge: Cambridge University Press, 2005), 222–37; Loveday Alexander, 'Madonna and Child: The Lucan Infancy Narrative and the Apologetic Agenda', unpublished paper read at the conference 'Evangiles de l'enfance/Infancy Gospels', University of Lausanne, October 2010.

30. Cf. Schaberg, 'Feminist Interpretations of the Infancy Narrative of Matthew', 238.

31. Schaberg, in *The Illegitimacy of Jesus*, proposes that Mary was the victim of seduction or rape or had willingly had sexual relations with a man other than her husband-to-be Joseph and that Luke knew this tradition.

at the way in Rossetti's painting Gabriel threatens Mary with the lily stem and the dove hovering over it. No, not by the Holy Spirit. By Luke the theologian.

The Levite's Wife

A more blatant and distressing use of a woman's body in the service of an androcentric agenda appears in Judges 19, the story of the Levite's wife, who is sacrificed in order to spare her husband from threatened abuse.[32] The story begins with the woman leaving her husband and returning to her father's house, an assertion of autonomy tantamount to divorce, since a woman did not have the right to divorce in ancient Israel.[33] Her husband goes after her to seek a reconciliation, and on their return journey they stop in Gibeah, where the nefarious men of the city surround the house in which they have lodged for the night and demand that the man be given over to them to be raped.[34] The Levite throws his wife out to be gang raped by the mob, after which he cuts her ravaged body into twelve pieces, which he sends throughout the territory of Israel as a call to arms.[35]

32. The woman is a *pilegesh*, a legal wife of secondary rank. The term is frequently translated in English as 'concubine', which gives the misleading impression that she is not a legitimate wife. An odd feature of this story is the absence of a primary wife.

33. Yair Zakovitch, 'The Woman's Rights in the Biblical Law of Divorce', *The Jewish Law Annual* 4 (1981): 39. According to the Hebrew text, the woman 'played the harlot' against her husband (19.2, the verb is *zanah*). Because an understanding of the woman as sexually promiscuous is not promoted by the story, which describes not the woman's involvement with other men but only her act of leaving her husband, many translations follow the versions in reading that she 'became angry with him' (e.g. LXX[AL], OL, followed by NRSV, NJB, REB). Zakovitch (38) points out that her relation to the Levite is described in terms of marriage: the technical use of 'to take' (v. 1); the description of the woman's father as the Levite's father-in-law (*hoten*, v. 4); and the fact that the term *pilegesh* is interchangeable with *shiphah* (the same term used of Hagar in Gen. 16) and *'ishshah* ('woman') in the case of Bilhah (Gen. 35.22; 32.22 [Heb. 32.23]; 30.4; 37.2). Similarly, Boling, *Judges*, 274: 'As Israelite law did not allow for divorce by the wife, she became an adulteress by walking out on him'. See also Exum, *Fragmented Women*, 141–42; Gale A. Yee, 'Ideological Criticism: Judges 17–21 and the Dismembered Body', in Yee, ed., *Judges and Method*, 153.

34. The Hebrew reads 'that we may know him', which most commentators understand to refer to rape, the point being to humiliate the man by placing him in the position of a woman. NRSV and NJB translate 'so that we may have intercourse with him'; JPS 'so that we can be intimate with him'.

35. The text, which reads, 'so the man seized his wife and put her out' in Judg. 19.25, does not specify the identity of the man who cast her out. Although the host

The story ends in civil war between the tribe of Benjamin, where the outrage takes place, and the other tribes. In *The Levite of Ephraim and his Dead Wife*, Jean-Jacques Henner pictures the scene just before the dismemberment (fig. 9.7). But whereas the biblical account represents the cutting up of the woman's body as an act seemingly carried out without forethought and in haste, Henner gives us a study in contemplation and deliberation that graphically draws attention to the scandal of the abused female body, even though the Levite has yet to lift the knife. In fact, we cannot see a knife in the picture.[36]

Fig. 9.7. Jean-Jacques Henner, *The Levite of Ephraim and his Dead Wife*, 1898, Private Collection

Why does the Levite treat his wife's abused body so violently rather than calling the tribes together by some other means?[37] I discuss her narrative punishment in the biblical account at length in my book *Fragmented Women*, where I argue that by leaving her husband the woman makes a gesture of sexual autonomy so threatening to patriarchal ideology that she must be punished sexually in the most extreme form.

has been the subject of the previous verses, 'his wife' points to the Levite as the perpetrator of the crime, which means that we see what a callous person he is even before he dismembers her body.

36. For a series of striking images and discussion of the molestation of the woman by the mob, the Levite's finding of her body and an especially grisly scene of the dismemberment, with messengers carrying off body parts, in the Morgan Picture Bible, c. 1240–55 (The Pierpont Morgan Library), see Schroeder, *Dinah's Lament*, 101–52.

37. His treatment of her dead, or possibly still alive body is not unlike the deity's response to his wayward wife Israel, whom he dismembers violently, as described in Ezek. 16 and 23.

The symbolic significance of dismembering the woman's body lies in its intent to de-sexualize her. Otherwise the act remains insufficiently motivated.[38] It is not enough that the woman who has offended sexually, by acting as if she and not the man owned her body, is abused sexually, by having her body possessed by many men. An even more radical punishment is called for. Because it has offended, the woman's sexuality must be destroyed and its threat diffused by scattering.[39]

38. Commentators are at a loss to explain its symbolic value. Susan Niditch sees the dissected body as a symbol of Israel's 'body politics', its divisions ('The "Sodomite" Theme in Judges 19–20: Family, Community, and Social Disintegration', *Catholic Biblical Quarterly* 44 [1982]: 371; similarly, *Judges*, 194); Stuart Lasine takes it as a sign of perversity in a topsy-turvy world. He comments, 'The "message" sent by the Levite by means of the severed body is made more bizarre because he is not quoted as declaring the exact significance of the message, unlike Saul, who makes it clear that the dismembered oxen represent what will happen to the oxen of those who do not rally to his call' ('Guest and Host in Judges 19: Lot's Hospitality in an Inverted World', *Journal for the Study of the Old Testament* 29 [1984]: 42). Also comparing Judg. 19 to 1 Sam. 11 Yairah Amit asks, '[W]hat was the person who received a piece of the concubine's body to understand?' (*Hidden Polemics in Biblical Narrative* [Leiden: Brill, 2000], 181); Susan Ackerman agrees that the dismemberment 'makes no sense within the Judges 19 tale' ('The Women of the Bible and Ancient Near Eastern Myth: The Case of the Levite's פילגש', in *Worship, Women, and War: Essays in Honor of Susan Niditch*, ed. John J. Collins, T. M. Lemos and Saul M. Olyan [Providence, RI: Brown University Press, 2015], 217). Soggin offers a typical response: 'However, in this instance the symbolism seems to be missing: the quartered limbs of the concubine are not a summons to arms, nor do they threaten the reluctant; they simply arouse horror. Such a macabre gesture is not only unnecessary for summoning the assembly; it does not even seem to serve a useful purpose' (*Judges*, 282).

39. *Fragmented Women*, 140–59; citation from 144. What I am describing in my analysis of this story is a gender-motivated subtext, not a conscious misogynistic design on the part of the narrator: 'In order to illustrate the social and moral disintegration of Israel before the monarchy, the narrator of Judges 19–21 tells a story in which the threatened abuse of the Levite and the actual treatment of his wife lead to internecine warfare, the near extinction of an Israelite tribe, and mass rape and murder. All of these events come under narrative censure, with violence against women treated merely as part of a larger social and moral problem – that is, as if the gender of the victims of violence were irrelevant. Yet the fact that the central act in the illustration is the rape and dismemberment of a woman foregrounds the important role gender plays, on a deeper level, in the presentation' (145). This is first and foremost a crime against a woman; to turn her into a political symbol is to perpetuate the crime. Ackerman brings further evidence of this gender bias to light by comparing the example of Tiamat in the *Enuma Elish* ('The Women of the Bible and Ancient Near Eastern Myth', 220–26).

Although Henner was probably influenced more by Jean-Jacques Rousseau's prose poem 'Le Lévite d'Ephraïm' than the account in Judges 19–21, his version does not challenge the story the biblical writer tells.[40] While it depicts a scene over which the biblical narrator does not linger, it treats the woman in much the same manner in a different medium. Echoing the verbal narrative, the visual narrative dehumanizes the woman; it appropriates her body, making it a focal part of its 'story'; and, like the Levite in our tale, it does not allow the body to tell its own story, a story of violation and brutality.

Let us consider first the Levite. Does he arouse our sympathy? It is hard to tell in this painting whether he is looking at the woman's body or staring beyond it, lost in thought, perhaps reflecting on the events or deciding what course of action he will take. In any event he shows no signs of grief or remorse for the part he played in her suffering. I see him as cold and calculating. His posture, with his chin resting upon his hand, suggests to me that he is deliberating very carefully how to divide the corpse into twelve parts, and perhaps thinking about how to distribute the severed body parts (not an easy question; who gets what?). In another version of this painting (fig. 9.8) we can see his face more clearly, and here he seems to be staring directly at the woman.

Fig. 9.8. Jean-Jacques Henner, *The Levite of Ephraim and his Dead Wife*, c. 1898, Princeton University Art Museum, Princeton, NJ

40. On Rousseau's story, see Judith Still, 'Rousseau's *Lévite d'Ephraïm*: The Imposition of Meaning (on Women)', *French Studies* 43 (1989): 12–30; Tanya Horeck, 'Body Politics: Rousseau's *Le Lévite d'Ephraïm*', in *Public Rape: Representing Violation in Fiction and Film* (Oxon: Routledge, 2004), 42–66; Michael S. Kochin, 'Living with the Bible: Jean-Jacques Rousseau Reads Judges 19–21', *Hebraic Political Studies* 2 (2007): 301–25.

I find the version in fig. 9.7, with its softer, hazy focus, more haunting than the painting in fig. 9.8, where both figures are more sharply delineated. It is more visually striking too, with the yellow cloth scarcely draped over the woman and the rich green of the Levite's cloak. Her body is whiter in this version, and her hair redder. The Levite's concentration on the body laid out before him on the table is reminiscent of a genre of painting popular since at least the time of Rembrandt, and the subject of much public interest in the late nineteenth century, when Henner was active: the anatomy lesson (figs. 9.9 and 9.10).[41] And, more pertinent, because of its date (around the same time as Henner) and its female subject, is a drawing of the dissection of a young woman by J. H. Hasselhorst (fig. 9.11). The body is opened up in order to discover its secrets, to understand its mystery and to gain mastery or a measure of control over it. When the body is female, cutting it open (or cutting it up, as in our story) can be viewed both as an expression of male fear of woman's sexuality, which must therefore be destroyed, and as an attempt to discover the secret of woman's sexuality. Because woman is the seductive and dangerous other, her mystery must be opened up by force.[42]

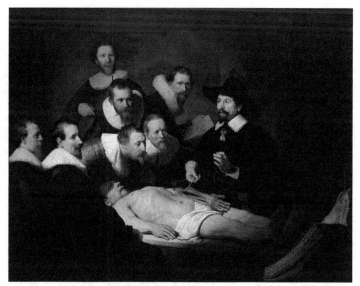

Fig. 9.9. Rembrandt, *The Anatomy Lecture of Dr Nicolaes Tulp*, 1632,
Royal Picture Gallery, Mauritshuis, The Hague

41. See the discussion in Elaine Showalter, *Sexual Anarchy: Gender and Culture at the Fin de Siècle* (New York: Penguin Books, 1990), 127–42.

42. My thinking on this issue owes much to Showalter, *Sexual Anarchy*, esp. 105–43.

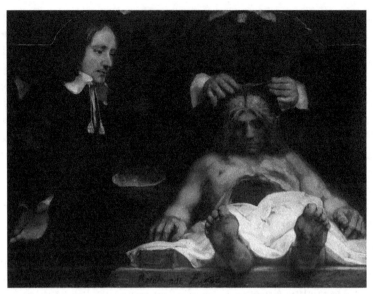

Fig. 9.10. Rembrandt, *The Anatomy Lesson of Dr Deijman*, 1656,
Amsterdam Museum

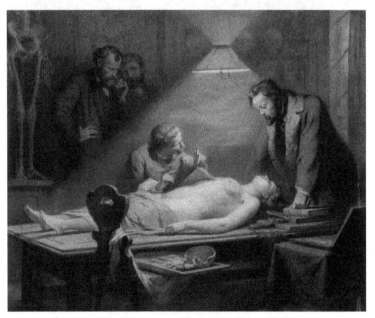

Fig. 9.11. *The Dissection of a Young, Beautiful Woman*,
directed by J. Ch. G. Lucae (1814–1885) in order to determine the ideal female
proportions. Chalk drawing by J. H. Hasselhorst, 1864,
Wellcome Institute Library, London

An interpretation of the Levite as callous finds ample support in the biblical story, where he destroys the evidence of the rape in a way that symbolically repeats it, by sharing the woman's body among men. What is more, he destroys the evidence of the crime against the woman by giving a different account of what happened when he offers his testimony to the Israelite assembly.

> To Gibeah that belongs to Benjamin I came, I and my wife, to spend the night. The men of Gibeah rose against me and surrounded the house against me by night. Me they meant to kill and my wife they raped, and she died. I took my wife and cut her in pieces and sent her throughout all the country of the inheritance of Israel, for they have committed abomination and wantonness in Israel (Judg. 20.4-6).

The Levite stresses the threat to himself: the men 'rose against *me*'; they 'surrounded the house against *me*'; '*me* [in first place for emphasis] they meant to kill'. In his version of the events, his life is at stake, and he does not mention the humiliating threat of homosexual rape. Indeed, it sounds as if the mob set out to kill him and only incidentally did it come about that they raped his wife. He neglects to mention that he and his host remained in the safety of the house while the woman was thrown out to the crowd to be raped all night. His statement, 'and she died', implies that her death resulted from the mob's abuse, whereas in the narrator's version whether she died from the rape or later is not clear.[43]

The fact that the biblical narrator is critical of the Levite does not mean that he is necessarily sympathetic to the woman.[44] As I have

---

43. In *Fragmented Women* I observe, 'By placing in the Levite's mouth an account so self-serving and so unlike the events described to us in ch. 19, the narrator reveals the Levite's baseness. Indeed, the narrator's sympathy does not lie with the Levite. He represents him as too irresolute to leave on his journey home at a reasonable hour and then too stubborn to remain another night at his father-in-law's house (19.5-10). Had he left early in the morning with his wife and servant as intended, they would not have needed to stop in Gibeah and the outrage might have been avoided. Moreover, it is surely a callous man who, upon finding his raped and battered wife lying at the door, can say, "Get up; let's go" (v. 28). But even though the Levite is a disreputable character, it is nonetheless the Levite's version of events to which the tribes respond. They go to war with Benjamin to avenge the threatened crime against the Levite and the actual abuse of his wife' (148–49).

44. The narrative does, however, acknowledge the crimes against the woman. After the Levite dismembers the woman and sends the parts of her body throughout Israelite territory, we read: 'All who saw it said, "Such a thing has never happened

already indicated, as part of her narrative punishment for asserting her sexual autonomy, the dismemberment functions to de-sexualize her and to diffuse her threat by scattering the parts. How does the painter's attitude to the woman compare to the biblical narrator's? Is this woman dead or only unconscious? In the Hebrew text, it is not entirely clear at what point the woman died or even that she is dead when her husband dismembers her, a detail the Septuagint and Vulgate translators apparently felt the need to clarify by adding 'and she was dead' after 'there was no answer' (v. 28).

> Her husband rose up in the morning and opened the door of the house. He went out to go on his way, and there was [*hinneh*] the woman, his wife, lying at the door of the house. He said to her, 'Get up so we can go', but *there was no answer*. He put her upon the donkey and he went at once to his place (Judg. 19.27-28).

The woman has been gang raped to the point of death or near death, yet there are no signs of such abuse on the body in Henner's painting. The body is not allowed to bear witness against the guilty parties, and thus

or been seen from the day that the people of Israel came up out of the land of Egypt until this day; consider it, take counsel, and speak"' (Judg. 19.30). Unless we assume that some explanation accompanied the body parts, 'such a thing' can refer only to the dismemberment and parcelling out of the woman's body, since only later do the tribes learn from the Levite what happened at Gibeah. When they assemble at Mizpah and ask the Levite to tell them 'how did this evil come to pass?' (20.4), the only obvious referent for 'this evil' is the dismemberment. Thus, in Judg. 19–21 we have a situation in which the narrator *tells* us that the tribes go to war to avenge what are certainly crimes against a man and his property. But he *shows* us horrible crimes against the woman, both the gang rape and the dismemberment; see Exum, *Fragmented Women*, 149–50. Julie Faith Parker ('Re-membering the Dismembered: Piecing Together Meaning from Stories of Women and Body Parts in Ancient Near Eastern Literature', *Biblical Interpretation* 23 [2015]: 179–81, 188–90) foregrounds the dismemberment's function to elicit revenge, with the ironic result that '[b]y cutting her body into pieces, [the Levite] brings the body of Israel together' (181). Francis Landy, in a brilliant analysis of Judg. 19 and its wider biblical context from new historical, psychoanalytical and literary perspectives, takes this a step further: '…all Israel once more comes together. At the same time, it is a catastrophe, a dissolution, as one tribe, a very important one, is almost annihilated; so…the end of an epoch, of Israel as a united people' but 'also a beginning, in fact two beginnings: Ruth and Samuel depending on which thread you want to pick up'; 'Between Centre and Periphery: Space and Gender in the Book of Judges in the Early Second Temple Period', in *Centres and Peripheries in the Early Second Temple Period*, ed. Ehud Ben Zvi and Christoph Levin (Tübingen: Mohr Siebeck, 2016), 141–42.

to tell its story. The woman's head is turned slightly away from us; we cannot make out any facial features, anything that would humanize her. The subject lying before the brooding man is more an 'it' than a 'she' – anonymous, as in the biblical story, where we do not learn her name.[45]

Henner's painting bears an arresting resemblance to that of another sacrificial victim, the Jesus of Hans Holbein the Younger's *The Body of the Dead Christ in the Tomb* (figs. 9.12 and 9.13). Henner too painted a *Christ Entombed*, but it is not nearly so harrowing as Holbein's.[46] Holbein's painting is claustrophobic; the tombstone presses in on the body. Henner's painting of the Levite's wife has a featureless backdrop that, like Holbein's, makes the body in the foreground and on which the light falls, the focus of attention, though here attention is shared with the Levite in the shadows, into whose deliberations the viewer is irresistibly drawn.

Fig. 9.12. Henner, *The Levite of Ephraim and his Dead Wife*

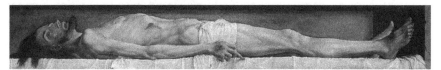

Fig. 9.13. Hans Holbein the Younger, *The Body of the Dead Christ in the Tomb*, 1521, Kunstmuseum, Basel

45. No one in the story is named, as if the events were too scandalous to identify the characters.

46. The painting is in the Musée Jean-Jacques Henner, Paris. Henner used Holbein's painting as a model; however the body of his Christ, like that of the Levite's wife, does not show the marks of his persecution.

The corpse is stretched out on a slab or table. Both figures are naked, draped almost casually with a bit of cloth. The position of the feet is similar, and in both paintings the right arm is in full view, resting at the side of the body. Christ's hand and middle finger extend over the side of the slab; the woman's hand, on the table, seems to be loosely closed and more relaxed. We cannot distinguish the fingers very well, though, interestingly, in the version of the painting in fig. 9.8, the index finger, pointing forward, is clearly visible. The hair of both figures hangs over the edge of the slab or table, and the face is slightly tilted: his toward us, hers away. He is humanized; she is not. Unlike her body, his emaciated body in death is all too disturbingly human. It bears the signs of torture – the wound in his side made by the spear and those of the nails in his hand and feet – and every detail testifies to the agony it has endured. Under the skin, the muscles, sinews and bones are clearly visible. And the face, with eyes staring vacantly and mouth open as though having emitted a final breath or a cry, is a study in anguish.

In Henner's painting, the woman's death, in contrast to Holbein's Christ's, is softened, her identity blurred and her suffering unacknowledged. It is her butcher's face we see, not hers. Her pallid body lies still, as though cold in death, but not bruised, not bloody and not broken. The crucial difference is that Holbein's *Dead Christ* is a painting of a willing sacrifice. Like his mother, Jesus surrenders his will to God's plan ('not my will but yours be done'). Unlike Jesus, who chooses to die for the sins of the world, the Levite's wife did not choose to die for her husband, to be thrown to her death so that he could remain safe and unharmed. She makes one choice – a wrong choice says our narrative: she leaves her husband, a crime the narrator cannot allow to go unpunished. In exposing her body to the viewer, does the painter expose the crime against her? The painting does anticipate chillingly the offense to come, the dismemberment. Nevertheless, although he draws attention to the victim, Henner repeats some of the biblical narrator's crimes against the woman: she is anonymous, she is not humanized, her agony is not shown (all in contrast to Holbein's Christ).

This is how a character in Dostoyevsky's *The Idiot* describes Holbein's painting:

> In the picture the face is terribly smashed with blows, tumefied, covered with terrible, swollen, and bloodstained bruises, the eyes open and squinting; the large, open whites of the eyes have a sort of dead and glassy glint. But, strange to say, as one looks at the dead body of this tortured man, one cannot help asking oneself the peculiar, arresting question: if such a corpse (and it must have been just like that) was seen by all His disciples, by His future

chief apostles, by the women who followed Him and stood by the cross, by all who believed in Him and worshipped Him, then how could they possibly have believed, confronted with such a sight, that this martyr would rise again?... And if, on the eve of the crucifixion, the Master could have seen what He would look like when taken from the cross, would he have mounted the cross and died as he did? This question, too, you can't help asking yourself as you look at the picture.

In an essay on this painting, Julia Kristeva suggests that Holbein may be inviting the viewer to participate in the death presented here, its finality, its grief and melancholia, its irony with regard to transcendence and its beauty.[47] I wonder, do viewers of Henner's painting feel inclined to participate in the woman's suffering and death?

47. Julia Kristeva, 'Holbein's Dead Christ', in *Black Sun: Depression and Melancholia*, trans. Leon S. Roudiez (New York: Columbia University Press, 1989), 113–14. I have taken the translation above from Kristeva's essay, 108–9. The last two occurrences of the word 'he' appear in lower case, I suspect as an oversight.

BIBLIOGRAPHY

Abasili, Alexander Izuchukwu. 'Was It Rape? The David and Bathsheba Pericope Re-examined'. *Vetus Testamentum* 61 (2011): 1–15.

Ackerman, Susan. *Warrior, Dancer, Seductress, Queen: Women in Judges and Biblical Israel*. New York: Doubleday, 1998.

———. 'The Women of the Bible and Ancient Near Eastern Myth: The Case of the Levite's פילגש'. In *Worship, Women, and War: Essays in Honor of Susan Niditch*, edited by John J. Collins, T. M. Lemos and Saul M. Olyan, 215–26. Providence, RI: Brown University Press, 2015.

Adelman, Rachel E. *The Female Ruse: Women's Deception and Divine Sanction in the Hebrew Bible*. Sheffield: Sheffield Phoenix Press, 2015.

Alexander, Loveday. 'The Four among Pagans'. In *The Written Gospel*, edited by Markus Bockmuehl and Donald A. Hagner, 222–37. Cambridge: Cambridge University Press, 2005.

———. 'Madonna and Child: The Lucan Infancy Narrative and the Apologetic Agenda'. Unpublished paper read at the conference 'Evangiles de l'enfance/Infancy Gospels'. University of Lausanne, October 2010.

Alexander, T. D. 'The Hagar Traditions in Genesis XVI and XXI'. In *Studies in the Pentateuch*, edited by J. A. Emerton, 131–48. Leiden: Brill, 1990.

Alter, Robert. *The Art of Biblical Poetry*. New York: Basic Books, 1985.

———. 'How Convention Helps Us Read: The Case of the Bible's Annunciation Type-Scene'. *Prooftexts* 3 (1983): 115–30.

Amit, Yairah. *Hidden Polemics in Biblical Narrative*. Leiden: Brill, 2000.

———. 'Judges 4: Its Contents and Form'. *Journal for the Study of the Old Testament* 39 (1987): 89–111.

Anderson, Gary A. *The Genesis of Perfection: Adam and Eve in Jewish and Christian Imagination*. Louisville, KY: Westminster John Knox Press, 2001.

Antony, Louise. 'Does God Love Us?'. In *Divine Evil? The Moral Character of the God of Abraham*, edited by Michael Bergmann, Michael J. Murray and Michael C. Rea, 29–46. Oxford: Oxford University Press, 2013.

Apostolos-Cappadona, Diane. 'Religion and the Arts: History and Method'. *Brill Research Perspectives in Religion and the Arts* 1 (2017): 1–80.

———. 'Toilet Scenes'. In *Encyclopedia of Comparative Iconography: Themes Depicted in Works of Art*, vol. 2, edited by Helene E. Roberts, 869–74. Chicago, IL: Fitzroy Dearborn Publishers, 1998.

Babcock-Abrahams, Barbara. '"A Tolerated Margin of Mess": The Trickster and His Tales Reconsidered'. *Journal of the Folklore Institute* 11 (1975): 147–86.

Bach, Alice. *Women, Seduction, and Betrayal in Biblical Narrative*. Cambridge: Cambridge University Press, 1997.

Bailey, Randall C. *David in Love and War: The Pursuit of Power in 2 Samuel 10–12*. Sheffield: JSOT Press, 1990.

Bakhos, Carol. *Ishmael on the Border: Rabbinic Portrayals of the First Arab*. Albany: State University of New York, 2006.

Bal, Mieke. *Death and Dissymmetry: The Politics of Coherence in the Book of Judges*. Chicago: University of Chicago Press, 1988.

———. *Double Exposures: The Subject of Cultural Analysis*. New York: Routledge, 1996.

———. 'Grounds of Comparison'. In Bal, ed., *The Artemisia Files*, 129–67.

———. *Looking In: The Art of Viewing*. London: Routledge, 2001.

———. *Loving Yusuf: Conceptual Travels from Present to Past*. Chicago: University of Chicago Press, 2008.

———. *Murder and Difference: Gender, Genre, and Scholarship on Sisera's Death*. Bloomington: Indiana University Press, 1988.

———. *Reading 'Rembrandt': Beyond the Word–Image Opposition*. Cambridge: Cambridge University Press, 1991.

Bal, Mieke, ed. *The Artemisia Files: Artemisia Gentileschi for Feminists and Other Thinking People*. Chicago: University of Chicago Press, 2005.

Barbiero, Gianni. *Song of Songs: A Close Reading*, translated by Michael Tait. Leiden: Brill, 2011.

Baxandall, Michael. *Painting and Experience in Fifteenth-Century Italy: A Primer in the Social History of Pictorial Style*. 2nd ed. Oxford: Oxford University Press, 1988.

Becking, Bob, and Susanne Hennecke, eds. *Out of Paradise: Eve and Adam and Their Interpreters*. Sheffield: Sheffield Phoenix Press, 2011.

Bekins, Peter. 'Tamar and Joseph in Genesis 38 and 39'. *Journal for the Study of the Old Testament* 40 (2016): 375–97.

Berdini, Paolo. *The Religious Art of Jacopo Bassano: Painting as Visual Exegesis*. Cambridge: Cambridge University Press, 1997.

Berger, John. *Ways of Seeing*. London: Penguin Books, 1972.

Black, Fiona C. *The Artifice of Love: Grotesque Bodies in the Song of Songs*. London: T&T Clark, 2009.

———. 'Beauty or the Beast? The Grotesque Body in the Song of Songs'. *Biblical Interpretation* 8 (2000): 302–23.

———. 'Nocturnal Egression: Exploring Some Margins of the Song of Songs'. In *Postmodern Interpretations of the Bible*, edited by A. K. M. Adam, 93–104. St Louis, MO: Chalice Press, 2001.

Black, Fiona C., and J. Cheryl Exum. 'Semiotics in Stained Glass: Edward Burne-Jones's Song of Songs'. In *Biblical Studies/Cultural Studies: The Third Sheffield Colloquium*, edited by J. Cheryl Exum and Stephen D. Moore, 315–42. Sheffield: Sheffield Academic Press, 1998.

Blyth, Caroline. *Reimagining Delilah's Afterlives as Femme Fatale: The Lost Seduction*. London: Bloomsbury T&T Clark, 2017.

Bohn, Babette. 'Death, Dispassion, and the Female Hero: Artemisia Gentileschi's *Jael and Sisera*'. In Bal, ed., *The Artemisia Files*, 107–27.

Boling, Robert G. *Judges: A New Translation with Introduction and Commentary*. Garden City, NY: Doubleday, 1975.

Bonfiglio, Ryan P. 'Choosing Sides in Judges 4–5: Rethinking Representations of Jael'. In *Joshua and Judges*, edited by Athalya Brenner and Gale A. Yee, 161–74. Minneapolis, MN: Fortress Press, 2013.

Boonen, Jacqueline. 'Die Geschichte von Israels Exil und Freiheitskampf'. In Tümpel, ed., *Im Lichte Rembrandts*, 106–21.

Bos, Johanna W. H. 'Out of the Shadows: Genesis 38; Judges 4:17–22; Ruth 3'. In *Reasoning with the Foxes: Female Wit in a World of Male Power*, edited by J. Cheryl Exum and Johanna W. H. Bos, 37–67. Atlanta, GA: Scholars Press, 1988.

Boyd, Jane, and Philip F. Esler. *Visuality and Biblical Text: Interpreting Velázquez' Christ with Martha and Mary as a Test Case*. Florence: Leo S. Olschki Editore, 2004.

Brenner, Athalya. 'Afterword'. In Brenner, ed., *A Feminist Companion to Judges*, 233–34.

———. '"Come Back, Come Back the Shulammite" (Song of Songs 7.1-10): A Parody of the *waṣf* Genre', in *A Feminist Companion to the Song of Songs*, edited by Athalya Brenner, 234–57. Sheffield: Sheffield Academic Press, 1993.

———. *The Israelite Woman: Social Role and Literary Type in Biblical Narrative*. 2nd ed. London: Bloomsbury, 2015.

Brenner, Athalya, ed. *A Feminist Companion to Judges*. Sheffield: Sheffield Academic Press, 1993.

Brenner, Athalya, and John Willem van Henten. 'Madame Potiphar through a Culture Trip, or, Which Side Are You On?'. In *Biblical Studies/Cultural Studies: The Third Sheffield Colloquium*, edited by J. Cheryl Exum and Stephen D. Moore, 203–19. Sheffield: Sheffield Academic Press, 1998.

Brett, Mark G. *Genesis: Procreation and the Politics of Identity*. London: Routledge, 2000.

Brison, Ora. 'Jael, *'eshet heber* the Kenite: A Diviner?' In *Joshua and Judges*, edited by Athalya Brenner and Gale A. Yee, 139–60. Minneapolis, MN: Fortress Press, 2013.

Bronner, Leila Leah. 'Valorized or Vilified? The Women of Judges in Midrashic Sources'. In Brenner, ed., *A Feminist Companion to Judges*, 72–95.

Brooks, Peter. *Body Work: Objects of Desire in Modern Narrative*. Cambridge, MA: Harvard University Press, 1993.

Brown, Raymond E. *The Birth of the Messiah: A Commentary on the Infancy Narratives in Matthew and Luke*. 2nd ed. London: Goeffrey Chapman, 1993.

Brueggemann, Walter. *Genesis*. Atlanta, GA: John Knox Press, 1982.

Burney, C. F. *The Book of Judges*. New York: Ktav, 1970 (1903).

Butts, Barbara. 'Drawings, Watercolours, Prints'. In Schuster, Vitali and Butts, eds., *Lovis Corinth*, 323–78.

Camp, Claudia V. 'Illustrations of the Sotah in Popular Printed Works in the Seventeenth–Nineteenth Centuries'. In Clines and van Wolde, eds., *A Critical Engagement*, 90–115.

———. 'The Wise Woman of 2 Samuel: A Role Model for Women in Early Israel?' *Catholic Biblical Quarterly* 43 (1981): 14–29.

Carlton, Wensday. 'Madonna and Child'. *TriQuarterly* 110/111 (2001): 490.

Clines, David J. A. 'Gendering the Magnificat'. In *Let the Reader Understand: Studies in Honor of Elizabeth Struthers Malbon*, edited by Edwin K. Broadhead, 175–82. London: T&T Clark, 2018.

———. *The Theme of the Pentateuch*. 2nd ed. Sheffield: Sheffield Phoenix Press, 1997.

Clines, David J. A., and Ellen van Wolde, eds. *A Critical Engagement: Essays on the Hebrew Bible in Honour of J. Cheryl Exum*. Sheffield: Sheffield Phoenix Press, 2011.

Coats, George W. *Genesis, with an Introduction to Narrative Literature*. Grand Rapids, MI: Eerdmans, 1983.

Cogan, Morton. 'A Technical Term for Exposure'. *Journal for Near Eastern Studies* 27 (1968): 133–35.

Collins, John J. *Daniel*. Minneapolis, MN: Fortress Press, 1993.

Collins, Sandra Ladick. *Weapons upon Her Body: The Female Heroic in the Hebrew Bible*. Newcastle upon Tyne: Cambridge Scholars Publishing, 2012.

Conway, Colleen M., 'The Malleability of Jael in the Dutch Renaissance'. *Biblical Reception* 2 (2013): 36–56.

———. *Sex and Slaughter in the Tent of Jael: A Cultural History of a Biblical Story*. Oxford: Oxford University Press, 2017.

Coogan, Michael David. 'A Structural and Literary Analysis of the Song of Deborah'. *Catholic Biblical Quarterly* 40 (1978): 143–66.

Corinth, Lovis. *Das Erlernen der Malerei. Ein Handbuch von Lovis Corinth*. 3rd ed. Berlin: Paul Cassirer, 1920 (originally published 1908). Repr. Hildesheim: Gerstenberg Verlag, 1979.

———. *Gesammelte Schriften*. Berlin: Fritz Gurlitt Verlag, 1920.

———. 'Januar 1913, Lovis Corinths Vorwort im Ausstellungskatalog'. In *Lovis Corinth: Eine Dokumentation*, edited by Thomas Corinth. Tübingen: Verlag Ernst Wasmuth, 1979.

———. *Selbstbiographie*. Leipzig: Hirzel, 1926.

Corinth, Thomas. 'Bericht von Thomas Corinth'. In *Lovis Corinth: Eine Dokumentation*, edited by Thomas Corinth. Tübingen: Verlag Ernst Wasmuth, 1979.

Crenshaw, James L. *Samson: A Secret Betrayed, a Vow Ignored*. Atlanta, GA: John Knox Press, 1978.

Darr, Katheryn Pfisterer. *Far More Precious than Jewels: Perspectives on Biblical Women*. Louisville, KY: Westminster John Knox Press, 1991.

[*DCH*] Clines, David J. A., ed. *The Dictionary of Classical Hebrew*. Sheffield: Sheffield Phoenix Press, 1993–.

Delaney, Carol. *Abraham on Trial: The Social Legacy of Biblical Myth*. Princeton, NJ: Princeton University Press, 1998.

Dijk-Hemmes, Fokkelien van. 'Mothers and a Mediator in the Song of Deborah'. In Brenner, ed., *A Feminist Companion to Judges*, 110–14.

Dillenberger, Jane. *Image and Spirit in Sacred and Secular Art*. New York: Crossroad, 1990.

Dowling Long, Siobhán. *The Sacrifice of Isaac: The Reception of a Biblical Story in Music*. Sheffield: Sheffield Phoenix Press, 2013.

Dozeman, Thomas B. 'The Wilderness and Salvation History in the Hagar Story'. *Journal of Biblical Literature* 117 (1998): 23–43.

Driver, G. R. 'Problems of Interpretation in the Heptateuch'. In *Mélanges bibliques rédigés en l'honneur de André Robert*, 66–76. Paris: Bloud & Gay, 1957.

Drury, John. *Painting the Word: Christian Pictures and Their Meanings*. New Haven, CT: Yale University Press, in association with National Gallery Publications, London, 1999.

Ebach, Jürgen. *Genesis 37–50*. Freiburg im Breisgau: Herder, 2007.

Edwards, Katie B. *Admen and Eve: The Bible in Contemporary Advertising*. Sheffield: Sheffield Phoenix Press, 2012.

Engel, Helmut. *Die Susanna-Erzählung: Einleitung, Übersetzung und Kommentar zum Septuaginta-Text und zur Theodotion-Bearbeitung* (Freiburg Schweiz: UniversitätsF verlag; Göttingen: Vandenhoeck & Ruprecht, 1985.

England, Yaffa [Jaffa]. 'The Expulsion of Hagar: Reading the Image, (Re)Viewing the Story'. *Religion and the Arts* 22 (2018): 261–93.

———. 'Ishmael Playing? Exegetical Understandings and Artistic Representations of the Verb *mᵉṣaḥēq* in Genesis 21.9'. *Biblical Reception* 2 (2013): 16–35.

Exum, J. Cheryl. 'The Accusing Look: The Abjection of Hagar in Art'. *Religion and the Arts* 11 (2007): 143–71.

———. 'Any Dream Will Do? Joseph from Text to Technicolor'. *Biblical Reception* 2 (2013): 202–26.

———. 'The Centre Cannot Hold: Thematic and Textual Instabilities in Judges'. *Catholic Biblical Quarterly* 52 (1990): 410–31.

———. 'Do You Feel Comforted? M. Night Shyamalan's *Signs* and the Book of Job'. In *Foster Biblical Scholarship: Essays in Honor of Kent Harold Richards*, edited by Frank Ritchel Ames and Charles William Miller, 251–67. Atlanta, GA: Society of Biblical Literature, 2010.

———. 'Feminist Criticism: Whose Interests Are Being Served?' In *Judges and Method: New Approaches in Biblical Studies*, edited by Gale A. Yee, 65–89. 2nd ed. Minneapolis, MN: Fortress Press, 2007.

———. *Fragmented Women: Feminist (Sub)versions of Biblical Narratives*. 2nd ed. London: Bloomsbury T&T Clark, 2016.

———. 'In the Eye of the Beholder: Wishing, Dreaming, and *double entendre* in the Song of Songs'. In *The Labour of Reading: Desire, Alienation, and Biblical Interpretation*, edited by Fiona C. Black, Roland Boer and Erin Runions, 71–86. Atlanta, GA: Scholars Press, 1999.

———. 'Israel's Ancestors: The Patriarchs and Matriarchs'. In *The Biblical World*, edited by Katharine Dell. Oxford: Routledge, forthcoming.

———. 'The Many Faces of Samson'. In Eynikel and Nicklas, eds., *Samson: Hero or Fool?*, 13–31.

———. *Plotted, Shot, and Painted: Cultural Representations of Biblical Women*. 2nd rev. ed. Sheffield: Sheffield Phoenix Press, 2012.

———. 'Samson and Delilah in Film'. In *The Bible in Motion: A Handbook of the Bible and Its Reception in Film*, Part 1, edited by Rhonda Burnette-Bletsch, 83–100. Berlin: W. de Gruyter, 2016.

———. 'Samson and His God: Modern Culture Reads the Bible'. In *Words, Ideas, Worlds: Essays in Honour of Yairah Amit*, edited by Athalya Brenner and Frank H. Polak, 70–92. Sheffield: Sheffield Phoenix Press, 2012.

———. *Song of Songs: A Commentary*. Louisville, KY: Westminster John Knox Press, 2005.

———. *Tragedy and Biblical Narrative: Arrows of the Almighty*. Cambridge: Cambridge University Press, 1992.

Exum, J. Cheryl, and David J. A. Clines, eds. *Biblical Reception* 1. Sheffield: Sheffield Phoenix Press, 2012.

———. *Biblical Reception* 2. Sheffield: Sheffield Phoenix Press, 2013.

———. *Biblical Reception* 3. Sheffield: Sheffield Phoenix Press, 2014.

Exum, J. Cheryl, and David J. A. Clines, eds. *Biblical Women and the Arts*. Guest ed. Diane Apostolos-Cappadona. *Biblical Reception* 5. London: Bloomsbury, 2018.

Exum, J. Cheryl, and Ela Nutu, eds. *Between the Text and the Canvas: The Bible and Art in Dialogue*. Sheffield: Sheffield Phoenix Press, 2007.

Eynikel, Erik, and Tobias Nicklas, eds. *Samson: Hero or Fool?* Leiden: Brill, 2014.

Fewell, Danna Nolan. 'Changing the Subject: Retelling the Story of Hagar the Egyptian'. In *Genesis: A Feminist Companion to the Bible (Second Series)*, edited by Athalya Brenner, 182–94. Sheffield: Sheffield Academic Press, 1998.

Fewell, Danna Nolan, and David M. Gunn. 'Controlling Perspectives: Women, Men, and the Authority of Violence in Judges 4 & 5'. *Journal of the American Academy of Religion* 58 (1990): 389–411.

Fokkelman, J. P. *Narrative Art and Poetry in the Books of Samuel*. I. *King David*. Assen: van Gorcum, 1981.

Foskett, Mary F. *A Virgin Conceived: Mary and Classical Representations of Virginity*. Bloomington: Indiana University Press, 2002.

Fox, Michael V. *The Song of Songs and the Ancient Egyptian Love Songs*. Madison: University of Wisconsin Press, 1985.

Freedman, H., trans. *Midrash Rabbah*, vol. 1, *Genesis*. London: Soncino Press, 1939.

Frolov, Serge, and Alexander Frolov. 'Sisera Unfastened: On the Meaning of Judges 4:21 aβ-γ'. *Biblische Notizen* 165 (2015): 55–61.

Frymer-Kensky, Tikva. 'Patriarchal Family Relationships and Near Eastern Law'. *Biblical Archaeologist* 44 (1981): 209–14.

Fuchs, Esther. 'The Literary Characterization of Mothers and Sexual Politics in the Hebrew Bible'. In *Feminist Perspectives on Biblical Scholarship*, edited by Adela Yarbro Collins, 117–36. Chico, CA: Scholars Press, 1985.

Gabler-Hover, Janet. *Dreaming Black/Writing White: The Hagar Myth in American Cultural History*. Lexington: University Press of Kentucky, 2000.

Garrard, Mary D. *Artemisia Gentileschi: The Image of the Female Hero in Italian Baroque Art*. Princeton, NJ: Princeton University Press, 1989.

——. 'Artemisia's Hand'. In Bal, ed., *The Artemisia Files*, 1–31.

Garrett, Duane. *Song of Songs*. Nashville, TN: Thomas Nelson, 2004.

Gaventa, Beverly. *Mary: Glimpses of the Mother of Jesus*. Minneapolis, MN: Fortress Press, 1999.

Gent, Judith van, and Gabriël M. C. Pastoor. 'Die Zeit der Richter'. In Tümpel, ed., *Im Lichte Rembrandts*, 66–87.

Gillmayr-Bucher, Susanne. 'Framework and Discourse in the Book of Judges'. *Journal of Biblical Literature* 128 (2009): 687–702.

——. 'A Hero Ensnared in Otherness? Literary Images of Samson'. In Eynikel and Nicklas, eds., *Samson: Hero or Fool?*, 33–51.

Glancy, Jennifer A. *Slavery in Early Christianity*. Oxford: Oxford University Press, 2002.

——. 'Text Appeal: Visual Pleasure and Biblical Studies'. In *In Search of the Present: The Bible through Cultural Studies*, edited by Stephen D. Moore, 63–78. Atlanta, GA: Society of Biblical Literature, 1998.

Goodman, Martin, George H. van Kooten and Jacques T.A.G.M. van Ruiten, eds. *Abraham, the Nations, and the Hagarites: Jewish, Christian, and Islamic Perspectives on Kinship with Abraham*. Leiden: Brill, 2010.

Gray, Alison. 'Reception of the Old Testament'. In *The Hebrew Bible: A Critical Companion*, edited by John Barton, 405–30. Princeton, NJ: Princeton University Press, 2016.

Gray, John. *Joshua, Judges, Ruth*. Grand Rapids, MI: Eerdmans, 1986.

Grillo, Jennie. 'Showing Seeing in Susanna: The Virtue of the Text'. *Prooftexts* 35 (2015): 250–70.

Grossfeld, Bernard. 'A Critical Note on Judg 4.21'. *Zeitschrift für die alttestamentliche Wissenschaft* 85 (1973): 348–51.

Grüneberg, Keith N. *Abraham, Blessing and the Nations: A Philological and Exegetical Study of Genesis 12:3 in Its Narrative Context*. Berlin: W. de Gruyter, 2003.

Guest, Deryn. 'From Gender Reversal to Genderfuck: Reading Jael through a Lesbian Lens'. In *Bible Trouble: Queer Reading at the Boundaries of Biblical Scholarship*, edited by Teresa J. Hornsby and Ken Stone, 9–43. Atlanta, GA: Society of Biblical Literature, 2011.

———. 'Looking Lesbian at the Bathing Bathsheba'. *Biblical Interpretation* 16 (2008): 227–62.

Gunkel, Hermann. *Genesis*. 6th ed. Göttingen: Vandenhoeck & Ruprecht, 1964.

Gunn, David M. *Judges*. Oxford: Blackwell, 2005.

———. 'Samson of Sorrows: An Isaianic Gloss on Judges 13–16'. In *Reading between Texts: Intertextuality and the Hebrew Bible*, edited by Danna Nolan Fewell, 225–53. Louisville, KY: Westminster John Knox Press, 1992.

Hackett, Jo Ann. 'In the Days of Jael: Reclaiming the History of Women in Ancient Israel'. In *Immaculate and Powerful: The Female in Sacred Image and Social Reality*, edited by Clarissa W. Atkinson, Constance H. Buchanan and Margaret R. Miles, 15–37. Boston: Beacon Press, 1985.

———. 'Rehabilitating Hagar: Fragments of an Epic Pattern'. In *Gender and Difference in Ancient Israel*, edited by Peggy L. Day, 12–27. Minneapolis, MN: Fortress Press, 1989.

Haag, Herbert, Dorothée Sölle, Joe H. Kirchberger, Anne-Marie Schnieper-Müller and Emil Bührer. *Great Women of the Bible in Art and Literature*. Grand Rapids, MI: Eerdmans, 1994.

Halpern, Baruch. *The First Historians: The Hebrew Bible and History*. San Francisco, CA: Harper & Row, 1988.

Hamilton, Victor P. *The Book of Genesis: Chapters 18–50*. Grand Rapids, MI: Eerdmans, 1995.

Harding, Kathryn. '"I sought him but I did not find him": The Elusive Lover in the Song of Songs'. *Biblical Interpretation* 16 (2008): 43–59.

Harvey, John. *The Bible as Visual Culture: When Text Becomes Image*. Sheffield: Sheffield Phoenix Press, 2013.

Heard, R. Christopher. *Dynamics of Diselection: Ambiguity in Genesis 12–36 and Ethnic Boundaries in Post-Exilic Judah*. Atlanta, GA: Society of Biblical Literature, 2001.

Hendel, Ronald. *Remembering Abraham: Culture, Memory, and History in the Hebrew Bible*. Oxford: Oxford University Press, 2005.

Hennecke, Susanne. 'A Different Perspective: Karl Barth and Luce Irigaray Looking at Michelangelo's *The Creation of Eve*'. In *Out of Paradise: Eve and Adam and Their Interpreters*, edited by Bob Becking and Susanne Hennecke, 124–39. Sheffield: Sheffield Phoenix Press, 2011.

Hertzberg, Hans Wilhelm. *I & II Samuel*, translated by J. S. Bowden. Philadelphia, PA: Westminster Press, 1964.

———. *Die Bücher Josua, Richter, Ruth*. Göttingen: Vandenhoeck & Ruprecht, 1969.

Hoke, James N. '"Behold, the Lord's Whore"? Slavery, Prostitution, and Luke 1:38'. *Biblical Interpretation* 26 (2018): 43–67.

Horeck, Tanya. 'Body Politics: Rousseau's *Le Lévite d'Ephraïm*'. In *Public Rape: Representing Violation in Fiction and Film*. Oxon: Routledge, 2004): 42–66.

Hornik, Heidi J., and Mikeal C. Parsons. *Acts of the Apostles through the Centuries*. Chichester, West Sussex, UK: Wiley Blackwell, 2016.

———. *Illuminating Luke: The Infancy Narrative in Italian Renaissance Painting*. Harrisburg, PA: Trinity Press International, 2003.

———. *Illuminating Luke: The Passion and Resurrection Narratives in Italian Renaissance and Baroque Painting*. London: T&T Clark, 2007.

———. *Illuminating Luke: The Public Ministry of Christ in Italian Renaissance and Baroque Painting*. New York: Continuum, 2005.

Humphreys, W. Lee. *The Tragic Vision and the Hebrew Tradition*. Philadelphia, PA: Fortress Press, 1985.

James, Elaine T. 'Battle of the Sexes: Gender and the City in the Song of Songs'. *Journal for the Study of the Old Testament* 42 (2017): 93–116.

———. *Landscapes of the Song of Songs: Poetry and Place*. New York: Oxford University Press, 2017.

Janzen. J. Gerald. *Abraham and All the Families of the Earth: A Commentary on the Book of Genesis 12–50*. Grand Rapids, MI: Eerdmans, 1993.

Jeter, Jr., Joseph R. *Preaching Judges*. St Louis, MO: Chalice Press, 2003.

Joshel, Sandra R. *Slavery in the Roman World*. Cambridge: Cambridge University Press, 2010.

Josipovici, Gabriel. *The Book of God: A Response to the Bible*. New Haven, CT: Yale University Press, 1988.

Jost, Renate. *Gender, Sexualität und Macht in der Anthropologie des Richterbuches*. Stuttgart: Kohlhammer, 2006.

Joyce, Paul M., and Diana Lipton, *Lamentations through the Centuries*. Oxford: Wiley-Blackwell, 2013.

Joynes, Christine E. 'A Place for Pushy Mothers? Visualizations of Christ Blessing the Children'. *Biblical Reception* 2 (2013): 117–33.

———. 'Visualizing Salome's Dance of Death: The Contribution of Art to Biblical Exegesis'. In Exum and Nutu, eds., *Between the Text and the Canvas*, 145–63.

Junior, Nyasha. 'Powerplay in Potiphar's House: The Interplay of Gender, Ethnicity, and Class in Genesis 39'. PhD diss., Princeton Theological Seminary, 2008.

———. *Reimagining Hagar: Blackness and Bible*. Oxford: Oxford University Press, 2019.

Kalimi, Isaac. 'Joseph between Potiphar and His Wife: The Biblical Text in the Light of a Comparative Study on Early Jewish Exegesis'. In *Early Jewish Exegesis and Theological Controversy: Studies in Scriptures in the Shadow of Internal and External Controversies*, 88–103. Assen: van Gorcum, 2002.

Kalmanofsky, Amy. *Gender-Play in the Hebrew Bible: The Ways the Bible Challenges Its Gender Norms*. Taylor & Francis, 2016. Accessed through ProQuest Ebook Central.

Kamp, Netty van de. 'Die Genesis: Die Urgeschichte und die Geschichte der Erzväter'. In Tümpel, ed., *Im Lichte Rembrandts*, 24–53, 234.

Kawashima, Robert S. 'Could a Woman Say "No" in Biblical Israel? On the Genealogy of Legal Status in Biblical Law and Literature'. *Association for Jewish Studies Review* 35 (2011): 1–22.

Klangwisan, Yael Cameron. *Jouissance: A Cixousian Encounter with the Song of Songs*. Sheffield: Sheffield Phoenix Press, 2015.

Klein, Lillian R. 'Bathsheba Revealed'. In *Samuel and Kings: A Feminist Companion to the Bible (Second Series)*, edited by Athalya Brenner, 47–64. Sheffield: Sheffield Academic Press, 2000.

Kochin, Michael S. 'Living with the Bible: Jean-Jacques Rousseau Reads Judges 19–21'. *Hebraic Political Studies* 2 (2007): 301–25.

Koenen, Klaus. 'Wer sieht wen? Zur Textgeschichte von Genesis XVI 13'. *Vetus Testamentum* 38 (1988): 468–74.

Kozar, Joseph Vlcek. 'Rereading the Opening Chapter of Luke from a Feminist Perspective'. In *Escaping Eden: New Feminist Perspectives on the Bible*, edited by Harold C. Washington, Susan Lochrie Graham and Pamela Thimmes, 53–68. Sheffield: Sheffield Academic Press, 1998.

Kramer, Phyllis Silverman. 'The Dismissal of Hagar in Five Art Works of the Sixteenth and Seventeenth Centuries'. In *Genesis: A Feminist Companion to the Bible (Second Series)*, edited by Athalya Brenner, 195–217. Sheffield: Sheffield Academic Press, 1998.

Krauss, Laura Greig. 'Restoring Hagar: Rembrandt van Rijn's Painting *Abraham Dismissing Hagar and Ishmael* in the Victoria and Albert Museum, London'. *Biblical Reception* 1 (2012): 65–87.

Krieger, Murry. *The Classic Vision: The Retreat from Extremity*, vol. 2 of *Visions of Extremity in Modern Literature*. Baltimore, MD: Johns Hopkins University Press, 1971.

Krinetzki, Leo. *Das Hohe Lied: Kommentar zu Gestalt und Kerygma eines alttestamentarischen Liebesliedes*. Düsseldorf: Patmos, 1964.

Kristeva, Julia. 'Holbein's Dead Christ'. In *Black Sun: Depression and Melancholia*, 105–38. Translated by Leon S. Roudiez. New York: Columbia University Press, 1989.

———. *Powers of Horror: An Essay on Abjection*. Translated by Leon S. Roudiez. New York: Columbia University Press, 1982.

Kugel, James L. *In Potiphar's House: The Interpretive Life of Biblical Texts*. San Francisco, CA: HarperSanFrancisco, 1990.

Kupka, František. *Illustrations to the Song of Songs*. Israel: The Israel Museum, 1980.

Landry, David T. 'Narrative Logic in the Annunciation to Mary (Luke 1:26–38)'. *Journal of Biblical Literature* 114 (1995): 65–79.

Landy, Francis. *Beauty and the Enigma and Other Essays on the Hebrew Bible*. Sheffield: Sheffield Academic Press, 2001.

———. 'Between Centre and Periphery: Space and Gender in the Book of Judges in the Early Second Temple Period'. In *Centres and Peripheries in the Early Second Temple Period*, edited by Ehud Ben Zvi and Christoph Levin, 133–62. Tübingen: Mohr Siebeck, 2016.

———. 'Erotic Words, Sacred Landscapes, Ideal Bodies: Love and Death in the Song of Songs'. *The Blackwell Companion to World Literature*, forthcoming.

———. 'Narrative Techniques and Symbolic Transactions in the Akedah'. In *Signs and Wonders: Biblical Texts in Literary Focus*, edited by J. Cheryl Exum, 1–40. Atlanta, GA: Society of Biblical Literature, 1989.

———. *Paradoxes of Paradise: Identity and Difference in the Song of Songs*. 2nd ed. Sheffield: Sheffield Phoenix Press, 2011.

Langer, Susanne. *Feeling and Form*. New York: Scribner's, 1953.

Lasine, Stuart. 'Guest and Host in Judges 19: Lot's Hospitality in an Inverted World'. *Journal for the Study of the Old Testament* 29 (1984): 37–59.

Latvus, Kari. 'Reading Hagar in Contexts: From Exegesis to Inter-Contextual Analysis'. In *Genesis*, edited by Athalya Brenner, Archie Chi Chung Lee and Gale A. Yee, 247–74. Minneapolis, MN: Fortress Press, 2010.

Leemhuis, Fred. 'Hājar in the Qur'ān and Its Early Commentaries'. In Goodman et al., *Abraham, the Nations, and the Hagarites*, 503–8.

Leneman, Helen. *Love, Lust, and Lunacy: The Stories of Saul and David in Music*. Sheffield: Sheffield Phoenix Press, 2010.

———. *Moses: The Man and the Myth in Music*. Sheffield: Sheffield Phoenix Press, 2014.

———. *The Performed Bible: The Story of Ruth in Opera and Oratorio*. Sheffield: Sheffield Phoenix Press, 2007.

Levenson, Jon D. *The Death and Resurrection of the Beloved Son: The Transformation of Child Sacrifice in Judaism and Christianity*. New Haven, CT: Yale University Press, 1993.

Levine, Amy-Jill. '"Hemmed in on Every Side": Jews and Women in the Book of Susanna'. In *A Feminist Companion to Esther, Judith and Susanna*, edited by Athalya Brenner, 303–23. Sheffield: Sheffield Academic Press, 1995.

Levinson, Joshua. 'An-Other Woman: Joseph and Potiphar's Wife: Staging the Body Politic'. *Jewish Quarterly Review* 87 (1997): 269–301.

Lindars, Barnabas. *Judges 1–5: A New Translation and Commentary*. Edinburgh: T. & T. Clark, 1995.

Lipton, Diana. *Longing for Egypt and Other Tales of the Unexpected*. Sheffield: Sheffield Phoenix Press, 2008.

Low, Katherine. *The Bible, Gender, and Reception History: The Case of Job's Wife*. London: T&T Clark, 2013.

———. 'Sharing a Mirror with Venus: Bathsheba and Susanna with Mirrors in Early Modern Venetian Art'. *Biblical Reception* 2 (2013): 57–74.

Matthews, Victor H., and Don C. Benjamin, *Social World of Ancient Israel 1250–587 BCE*. Peabody, MA: Hendrickson, 1993.

Matskevich, Karalina. *Construction of Gender and Identity in Genesis: The Subject and the Other*. London: T&T Clark, 2019.

Mazar, Benjamin. 'The Sanctuary of Arad and the Family of Hobab the Kenite'. *Journal of Near Eastern Studies* 24 (1965): 297–303.

McKinlay, Judith E. *Reframing Her: Biblical Women in Postcolonial Focus*. Sheffield: Sheffield Phoenix Press, 2004.

———. 'Sarah and Hagar: What Have I to Do with Them?'. In *Her Master's Tools? Feminist and Postcolonial Engagements of Historical-Critical Discourse*, edited by Caroline Vander Stichele and Todd Penner, 159–77. Atlanta, GA: Society of Biblical Literature, 2005.

———. *Troubling Women and Land: Reading Biblical Texts in Aotearoa New Zealand*. Sheffield: Sheffield Phoenix Press, 2014.

Meredith, Christopher. '"Eating Sex" and the Unlovely Song of Songs: Reading Consumption, Excretion and D. H. Lawrence'. *Journal for the Study of the Old Testament* 42 (2018): 341–62.

———. *Journeys in the Songscape: Space and the Song of Songs*. Sheffield: Sheffield Phoenix Press, 2013.

Mettinger, Tryggve N. D. *The Eden Narrative: A Literary and Religio-historical Study of Genesis 2–3*. Winona Lake, IN: Eisenbrauns, 2007.

Meyers, Carol L. 'Was Ancient Israel a Patriarchal Society?' *Journal of Biblical Literature* 113 (2014): 8–27.

Miles, Margaret R. *Carnal Knowing: Female Nakedness and Religious Meaning in the Christian West*. New York: Vintage Books, 1991.

Miller, Geoffrey P. 'A Riposte Form in the Song of Deborah'. In *Gender and Law in the Hebrew Bible and the Ancient Near East*, edited by Victor H. Matthews, Bernard M. Levinson and Tikva Frymer-Kensky, 113–27. Sheffield: Sheffield Academic Press, 1998.

Miller, R., E. McEwen and C. Bergman. 'Experimental Approaches to Ancient Near Eastern Archery'. *World Archaeology* 18 (1986): 178–95.

Mitchell, W. J. T. *Iconology: Image, Text, Ideology*. Chicago: University of Chicago Press, 1986.

Mobley, Gregory. *Samson and the Liminal Hero in the Ancient Near East*. New York: T&T Clark, 2006.

———. 'The Wild Man in the Bible and the Ancient Near East'. *Journal of Biblical Literature* 116 (1997): 217–33.

Moore, Carey A. *Daniel, Esther, and Jeremiah: The Additions*. Garden City, NY: Doubleday, 1977.

Moore, George F. *A Critical and Exegetical Commentary on Judges*. Edinburgh: T. & T. Clark, 1895.

Morris, Paul, and Deborah Sawyer, eds. *A Walk in the Garden: Biblical, Iconographical and Literary Images of Eden*. Sheffield: Sheffield Academic Press, 1992.

Müller, Hans-Peter. *Das Hohelied*. Göttingen: Vandenhoeck & Ruprecht, 1992.

Murray, D. F. 'Narrative Structure and Technique in the Deborah–Barak Story (Judges IV:4–22)'. In *Studies in the Historical Books of the Old Testament*, edited by J. A. Emerton, 155–89. Leiden: Brill, 1979.

Musée National Message Biblique Marc Chagall. *Marc Chagall (1887–1985)*. Paris: Editions de la Réunion des musées nationaux, 1998.

Myrone, Martin. 'Prudery, Pornography and the Victorian Nude (Or, what do we think the butler saw?)'. In *Exposed: The Victorian Nude*, edited by Alison Smith, 23–35. London: The Tate Trustees, 2001.

Nead, Lynda. *The Female Nude: Art, Obscenity and Sexuality*. London: Routledge, 1992.

Nelson, Richard D. *Judges: A Critical and Rhetorical Commentary*. London: Bloomsbury T&T Clark, 2017.

Nicholls, Rachel. '"What kind of woman is this?" Reading Luke 7.36–50 in the Light of Dante Rossetti's Drawing *Mary Magdalene at the Door of Simon the Pharisee, 1853–89*'. In *From the Margins 2: Women of the New Testament and Their Afterlives*, edited by Christine E. Joynes and Christopher C. Rowland, 114–28. Sheffield: Sheffield Phoenix Press, 2009.

Nicol, George G. 'The Alleged Rape of Bathsheba: Some Observations on Ambiguity in Biblical Narrative'. *Journal for the Study of the Old Testament* 73 (1997): 43–54.

———. 'Bathsheba, a Clever Woman?'. *Expository Times* 99 (1988): 360–63.

Niditch, Susan. 'Eroticism and Death in the Tale of Jael'. In *Gender and Difference in Ancient Israel*, edited by Peggy L. Day, 43–57. Minneapolis, MN: Fortress Press, 1989.

———. 'Genesis'. In *Women's Bible Commentary*, edited by Carol A. Newsom, Sharon H. Ringe and Jacqueline E. Lapsley, 27–45. 3rd rev. ed. Louisville, KY: Westminster John Knox Press, 2012.

———. *Judges: A Commentary*. Louisville, KY: Westminster John Knox Press, 2008.

————. 'Samson as Culture Hero, Trickster, and Bandit: The Empowerment of the Weak'. *Catholic Biblical Quarterly* 52 (1990): 608–24.

————. 'The "Sodomite" Theme in Judges 19–20: Family, Community, and Social Disintegration'. *Catholic Biblical Quarterly* 44 (1982): 365–78.

Nikaido, S. 'Hagar and Ishmael as Literary Figures: An Intertextual Study'. *Vetus Testamentum* 51 (2001): 219–42.

Nochlin, Linda. *Bathers, Bodies, Beauty: The Visceral Eye*. Cambridge, MA: Harvard University Press, 2006.

————. *The Politics of Vision: Essays on Nineteenth-Century Art and Society*. Boulder, CO: Westview Press, 1989.

Norris, Pamela. *Eve: A Biography*. New York: New York University Press, 1998.

Noth, Martin. *A History of Pentateuchal Traditions*. Translated by Bernhard W. Anderson; Englewood Cliffs, NJ: Prentice-Hall, 1972.

Nutu, Ela. 'Framing Judith: Whose Text, Whose Gaze, Whose Language?' In Exum and Nutu, eds., *Between the Text and the Canvas*, 117–44.

O'Kane, Martin. 'The Bible in Orientalist Art'. In Clines and van Wolde, eds., *A Critical Engagement*, 288–308.

————. 'The Biblical Elijah and His Visual Afterlives'. In Exum and Nutu, eds., *Between the Text and the Canvas*, 60–79.

————. *Painting the Text: The Artist as Biblical Interpreter*. Sheffield: Sheffield Phoenix Press, 2007.

————. '*Wirkungsgeschichte* and Visual Exegesis: The Contribution of Hans-Georg Gadamer'. *Journal for the Study of the New Testament* 33 (2010): 147–59.

O'Kane, Martin, and Talha Bhamji. 'Islamic Tradition and the Reception History of the Bible'. In *Reading the Bible in Islamic Context: Qur'anic Conversations*, edited by Daniel J. Crowther, Shirin Sahfaie, Ida Glaser and Shabbir Akhtar, 148–66. London: Routledge, 2018.

Padgett, Jacqueline Olson. 'Ekphrasis, Lorenzo Lotto's *Annunciation*, and the Hermeneutics of Suspicion'. *Religion and the Arts* 10 (2006): 191–218.

Pardes, Ilana. '"I Am a Wall, and My Breasts like Towers": The Song of Songs and the Question of Canonization'. In *Countertraditions in the Bible: A Feminist Approach*, 118–43. Cambridge, MA: Harvard University Press, 1992.

Parker, Julie Faith. 'Re-membering the Dismembered: Piecing Together Meaning from Stories of Women and Body Parts in Ancient Near Eastern Literature'. *Biblical Interpretation* 23 (2015): 174–90.

Plummer, Alfred. *The Gospel according to S. Luke*. 4th ed. Edinburgh: T. & T. Clark, 1913.

Polaski, Donald C. '"What Will Ye See in the Shulammite?" Women, Power and Panopticism in the Song of Songs'. *Biblical Interpretation* 5 (1997): 64–81.

Pollock, Griselda, and Deborah Cherry. 'Woman as Sign in Pre-Raphaelite Literature: The Representation of Elizabeth Siddall'. In Griselda Pollock, *Vision and Difference: Femininity, Feminism and the Histories of Art*, 91–114. London: Routledge, 1988.

Pope, Michael. 'Gabriel's Entrance and Biblical Violence in Luke's Annunciation Narrative'. *Journal of Biblical Literature* 137 (2018): 701–10.

Prettejohn, Elizabeth. *The Art of the Pre-Raphaelites*. London: Tate Publishing, 2007.

Pyper, Hugh S. 'Love beyond Limits: The Debatable Body in Depictions of David and Jonathan'. In Exum and Nutu, eds., *Between the Text and the Canvas*, 38–59.

Raban, Ze'ev. *The Song of Songs*. Jerusalem: Korén Publishers, 1994.

Rad, Gerhard von. *Genesis: A Commentary*. Translated by John H. Marks. Philadelphia, PA: Westminster Press, 1961.

Reid, Barbara E. 'Prophetic Voices of Elizabeth, Mary, and Anna in Luke 1–2'. In *New Perspectives on the Nativity*, edited by Jeremy Corley, 37–46. London: T&T Clark, 2009.

Reis, Pamela Tamarkin. 'Hagar Requited'. *Journal for the Study of the Old Testament* 87 (2000): 75–109.

———. 'Uncovering Jael and Sisera: A New Reading'. *Scandinavian Journal of the Old Testament* 19 (2005): 24–47.

Robbins, Vernon K., Walter S. Melion and Roy R. Jeal, eds. *The Art of Visual Exegesis: Rhetoric, Texts, Images*. Atlanta, GA: SBL Press, 2017.

Roberts, M. J. D. 'Morals, Art, and the Law: The Passing of the Obscene Publications Act, 1857'. *Victorian Studies* 28 (1985): 609–29.

Rooke, Deborah W. *Handel's Israelite Oratorio Libretti: Sacred Drama and Biblical Exegesis*. Oxford: Oxford University Press, 2012.

Rooney, Ellen. '"A Little More than Persuading": Tess and the Subject of Sexual Violence'. In *Rape and Representation*, edited by Lynn A. Higgins and Brenda R. Silver, 87–114. New York: Columbia University Press, 1991.

Rosenberg, Joel. *King and Kin: Political Allegory in the Hebrew Bible*. Bloomington: Indiana University Press, 1986.

Salomon, Nanette. 'Judging Artemisia: A Baroque Woman in Modern Art History'. In Bal, ed., *The Artemisia Files*, 33–61.

Sasson, Jack M. '"A Breeder or Two for Each Leader": On Mothers in Judges 4 and 5'. In Clines and van Wolde, eds., *A Critical Engagement*, 333–54.

———. *Judges 1–12*. New Haven, CT: Yale University Press, 2014.

———. 'Who Cut Samson's Hair? (And Other Trifling Issues Raised by Judges 16)'. *Prooftexts* 8 (1988): 333–39.

Sawyer, John F. A. 'A Critical Review of Recent Projects and Publications'. *Hebrew Bible and Ancient Israel* 1 (2012): 298–326.

———. 'Interpreting Hebrew Writing in Christian Art'. In Clines and van Wolde, eds., *A Critical Engagement*, 355–71.

Scarry, Elaine. *The Body in Pain: The Making and Unmaking of the World*. New York: Oxford University Press, 1985.

Schaberg, Jane. 'Feminist Interpretations of the Infancy Narrative of Matthew'. In Shaberg, *The Illegitimacy of Jesus*, 231–57.

———. *The Illegitimacy of Jesus: A Feminist Theological Interpretation of the Infancy Narratives*. Expanded Twentieth Anniversary Edition, with contributions by David T. Landry and Frank Reilly. Sheffield: Sheffield Phoenix Press, 2006.

Schearing, Linda S., and Valarie H. Ziegler. *Enticed by Eden: How Western Culture Uses, Confuses, (and Sometimes Abuses) Adam and Eve*. Waco, TX: Baylor University Press, 2013.

Schneider, Tammi J. *Sarah: Mother of Nations*. New York: Continuum, 2004.

Scholz, Susanne. *Sacred Witness: Rape in the Hebrew Bible*. Minneapolis, MN: Fortress Press, 2010.

Schöpflin, Karin. 'Samson in European Literature: Some Examples from English, French and German Poetry'. In Eynikel and Nicklas, eds., *Samson: Hero or Fool?*, 177–96.

Schroeder, Joy A. *Dinah's Lament: The Biblical Legacy of Sexual Violence in Christian Interpretation*. Minneapolis, MN: Fortress Press, 2007.

Schuster, Peter-Klaus, Christoph Vitali and Barbara Butts, eds. *Lovis Corinth*. Munich: Prestel Verlag, 1996.

Seebass, Horst. *Genesis II: Vätergeschichte I (11,27–22,24)*. Neukirchen-Vluyn: Neukirchener Verlag, 1997.

Sellin, Christine Petra. *Fractured Families and Rebel Maidservants: The Biblical Hagar in Seventeenth-Century Dutch Art and Literature*. New York: T&T Clark, 2006.

Sheaffer, Andrea M. *Envisioning the Book of Judith: How Art Illuminates Minor Characters*. Sheffield: Sheffield Phoenix Press, 2014.

Sherwood, Yvonne. 'Binding–Unbinding: Divided Responses of Judaism, Christianity, and Islam to the "Sacrifice" of Abraham's Beloved Son'. *Journal of the American Academy of Religion* 72 (2004): 821–61.

———. 'Hagar and Ishmael: The Reception of Expulsion'. *Interpretation* 68 (2014): 286–304.

Showalter, Elaine. *Sexual Anarchy: Gender and Culture at the Fin de Siècle*. New York: Penguin Books, 1990.

Skinner, John. *A Critical and Exegetical Commentary on Genesis*. 2nd ed. Edinburgh: T. & T. Clark, 1930.

Smith, Alison, ed., with contributions by Robert Upstone, Michael Hatt, Martin Myrone, Virginia Dodier and Tim Batchelor. *Exposed: The Victorian Nude*. London: Tate Publishing, 2001.

Soggin, J. Alberto. *Judges: A Commentary*. Translated by John Bowden. Philadelphia, PA: Westminster Press, 1981.

Speiser, E. A. *Genesis*. Garden City, NY: Doubleday, 1964.

Spijkerboer, Anne Marijke. 'Rembrandt und Hagar'. In *Unless Some One Guide Me* [Festschrift K. A. Duerloo], edited by Janet W. Dyk et al., 21–31. Maastricht: Shaker, 2001.

Steinberg, Naomi. *Kinship and Marriage in Genesis: A Household Economics Perspective*. Minneapolis, MN: Fortress Press, 1993.

———. *The World of the Child in the Hebrew Bible*. Sheffield: Sheffield Phoenix Press, 2013.

———. 'The World of the Family in Genesis'. In *The Book of Genesis: Composition, Reception, and Interpretation*, edited by Craig A. Evans, Joel N. Lohr and David L. Petersen, 279–300. Leiden: Brill, 2012.

Sternberg, Meir. *The Poetics of Biblical Narrative: Ideological Literature and the Drama of Reading*. Bloomington: Indiana University Press, 1985.

Still, Judith. 'Rousseau's *Lévite d'Ephraïm*: The Imposition of Meaning (on Women)'. *French Studies* 43 (1989): 12–30.

Stocker, Margarita. *Judith, Sexual Warrior: Women and Power in Western Culture*. New Haven, CT: Yale University Press, 1998.

Tamber-Rosenau, Caryn. 'Biblical Bathing Beauties and the Manipulation of the Male Gaze: What Judith Can Tell Us about Bathsheba and Susanna'. *Journal of Feminist Studies in Religion* 33 (2017): 55–72.

Taschner, Johannes. 'Mit wem ringt Jakob in der Nacht? Oder: Der Versuch, mit Rembrandt eine Leerstelle auszuleuchten'. In *Beyond the Biblical Horizon: The Bible and the Arts*, edited by J. Cheryl Exum, 109–22. Leiden: Brill, 1999.

Thompson, John L. *Reading the Bible with the Dead: What You Can Learn from the History of Exegesis that You Can't Learn from Exegesis Alone*. Grand Rapids, MI: Eerdmans, 2007.

———. *Writing the Wrongs: Women of the Old Testament among Biblical Commentators from Philo through the Reformation*. Oxford: Oxford University Press, 2001.

Tollerton, David. 'Divine Violence Caught on Camera: Negotiating Text and Photography in Broomberg and Chanarin's *Holy Bible*'. *Biblical Reception* 3 (2014): 146–60.

Tongue, Samuel. *Between Biblical Criticism and Poetic Rewriting: Interpretative Struggles over Genesis 32:22–32*. Leiden: Brill, 2014.

Treuherz, Julian. *Pre-Raphaelite Paintings from Manchester City Art Galleries*. Manchester: Manchester City Art Gallery, 1993.

Trible, Phyllis. 'Depatriarchalizing in Biblical Interpretation'. *Journal of the American Academy of Religion* 41 (1973): 30–48.

———. *God and the Rhetoric of Sexuality*. Philadelphia, PA: Fortress Press, 1978.

———. 'Ominous Beginnings for a Promise of Blessing'. In Trible and Russell, eds., *Hagar, Sarah, and Their Children: Jewish, Christian, and Muslim Perspectives*, 33–69.

———. *Texts of Terror: Literary-Feminist Readings of Biblical Narratives*. Philadelphia, PA: Fortress Press, 1984.

Trible, Phyllis, and Letty M. Russell, eds., *Hagar, Sarah, and Their Children: Jewish, Christian, and Muslim Perspectives*. Louisville, KY: Westminster John Knox, 2006.

Tümpel, Christian, ed. *Im Lichte Rembrandts: Das Alte Testament im Goldenen Zeitalter der niederländischen Kunst*. Zwolle: Waanders, n.d.

Vawter, Bruce. *On Genesis: A New Reading*. London: Geoffrey Chapman, 1977.

Verdi, Richard. *Matthias Stom: Isaac Blessing Jacob*. Birmingham: The Trustees of the Barber Institute of Fine Arts, 1999.

Vergo, Peter. 'Impressions of a Suicide Postponed'. *Times Literary Supplement* (14 March 1997): 18.

Vickery, John. 'In Strange Ways: The Story of Samson'. In *Images of Man and God*, edited by Burke O. Long, 58–73. Sheffield: Almond Press, 1981.

Waltke, Bruce K. *Genesis: A Commentary*. Grand Rapids, MI: Eerdmans, 2001.

Webb, Barry G. *The Book of the Judges*. Grand Rapids, MI: Eerdmans, 2012.

———. *The Book of the Judges: An Integrated Reading*. Sheffield: JSOT Press, 1987.

Weems, Renita J. *Just a Sister Away: A Womanist Vision of Women's Relationships in the Bible*. San Diego, CA: LuraMedia, 1988.

Weis, Richard D. 'Stained Glass Window, Kaleidoscope or Catalyst: The Implications of Difference in Readings of the Hagar and Sarah Stories'. In *A Gift of God in Due Season: Essays on Scripture and Community in Honor of James A. Sanders*, edited by Richard D. Weis and David M. Carr, 253–73. Sheffield: Sheffield Academic Press, 1996.

Wenham, Gordon J. *Genesis 1–15*. Waco, TX: Word Books, 1987.

———. *Genesis 16–50*. Dallas, TX: Word Books, 1994.

Westermann, Claus. *Genesis 12–36: A Commentary*. Translated by John J. Scullion. London: SPCK, 1985.

———. *Genesis 37–50: A Commentary*. Translated by John J. Scullion. Minneapolis, MN: Augsburg, 1986.

———. *The Promises to the Fathers: Studies on the Patriarchal Narratives*. Translated by David E. Green. Philadelphia, PA: Fortress Press, 1980.

Wharton, James A. 'The Secret of Yahweh: Story and Affirmation in Judges 13–16'. *Interpretation* 27 (1973): 48–65.

Whedbee, J. William. 'Paradox and Parody in the Song of Solomon'. In *The Bible and the Comic Vision*, 263–77. Minneapolis, MN: Fortress Press, 1998.

White, Hugh C. *Narration and Discourse in the Book of Genesis*. Cambridge: Cambridge University Press, 1991.

Williams, Delores S. 'Hagar in African American Biblical Appropriation'. In Trible and Russell, eds., *Hagar, Sarah, and their Children: Jewish, Christian, and Muslim Perspectives*, 171–84.

Wisse, Kees. 'Samson in Music'. In Eynikel and Nicklas, eds., *Samson: Hero or Fool?*, 161–76.

Wolde, Ellen van. 'The Bow in the Clouds in Genesis 9.12–17: When Cognitive Linguistics Meets Visual Criticism'. In Clines and van Wolde, eds., *A Critical Engagement*, 380–400.

———. 'Does *'innâ* Denote Rape? A Semantic Analysis of a Controversial Word'. *Vetus Testamentum* 52 (2002): 528–44.

———. *Reframing Biblical Studies: When Language and Text Meet Culture, Cognition, and Context*. Winona Lake, IN: Eisenbrauns, 2009.

———. 'Ya'el in Judges 4'. *Zeitschrift für die alttestamentliche Wissenschaft* 107 (1995): 240–46.

Yee, Gale A. 'By the Hand of a Woman: The Metaphor of the Woman Warrior in Judges 4'. In *Women, War, and Metaphor: Language and Society in the Study of the Hebrew Bible*, edited by Claudia V. Camp and Carole R. Fontaine, 99–132. Atlanta, GA: Society of Biblical Literature, 1993.

———. 'Ideological Criticism: Judges 17–21 and the Dismembered Body'. In *Judges and Method: New Approaches in Biblical Studies*, edited by Gale A. Yee, 138–60. 2nd ed. Minneapolis, MN: Fortress Press, 2007.

Yoo, Philip Y. 'Hagar the Egyptian: Wife, Handmaid, and Concubine'. *Catholic Biblical Quarterly* 78 (2016): 215–35.

Zakovitch, Yair. '∪ and ∩ in the Bible'. In *Tragedy and Comedy in the Bible*, edited by J. Cheryl Exum, 107–14. Decatur, GA: Scholars Press, 1984.

———. 'Sisseras Tod'. *Zeitschrift für die alttestamentliche Wissenschaft* 93 (1981): 364–74.

———. 'The Woman's Rights in the Biblical Law of Divorce'. *The Jewish Law Annual* 4 (1981): 28–46.

Zwick, Reinhold. 'Obsessive Love: Samson and Delilah Go to the Movies'. In Eynikel and Nicklas, eds., *Samson: Hero or Fool?*, 211–35.

Index of References

INDEX OF AUTHORS

CPSIA information can be obtained
at www.ICGtesting.com
Printed in the USA
LVHW080833290121
677760LV00004B/14